Vocabulary
for the
College-Bound
Student

Vocabulary books by the authors

Vocabulary and Composition Through Pleasurable Reading, Books I–VI
Vocabulary for Enjoyment, Books I–III
Vocabulary for the High School Student, Books A, B
Vocabulary for the High School Student
Vocabulary for the College-Bound Student
The Joy of Vocabulary

THIRD EDITION

Vocabulary for the College-Bound Student

HAROLD LEVINE
Chairman Emeritus of English,
Benjamin Cardozo High School, New York

NORMAN LEVINE
Associate Professor of English,
City College of the City University of New York

ROBERT T. LEVINE
Professor of English,
North Carolina A & T State University

When ordering this book, please specify:
either **R 573 W** or
VOCABULARY FOR THE COLLEGE-BOUND
STUDENT, WORKBOOK

AMSCO SCHOOL PUBLICATIONS, INC.
315 Hudson Street / New York, N.Y. 10013

ISBN 0-87720-768-2

Printed in the United States of America

5 6 7 8 9 10   99 98 97 96

PREFACE

The aim of this updated and enlarged edition is to help high school students build a superior vocabulary and use it effectively. About two hundred new lesson words have been incorporated into the text. The exercises, to an even greater extent than in the previous edition, teach close reading and concise writing at the same time as vocabulary. Some exercises ask students to write "minicompositions" of no more than three sentences, in which they not only use their new lesson words, but also learn an important composition skill, like stating an opinion and supporting it with reasons or examples.

Except for the above changes, the vocabulary-building procedures of the previous edition have been retained.

Learning New Words From the Context (Chapter 2) is an adventure in critical thinking. It presents eighty short passages in which possibly unfamiliar words can be defined with help from clues in the context. By teaching students how to interpret such clues, this chapter provides them with a lifelong tool for vocabulary growth, *and at the same time, it makes them better readers.*

Building Vocabulary Through Central Ideas (Chapter 3) involves students in studying twenty-five groups of related words. In the FLATTERY group, they will learn *adulation, cajole, obsequious,* etc.—and in the REASONING group, *analogy, axiomatic, specious,* etc.

Words Derived From Greek (Chapter 4) teaches derivatives from twenty-five Ancient Greek word elements. For example, from EU, meaning "good," we get *euphemism, euphoria, euthanasia,* etc.—and from DYS, meaning "bad," *dysfunction, dyspepsia, dystrophy,* etc.

Words Derived From Latin (Chapter 5), the largest source of English words, teaches derivatives from thirty Latin roots. The root VOR, for example, meaning "eat," gives us *carnivorous, frugivorous, voracious,* etc.—and the root FRACT, meaning "break," yields *fractious, infraction, refractory,* etc.

Words From Classical Mythology and History (Chapter 6) teaches not only derivatives from the myths of the Ancient Greeks and Romans, like *amazon, hector, narcissistic,* etc. It also teaches derivatives from classical history, like *Draconian, Lucullan, marathon,* etc.

Anglo-Saxon Vocabulary (Chapter 7) teaches derivatives from prefixes like WITH, meaning "back,": *withdraw, withhold,* etc.—and suffixes like LING, meaning "little,": *sapling, stripling,* etc. It also pairs some Anglo-Saxon words with nearly synonymous Latin-derived words—for example, *flay* with *excoriate*—to help students enrich their vocabularies.

French Words in English (Chapter 8) teaches about one hundred fifty loanwords integrated into English from French—*clairvoyant, canard, concierge, martinet, nonpareil,* etc.

Italian Words in English (Chapter 9) teaches similar borrowings from Italian—*alfresco, crescendo, diva, imbroglio, impresario,* etc.

Spanish Words in English (Chapter 10) teaches such loanwords from Spanish as *aficionado, barrio, bodega, bonanza, macho,* etc.

Expanding Vocabulary Through Derivatives (Chapter 11) offers instruction in forming derivatives, so that when students learn *plausible,* for example, they may convert it, when necessary, to *implausible, plausibly, implausibly, plausibility,* or *implausibility.* The chapter also reviews some pertinent spelling rules.

Sample Vocabulary Questions in Pre-College Tests (Chapter 12) reprints, with permission, a total of sixty-three sentence completion, antonym, and word analogy questions intended to acquaint students with the following pre-college tests:

1. PSAT/NMSQT (The Preliminary Scholastic Aptitude Test/National Merit Scholarship Qualifying Test), and
2. SAT (The Scholastic Aptitude Test)

Of the reprinted questions, twenty-one are sample questions with accompanying explanations, and forty-two are practice-test questions, for which the official answer keys are provided.

Dictionary of Words Taught in This Text (Chapter 13) is appended for ease of reference and review.

Students should be encouraged to use their newly learned words whenever appropriate in their writing and classroom discussions. Only through actual use will they be able to incorporate such words into their vocabularies. They should also be encouraged to own a good dictionary and to develop the dictionary habit.

The Authors

CONTENTS

Chapter 6   Words From Classical Mythology and History   180

Chapter 7   Anglo-Saxon Vocabulary   191

Chapter 12   Sample Vocabulary Questions in Pre-College Tests   273

Chapter 13   Dictionary of Words Taught in This Text   287

CHAPTER 1

The Importance of Vocabulary to <u>You</u>

Vocabulary and thinking

Words stand for ideas. Words are the tools of thought. If your word power is limited, your ability to think will also be limited, since you can neither receive ideas nor communicate with others except within the confines of an inadequate vocabulary. But if you broaden your vocabulary, you will find it easier to do the thinking that success in life often demands.

Vocabulary and college admission

College admissions officers will be interested in the extent of your vocabulary, for a good vocabulary will suggest that you are likely to do well in college. It will suggest, too, that you have done wide reading, since reading is the principal way of developing a good vocabulary. In the college entrance and scholarship tests you are likely to take, you will find vocabulary a major ingredient.

Vocabulary growth through reading

Persons who read widely gradually build up extensive vocabularies, especially if they have a curiosity about words. This curiosity, compelling them to regard every unfamiliar word as a breakdown in communication between author and reader, sends them thumbing through the dictionary. Should you, too, develop such word curiosity, you will be assured a lifetime of vocabulary growth.

Though reading is the basic means of vocabulary growth, it is a relatively slow means. For the college-bound student who has not yet achieved a superior vocabulary, reading needs to be supplemented by a direct attack that will yield comparatively rapid growth—and that is the purpose of this book.

Vocabulary growth through this book

This book will involve you in a five-pronged attack on vocabulary.

Attack #1: Learning New Words From the Context

Often, we can discover the meaning of an unfamiliar word from its *context*—the other words with which it is used. Note, for example, how we can determine the meaning of *parsimonious* in the following sentence:

People vary in their tipping habits from the very generous to the very *parsimonious*.

Obviously, from the above context, *parsimonious* is the opposite of *generous*; *parsimonious* means "stingy."

Chapter II will teach you the various clues for learning the meaning of a possibly unfamiliar word, like *parsimonious*, from its context. As you learn to use these clues, you will be broadening your vocabulary and—what is even more important—becoming a more skillful reader.

Attack #2: Learning Vocabulary in Groups of Related Words

Vocabulary growth that evolves from a day's reading has one serious disadvantage: it is poorly organized. The new words you encounter as you read usually bear little relationship to one another. This, of course, does not mean that you should think any the less of reading as a means of vocabulary building. It does, however, suggest that you may achieve relatively rapid vocabulary growth by studying *groups of related words*.

In the "central-ideas" chapter you will find twenty-five groups of related words. Each group presents words revolving about one idea—*joy, sadness, flattery, age, relatives, reasoning*, etc. The new words are further explained in hundreds of illustrative sentences that have one feature in common: they present new vocabulary in such context as will make the meaning obvious and easy to remember.

Attack #3: Learning Vocabulary Derived From Greek and Latin

The principle of the lever has enabled humans, using relatively little effort, to do a great amount of work. You can apply the same principle to learning vocabulary. If you study certain productive Greek and Latin prefixes and roots, you can gain word leverage. Each prefix or root adequately understood will help you learn the meanings of the many English words it has produced. In the Greek and Latin chapters, you will meet important prefixes and roots, each with numerous English offspring.

Rounding out the attack on Greek and Latin are two briefer chapters. One will teach you useful English words derived from classical (Latin and Greek) mythology and history. The other, dealing with the interplay of Latin and Anglo-Saxon, will contribute further to your word hoard.

Attack #4: Learning Vocabulary Borrowed From French, Italian, and Spanish

Since English has borrowed heavily from French, you are sure to encounter adopted French words in books, newspapers, and magazines. Such words are considered a part of our English vocabulary and are often key words in the passages in which they occur. Not to know the meanings of common French borrowings is therefore a serious vocabulary deficiency.

The French chapter presents more than one hundred fifty commonly used loanwords, divided into small, easy-to-learn groups. To give you confidence in your understanding of each word, care has been taken to make the definitions and illustrative sentences as helpful as possible. You will find similar treatment in the briefer chapters on important Italian and Spanish loanwords.

Attack #5: Learning to Form Derivatives

Suppose you have just learned a new word—*fallible*, meaning "liable to be mistaken." If you do not know how to form derivatives, all you have added to your vocabulary is *fallible*—just one word.

But if you know how to form derivatives, you have learned not one but several new words. You have learned *fallible* and *infallible; fallibly* and *infallibly; fallibility* and *infallibility*, etc.

Chapter XI will teach you how to form and spell derivatives so that you may know how to add many new words to your vocabulary whenever you learn one new word.

"Exercising" new vocabulary

Muscular exercise is essential, especially during your years of physical growth. Vocabulary exercise, too, is essential in your periods of word growth.

To learn new words effectively, you must put them to use early and often. The challenging drills and tests in this book will give you abundant opportunities for varied vocabulary exercise. But you should do more on your own.

In your reading and listening experiences, be conscious of vocabulary. In your speaking and writing, take the initiative on suitable occasions to use new vocabulary. Such follow-up is a *must* if you are to make new words securely yours.

CHAPTER 2

Learning New Words
From the Context

What is the context?

Most of the time, a word is used not by itself but with other words. These other words are its *context*. The meaning of a word is often found in its context—the other words with which it is used.

Suppose, for example, we were asked for the meaning of *strike*. We would not be able to give a definite answer because *strike*, as presented to us, is all by itself; it has no context.

But if we were asked to define *strike* in one of the following sentences, we would have no trouble telling its meaning from its *context*—the other words with which it is used.

1. *Strike* three! You're out!
   (*Strike* means "a ball pitched over the plate between a batter's knees and shoulders.")

2. There were no milk deliveries because of a *strike*.
   (*Strike* means "a work stoppage because of a labor dispute.")

3. He made a fist as if to *strike* me.
   (*Strike* means "hit.")

How can the context help you expand your vocabulary?

Here is an amazing fact: the context can often give you the meaning not only of common words like *strike*, **but also of unfamiliar words, including words you have never before seen or heard!**

"What," asks a friend, "is *xenophobic*?"
"How should I know?" you say. "I never heard of it."
"It's in today's paper," says the friend. "Here it is."

You take the newspaper and read the sentence with the strange word: "The new ruler is *xenophobic*; he has ordered all foreigners to leave the country."

"Aha!" you say. "Now I know: *xenophobic* means '*afraid or distrustful of foreigners*.' The context gives us the meaning."

Of course, you are right.

What can this chapter do for you?

This chapter will teach you how to use the context to get the meaning of unfamiliar words. Once you learn this skill, it will serve you for the rest of your life in two important ways: (1) it will keep enlarging your vocabulary; and (2) it will make you an ever better reader.

Part 1.
Contexts With Contrasting Words

Each passage below contains a word in italics. If you read the passage carefully, you will find a clue to the meaning of this word in an opposite word (**antonym**) or a contrasting idea.

Below each passage, write (*a*) the clue that led you to the meaning, and (*b*) the meaning itself. The answers for the first two passages have been filled in for you as examples.

1. ''That you, Joe?'' he asked . . .
   ''Who else could it be?'' I *retorted*.—William R. Scott

   a. CLUE: _____*Retorted* is the opposite of ''asked.''_____

   b. MEANING: _____*Retorted* means ''answered.''_____

2. Some substances that cause cancer were once regarded as *noncarcinogenic*.

   a. CLUE: _____*Noncarcinogenic* is in contrast with ''that cause cancer.''_____

   b. MEANING: _____*Noncarcinogenic* means ''not cancer-causing.''_____

3. At this stage we cannot tell whether the new regulations will be to our advantage or *detriment*.

   a. CLUE: _____

   b. MEANING: _____

4. If his health *ameliorates*, he will stay on the job; if it becomes worse, he will have to resign.

   a. CLUE: _____

   b. MEANING: _____

5. In this firm the industrious are promoted and the *indolent* are encouraged to leave.

   a. CLUE: _____

   b. MEANING: _____

6. Parents, I suppose, were as much a problem *formerly* as they are today.—Gretchen Finletter

   a. CLUE: _____

   b. MEANING: _____

7. If you are going to get up before dawn tomorrow, you had better *retire* by 11 P.M.

   a. CLUE: _____

   b. MEANING: _____

8. Evidence presented at the trials of the two public officials showed that they had *subverted* the laws they were supposed to uphold.

    a. CLUE: _____

    b. MEANING: _____

9. Many who used to waste fuel are *conserving* it, now that it has become so much more expensive.

    a. CLUE: _____

    b. MEANING: _____

10. Only one lower wing and the landing gear had been completely demolished. The rest of the machine was virtually *intact.*—Edwin Way Teale

    a. CLUE: _____

    b. MEANING: _____

11. Those who volunteered to help turned out to be more of an *impediment* than an aid.

    a. CLUE: _____

    b. MEANING: _____

12. The Sullivan home, which used to stand on this corner, was erected in 1929 and *razed* in 1992.

    a. CLUE: _____

    b. MEANING: _____

13. Time has proved that Seward's purchase of Alaska from Russia in 1867 for $7,200,000 was wisdom, not *folly.*

    a. CLUE: _____

    b. MEANING: _____

14. When millions face starvation, we cannot be *parsimonious* in doling out aid; we must be generous.

    a. CLUE: _____

    b. MEANING: _____

15. . . . A wave of rebelliousness ran through the countryside. Bulls which had always been *tractable* suddenly turned savage, sheep broke down hedges and devoured clover, cows kicked the pail over . . .—George Orwell

    a. CLUE: _____

    b. MEANING: _____

16. Children will tell how old they are, but older people are inclined to be *reticent* about their age.

    a. CLUE: _____

    b. MEANING: _____

17. The organization is trying to put on a show of *harmony* though there is deep conflict within its ranks.

    a. CLUE: _____

    b. MEANING: _____

18. Those who heeded our advice did well; those who *ignored* it did not.

    a. CLUE: _____

    b. MEANING: _____

19. Her learner's permit is still in effect but mine is *invalid*.

    a. CLUE: _____

    b. MEANING: _____

20. There once was a society in Hawaii for the special purpose of introducing *exotic* birds. Today when you go to the islands, you see, instead of the exquisite native birds that greeted Captain Cook, mynas from India, cardinals from the United States or Brazil, doves from Asia . . .

                                                              —Rachel Carson

    a. CLUE: _____

    b. MEANING: _____

Study Your New Words, **Group 1**

You have just defined twenty new words simply by contrasting them with other words or expressions in the context. Now, to reinforce your grasp of these words and make them a part of your active vocabulary, study the following:

WORD	MEANING	TYPICAL USE
ameliorate (*v.*) ə-'mēl-yə-ˌrāt	become better; make better; improve (*ant.* **worsen**)	We expected business conditions to *ameliorate*, but they grew worse.
***amelioration** (*n.*) ə-ˌmēl-yə-'rā-shən	improvement	
conserve (*v.*) kən-'sərv	keep from waste, loss, or decay; save (*ant.* **waste**)	One way to *conserve* water is to repair leaking faucets.
conservation (*n.*) ˌkän-sər-'vā-shən	preservation from loss, injury, or waste	
conservationist (*n.*) ˌkän-sər-'vā-shə-nəst	one who advocates the conservation of natural resources	
detriment (*n.*) 'de-trə-mənt	injury, damage, or something that causes it; disadvantage (*ant.* **advantage**)	Skipping meals can be a *detriment* to your health.
detrimental (*adj.*) ˌde-trə-'ment-'l	harmful; damaging	
exotic (*adj.*) ig-'zät-ik	1. introduced from another country; foreign (*ant.* **native**)	The chrysanthemum is an *exotic* plant; it was introduced from the Orient.
	2. strikingly unusual; strange	This wallpaper has an *exotic* charm.

*Note that *amelioration* is a bonus word—you can understand it instantly if you know *ameliorate*. Useful bonus words, like *amelioration*, will be introduced from now on.

folly (*n.*)
'fäl-ē

lack of good sense; foolish action or undertaking (*ant.* **wisdom**)

It is *folly* to go on a long drive with a nearly empty gas tank.

formerly (*adv.*)
'fȯr-mər-lē

in an earlier period; previously (*ant.* **now**)

Our physics instructor was *formerly* an engineer.

former (*adj.*)
'fȯr-mər

preceding; previous (*ant.* **latter**)

harmony (*n.*)
'här-mə-nē

peaceable or friendly relations; accord; agreement; tranquillity (*ant.* **conflict; disharmony**)

A boundary dispute is making it impossible for the neighbors to live in *harmony*.

harmonious (*adj.*)
här-'mō-nē-əs

friendly; amicable

ignore (*v.*)
ig-'nȯ(ə)r

refuse to take notice of; disregard (*ant.* **heed**)

You may get into a serious accident if you *ignore* a full-stop sign.

ignoramus (*n.*)
,ig-nə-'rā-məs

ignorant, stupid person; dunce

impediment (*n.*)
im-'ped-ə-mənt

something that hinders or obstructs; hindrance; obstacle (*ant.* **aid**)

A person's lack of education is often an *impediment* to advancement.

impede (*v.*)
im-pēd

interfere with or slow the progress of; hinder; obstruct

indolent (*adj.*)
'in-də-lənt

disposed to avoid exertion; lazy; idle; lethargic (*ant.* **industrious**)

I was so comfortable in the reclining chair that I became *indolent* and did not feel like studying.

indolence (*n.*)
'in-də-ləns

idleness; laziness

intact (*adj.*)
in-'takt

untouched by anything that damages or diminishes; left complete or entire; uninjured (*ant.* **imperfect**)

The tornado demolished the barn but left the farmhouse *intact*.

invalid (*adj.*)
in-'val-əd

not valid; having no force or effect; void (*ant.* **valid**, binding in law)

The courts have ruled that a forced confession is *invalid* and cannot be introduced as evidence.

invalidate (*v.*)
in-'val-ə-,dāt

abolish; annul

invalid (*n.*)
'in-və-ləd

sickly or disabled person

noncarcinogenic (*adj.*)
'nän-,kär-sə-nō-'jen-ik

not producing, or tending to produce, cancer (*ant.* **carcinogenic**)

Cancer-causing ingredients must be replaced by others that are *noncarcinogenic*.

parsimonious (*adj.*)
,pär-sə-'mō-nē-əs

unduly sparing in the spending of money; stingy (*ant.* **generous**)

Some accuse the government of being too *generous* in funding road improvement and too *parsimonious* in financing education.

parsimony (n.) 'pär-sə-ˌmō-nē	stinginess; parsimoniousness (*ant.* **generosity**)	
raze (v.) 'rāz	destroy utterly by tearing down; de-molish; level to the ground (*ant.* **erect**)	The building was so badly damaged in the fire that it had to be *razed*.
reticent (adj.) 'ret-ə-sənt	inclined to be silent or secretive; un-communicative (*ant.* **frank**)	Have you noticed that people who boast about their successes are *reticent* about their failures?
reticence (n.) 'ret-ə-səns	restraint in communicating (*ant.* **frankness**)	
retire (v.) ri-'tī(ə)r	1. withdraw from active duty or business	Does your grandfather plan to *retire* at 65 or continue to work?
	2. go to bed (*ant.* **rise**)	Please do not phone after 10 P.M. because my folks *retire* early.
retort (v.) ri-'tȯrt	answer; reply sharply or angrily (*ant.* **ask**)	"Giving up?" she asked. "Absolutely not!" I *retorted*.
retort (n.) ri-'tȯrt	quick, witty, or sharp reply; answer	
subvert (v.) səb-'vərt	overturn or overthrow from the foundation; undermine (*ant.* **uphold**)	We are *subverting* our fuel-conser-vation efforts when we heat rooms that are not occupied.
subversion (n.) səb-'vər-zhən	sabotage; undermining	
tractable (adj.) 'trak-tə-bəl	easily led, taught, or controlled; yielding; docile (*ant.* **unruly; intractable**)	A child who misbehaves may be more *tractable* in a small group than in a large one.
tractability (n.) ˌtrak-tə-'bil-ət-ē	obedience	

Apply What You Have Learned

EXERCISE 2.1: SENTENCE COMPLETION

Which choice, A or B, makes the sentence correct? Write the *letter* of your answer in the space provided.

1. When I heard the noise, I ignored it. I went _____.

(A) on with my work   (B) to investigate

2. The more we conserve heat, the _____ fuel we have for future use.

(A) more   (B) less

3. It is folly to _____ .

   (A) apply your brakes suddenly on   (B) reduce your speed drastically in
      an icy road   a thick fog

4. The reticent witness provided _____ details.

   (A) few   (B) abundant

5. I like _____ food, but I also have a craving for exotic dishes.

   (A) foreign   (B) American

6. You would not expect parsimonious persons to _____ .

   (A) collect bits of string   (B) spend freely

7. Because of _____ , the company is doing its utmost to ameliorate service.

   (A) a shortage of raw materials   (B) customer complaints

8. The stolen jewels were found intact; _____ was missing.

   (A) nothing   (B) a diamond ring

9. Most of the listeners were tractable; they _____ the speaker's instructions.

   (A) readily followed   (B) totally disregarded

10. Carcinogenic materials _____ to our health.

   (A) are a threat   (B) pose no danger

EXERCISE 2.2: CONCISE WRITING

Express the thought of each sentence below in no more than four words. The first two sentences have been rewritten as examples.

1. "Wait outside!" he replied in a sharp and angry tone of voice.

   "Wait outside!" he retorted. _____

2. We are opposed to the waste, mismanagement, and destruction of our natural resources.

   We are conservationists. _____

3. The advice that they have been giving is doing more harm than good.

   _____

4. His inclination to exert himself as little as possible is self-defeating.

   _____

5. Is there a possibility that friendly relations can be restored?

   _____

6. The house that they lived in was leveled to the ground.

   _____

7. All the things that belonged to her arrived with nothing missing or damaged.

_____

8. At an earlier period of time, land could be bought for very little money.

_____

9. Wills that have not been signed are not binding in law.

_____

10. What time was it when you went to bed for the night?

_____

EXERCISE 2.3: CLOSE READING

Carefully read the statements below and answer the questions.

STATEMENTS

A fallen tree was blocking traffic on Bainbridge Road.

The Z Company had a disastrous year but decided to stay in business.

Russ has said very little about what had happened.

Angela's motto was "Take it easy." She could have done much more if she had wanted, but she kept saying, "Why kill myself?"

Our new storm door has reduced heat loss.

The ABC Company's employees had never gone on strike.

Billy refused to remain in his seat, despite the pleas of his parents and the usher.

While the rest of us were trying to sell tickets, one member of the cast was privately telling people that the play was not worth seeing.

Despite her large income, Alicia bought only the barest necessities.

The refugees perished in the avalanche, but the inn from which they had fled suffered no damage.

QUESTIONS

1. What was impeding something? _____

2. Who was intractable? _____

3. Who seemed indolent? _____

4. Who was reticent? _____

5. Who appeared to be parsimonious? _____

6. What was helping to conserve something? _____

7. Who probably expected some amelioration? _____

8. Who was subversive? _____

9. Who seemed to be enjoying harmony? _____

10. What was left intact? _____

EXERCISE 2.4: ANTONYMS

Complete the sentence by inserting the antonym of the italicized word. Select your antonyms from pages 7–9.

1. Truly, I do not care whether you *heed* my suggestion or _____ it.

2. Now that the *conflict* is over, _____ may soon be restored.

3. As an officer of the club, you should *uphold* the constitution, not_____ it.

4. I cannot see the *wisdom* of your actions; they are pure _____ .

5. Usually I *rise* at 6:45 A.M. and _____ by 11 P.M.

6. The newcomer, *unruly* at first, is becoming more _____ .

7. Not all the trees on the school grounds are *native* to our soil. Some are _____ .

8. An early start, we thought, would work to our *advantage*, but it turned out to be to our

    _____ .

9. _____ , she worked as a bookkeeper. *Now* she is studying for a law degree.

10. Did the medicine _____ your condition or *worsen* it?

EXERCISE 2.5: COMPOSITION

Answer in a sentence or two.

1. What is one way to conserve energy that many people ignore?

    _____

    _____

    _____

2. Is it always folly to raze a structurally sound building? Explain.

_____

_____

_____

3. Why do conservationists want to prevent even the most exotic plants and animals from disappearing from the face of the earth?

_____

_____

_____

4. Give an example of how a reticent witness can subvert the process of justice.

_____

_____

_____

5. Would you rather have a parsimonious friend or an indolent one? Why?

_____

_____

_____

EXERCISE 2.6: BRAINTEASERS

Fill in the missing letters, as in the following sample:

He knows math, but in art and literature he is a(n) i g n o r a m u s.

1. Skipping breakfast may be _ _ _ _ _ **m e n** _ _ _ to your health.

2. Please step aside. You are **i m p** _ _ _ _ _ our progress.

3. Turn off that noise. Let's have some peace and _ _ _ _ _ _ **i l l** _ _ _.

4. When its own crops fail, a nation must buy food from _ _ _ **t i c** sources.

5. A license that expired yesterday is no longer _ _ **l i d**.

6. _ _ _ _ _ _ **v a t** _ _ _ can help prevent future shortages.

7. Though formerly enemies, they are now on _ **a r m** _ _ _ _ _ _ terms.

8. Our sugar is _ _ **d i g** _ _ _ _ _, but our tea is imported.

9. Did he tell you anything, or is he still _ _ _ _ _ _ _ _ _ **c a t** _ _ _?

10. _ _ **d u s t** _ _ _ _ _ workers deserve higher pay than indolent ones.

Part 2.
Contexts With Similar Words

Often you can learn the meaning of an unfamiliar word from a *similar* word or expression in the context. Do you know what *castigated* means? If not, you should be able to find out from the following:

> The candidate denounced his opponent for her views on foreign policy, and she *castigated* him for his attitude toward education.

Here, the meaning of *castigated* is given to us by a similar word in the context, *denounced*.

Do you know what *remote* means? If not, you can learn it from the following passage:

> There lay a young man, fast asleep—sleeping so soundly, so deeply, that he was far, far away from them both. Oh, so *remote* . . .—Katherine Mansfield

The context teaches us that *remote* means "far."

Let's try one more. Find the meaning of *reluctantly* in the next passage.

> My mother scolded me for my thoughtlessness and bade me say good-bye to them. *Reluctantly* I obeyed her, wishing that I did not have to do so.—Richard Wright

The clue here is in the words *wishing that I did not have to do so*. They suggest that *reluctantly* means "unwillingly."

Pretest 2

Write the meaning of the italicized word. (Hint: Look for a *similar* word or expression in the context.)

1. Mr. Smith had already become acquainted with British *cinemas* in small towns. Also, he was a Southern Californian and had that familiarity with movies that belongs to all Southern Californians.

   —Eric Knight

   cinemas means _____

2. Burke tossed the circular into the wastebasket without *perusing* it. He never reads junk mail.

   perusing means _____

3. The dealer asked for $1200. He *spurned* my offer of $1100, and when I went to $1150, he refused that too.

   spurned means _____

4. Your whistling *galls* me. In fact, your entire behavior irritates me.

   galls means _____

5. I said the water was *tepid*. She didn't believe me. She tested it herself to see if it was lukewarm.

   tepid means _____

6. Eileen and I hated the book [*Bird Life for Children*], so we were quite prepared to *despise* birds when we started off that morning on our first bird walk.—Ruth McKenney

   despise means _____

7. Everyone brimmed with enthusiasm. Carl was particularly *ebullient*.

   ebullient means _____

8. She is eager to bet me she will win the match, but I told her I do not *wager*.

   wager means _____

9. A fight started between two of the opposing athletes. Several of their teammates joined in. It was quite a *scuffle*.

   scuffle means _____

10. . . . the picture changed and sport began to *wane*.
    A good many factors contributed to the decline of sport.—E. B. White

    wane means _____

11. Later I realized I had made some *inane* remarks, and I was ashamed of myself for having been so silly.

    inane means _____

12. She was supposed to be *indemnified*—the repair bill came to $180—but she has not yet been repaid.

    indemnified means _____

13. Dorene is quite *finicky* about her penmanship. I am much less fussy.

    finicky means _____

14. The fact is, we have all been a good deal puzzled because the affair is so simple, and yet *baffles* us altogether.—Edgar Allan Poe

    baffles means _____

15. Though the starting salary is only $300 a week, Roberta has been promised an early promotion and a higher *stipend*.

    stipend means _____

16. They *exhorted* us to join them for dinner, but we resisted their urging and thanked them very much.

    exhorted means _____

17. When an Englishman has anything surprising to tell he never *exaggerates* it, never overstates it
    . . .

    —Stephen B. Leacock

    exaggerates means _____

18. I know how to change a tire, but tuning an engine is beyond my *expertise*.

     expertise means _____

19. Asians who have never been to the *Occident* learn much about Western culture from films and television.

     Occident means _____

20. Gerald suspected we were being watched. "Really?" I asked. "What makes you think we are under *surveillance*?"

     surveillance means _____

Study Your New Words, *Group 2*

You have just tried to define twenty new words with the help of similar words or expressions in the context. To strengthen your grasp of these new words, study the following:

WORD	MEANING	TYPICAL USE
baffle (*v.*) 'baf-əl	bewilder; perplex; fill with confusion; puzzle; frustrate	At last, we have found a solution to a problem that has been *baffling* us.
baffling (*adj.*) 'baf-liŋ	frustrating; bewildering	
cinema (*n.*) 'sin-ə-mə	movies; motion picture industry	Which do you like better, TV or the *cinema*?
cinematography (*n.*) ˌsin-ə-mə-'täg-rə-fē	art of making motion pictures	
despise (*v.*) di-'spīz	look down on with contempt or disgust; loathe; regard as inferior (*ant.* **admire**)	The world *admires* heroes and *despises* cowards.
despicable (*adj.*) 'des-pik-ə-bəl	worthy of contempt; contemptible (*ant.* **laudable**)	
ebullient (*adj.*) i-'bul-yənt	overflowing with enthusiasm; exuberant	Hundreds of *ebullient* fans thronged the airport to greet the new champions.
ebullience (*n.*) i-'bul-yəns	exuberance	
exaggerate (*v.*) ig-'zaj-ə-ˌrāt	overstate; go beyond the limits of the actual truth (*ant.* **minimize**)	You *exaggerated* when you called me an excellent cook. I can't make anything except chocolate pudding.
exaggeration (*n.*) ig-ˌzaj-ə-'rā-shən	overstatement (*ant.* **understatement**)	

exhort (*v.*) ig-'zȯrt	arouse by words; advise strongly; urge	The newscaster *exhorted* drivers to leave their cars at home because of the slippery roads.
exhortation (*n.*) ‚eks-‚ȯr-'tā-shən	urgent recommendation or advice	
expertise (*n.*) ‚ek-spər-'tēz	specialized skill or technical knowledge; know-how; expertness	The Waldos hire an accountant to prepare their tax return because they lack the *expertise* to do it themselves.
finicky (*adj.*) 'fin-i-kē	excessively concerned with trifles or details; hard to please; fussy; particular	Abe showed me I had forgotten to dot one of my i's. He is very *finicky* about such matters.
gall (*v.*) 'gȯl	make sore; irritate mentally; annoy; vex	Why are you in such a bad mood? What is *galling* you?
gall (*n.*) 'gȯl	brazen boldness; nerve (*ant.* **meekness**)	
inane (*adj.*) in-'ān	lacking significance or sense; pointless; silly; insipid (*ant.* **deep; profound**)	I asked him how the water was, and he said ''wet.'' Now isn't that *inane*?
inanity (*n.*) in-'an-ət-ē	foolishness; shallowness	
indemnify (*v.*) in-'dem-nə-‚fī	compensate for loss, damage, or injury; reimburse; repay	Some of the tenants were not *indemnified* for their losses in the fire, as they carried no insurance.
Occident (*n.*) 'äk-sə-dənt	west; countries of America and Europe (*ant.* **Orient**)	The plane that landed in Shanghai brought tourists from the United States, Canada, Brazil, Italy, and other countries in the *Occident*.
occidental (*adj.*) ‚äk-sə-'dent'l	western (*ant.* **oriental**)	
peruse (*v.*) pə-'rüz	read; look at fairly attentively; study	Before signing a contract, you should *peruse* its contents and discuss any questions you may have with your attorney.
perusal (*n.*) pə-'rü-zəl	reading; study	
scuffle (*v.*) 'skəf-əl	struggle at close quarters in a rough and confused manner; wrestle; grapple	The players who *scuffled* with the umpires were suspended and heavily fined.
scuffle (*n.*) 'skəf-əl	brawl; fight	

spurn (*v.*) 'spərn	thrust aside with disdain or contempt; reject (*ant.* **accept**)	We wanted to assist, but they *spurned* all offers of aid.
stipend (*n.*) 'stī-ˌpend	fixed pay for services; salary; regular allowance awarded a scholarship winner	My sister's scholarship will pay her an annual *stipend* of $1000 for four years.
surveillance (*n.*) sər-'vā-ləns	close watch over a person, group, or area; supervision	The patients in the intensive care ward are under continuous *surveillance*.
tepid (*adj.*) 'tep-əd	moderately warm; lukewarm	The soup was served hot, but I didn't get to it for about five minutes, and by then it was *tepid*.
tepidly (*adv.*) 'tep-əd-lē	unenthusiastically; lukewarmly	
wager (*v.*) 'wā-jər	risk (something) on the outcome of a contest or uncertain event; gamble; bet	Those who had *wagered* we would win are out of some money; we lost the game.
wager (*n.*) 'wā-jər	bet	
wane (*v.*) 'wān	decrease in power or size; dwindle; decline; sink	The senator may not be reelected. His popularity is *waning*.

Apply What You Have Learned

EXERCISE 2.7: SENTENCE COMPLETION

Which choice, A or B, makes the sentence correct? Write the *letter* of your answer in the space provided.

1. They spurned my suggestion and did as _____ .

    (A) they pleased   (B) I advised

2. To send someone a birthday card _____ her or his birthday is absolutely inane.

    (A) six months after   (B) three days before

3. The Independents have just _____ two more seats; their influence is waning.

    (A) won   (B) lost

4. After four years of service in the American embassy in _____ , Williams is longing to return to the Occident.

    (A) Tokyo   (B) Madrid

5. Our guests are not finicky; they are _____ to please.

 (A) hard   (B) easy

6. Asked if she were coming to Class Night, an ebullient senior answered: _____ .

 (A) "I guess so."   (B) "I wouldn't miss it for the world!"

7. The _____ provides live entertainment.

 (A) theater   (B) cinema

8. He is just under five eleven, and when he gives his height, he says: _____ . He does not exaggerate.

 (A) "six feet"   (B) "five ten"

9. We are keeping _____ the suspects; they are under surveillance.

 (A) a lookout for   (B) an eye on

10. Surely you would not want to _____ someone you despise.

 (A) ignore   (B) associate with

EXERCISE 2.8: CONCISE WRITING

Express the thought of each sentence below in no more than four words.

1. Stephanie sometimes makes a statement that goes beyond the limits of the actual truth.

   _____

2. We were greeted in a manner that was lacking in enthusiasm.

   _____

3. Those who hold insurance policies will be compensated for their losses.

   _____

4. A close watch is being kept over our comings and goings.

   _____

5. We pay no attention to remarks that have no sense or significance.

   _____

6. He does not have the specialized skills that she has.

   _____

7. Don't be so overly concerned with trifles and minor details.

   _____

8. They were seen struggling at close quarters in a rough and confused manner.

   _____

9. Michael looks down with contempt on people who are inclined to avoid exertion.

_____

10. People from the United States visit the countries of Asia.

_____

EXERCISE 2.9: CLOSE READING

Carefully read the statements below and answer the questions.

STATEMENTS

A closed-circuit TV screen enabled the security guard to watch the three visitors as they rode up in the elevator.

Joyce was dissatisfied with the way George had set the table because some of the spoons and forks were not exactly parallel.

It took five minutes for Armand to replace the washer of the leaking faucet.

Dan's insurance company paid in full for the damage to Barbara's car.

Roger urged the audience to contribute generously for the relief of the earthquake victims.

The producer said the play had opened to a full house, but Emily, who attended the performance, recalls seeing a number of vacant seats.

Susan protested that Denny's conclusions made no sense at all.

Many residents enthusiastically supported the mayor's program.

The pushing and shoving began when a latecomer tried to get in at the head of the line. Two people were hurt.

Before the match, both rivals had agreed that the loser would pay for the refreshments.

QUESTIONS

1. Who detected an exaggeration? _____

2. Who was finicky? _____

3. Who made a wager? _____

4. Who indemnified someone? _____

5. Who started a scuffle? _____

6. Who was under surveillance? _____

7. Who was ebullient? _____

8. Who was exhorted? _____

9. Who demonstrated mechanical expertise? _____

10. Who stated that something was inane? _____

EXERCISE 2.10: SYNONYMS AND ANTONYMS

A. In the blank space, insert a SYNONYM from pages 16–18 for the italicized word.

_____ 1. These bills *annoy* me.

_____ 2. Charlie Chaplin was a star of the silent *movies*.

_____ 3. The crowd was *exuberant*.

_____ 4. The water was *lukewarm*.

_____ 5. You are acquiring *know-how* in carpentry.

B. In the blank space, insert an ANTONYM from pages 16–18 for the italicized word.

_____ 6. Do not *minimize* your achievements.

_____ 7. The freighter is bound for the *Orient*.

_____ 8. Their behavior was *admirable*.

_____ 9. She said something very *profound*.

_____ 10. The winner will probably *accept* the award.

EXERCISE 2.11: COMPOSITION

Answer in a sentence or two.

1. What is one thing that might baffle a visitor from the Orient. Why?

_____

_____

_____

2. Why should a bank maintain surveillance over an employee with an excessive fondness for wagering?

_____

_____

_____

3. What would you say to someone who exaggerates the damage you did to his or her property and asks to be indemnified?

_____

_____

_____

4. If you are hurt in an accident, why would it be inane to minimize your injury?

_____

_____

_____

5. Does a married employee deserve a higher stipend than an unmarried one with the same expertise? Explain.

_____

_____

_____

EXERCISE 2.12: BRAINTEASERS

Fill in the missing letters.

1. Infants learning to walk need continuous __ __ __ **v e i l** __ __ __ __ __.

2. The problem baffles us. We are bewildered and __ **r u s t** __ __ __ __ __.

3. I noticed the article, but I had no time to __ __ __ **u s e** it.

4. Marco Polo's travels led to trade between China and the __ __ __ __ **d e n** __.

5. If the offer had been reasonable, it would not have been __ __ **u r n** __ __.

6. We cannot praise what you have done because it is not __ __ __ __ **a b l e**.

7. The unemployed watched their savings __ **w i n** __ __ __.

8. Making a movie requires some __ __ **p e r** __ __ __ __ in cinematography.

9. Many remained in their homes, despite repeated __ __ __ __ __ **t a t** __ __ __ s that they leave for higher ground.

10. Stop fussing over petty details. Don't be so __ **a r t** __ __ __ __ __ __.

Part 3.

"Commonsense" Contexts

Do you know what *reel* means in the following sentence?

> It weighs a ton, and strong porters *reel* under its weight.—W. Somerset Maugham

Note that the context contains neither a contrasting nor a similar word to help with the meaning of *reel*. Yet you can tell what it means just by using a bit of **common sense.** You ask yourself:

> "How would I behave if I were to carry, or try to carry, something that feels like a ton?"

You realize that you would "sway dizzily," or "stagger." That is exactly what *reel* means.

Can you give a definition of *severed*? Do you know what *pinioned* means? If not, you should be able to discover their meanings from the following context by applying common sense.

> ". . . I whirled about, grabbing the razor-sharp knife from my belt sheath, and slashed three or four times with a full sweep of my arms in the direction of the touch. By luck I *severed* two of the lassoing arms that were gripping me; in another instant the octopus would have had my two arms *pinioned* and I should have been helpless."
>
> —Victor Berge and Henry W. Lanier

What would you do to the arms of an octopus if you slashed them three or four times with a razor-sharp knife with a full sweep of your arms? You would *cut them off*, of course. *Severed* means "cut off."

And what would happen to your own arms if they were lassoed and gripped by the arms of an octopus? Obviously, they would be *bound fast*, so that you would not be able to use them. *Pinioned* means "bound fast."

The term *"commonsense" context,* as used in this book, means a context that yields the meaning of an unfamiliar word through clues other than a synonym or antonym. Such contexts, as we have seen, involve a bit of reasoning on your part.

Pretest 3

Try to discover the meaning of the italicized word in each of the following "commonsense" contexts:

1. A child wandering through a department store with its mother is *admonished* over and over again not to touch things.—Paul Gallico

   admonished means _____

2. My simple *repast* consisted of a sandwich and an apple.

   repast means _____

3. Restrictions on the use of water will end as soon as our reservoirs are *replenished*.

   replenished means _____

4. A sufferer from *insomnia*, she lies awake most of the night.

   insomnia means _____

5. The judge listened to the arguments of both attorneys before *rendering* her decision.

   rendering means _____

6. And take from seventy springs a *score*,
   It only leaves me fifty more.—A. E. Housman

   score means _____

7. In another year my father will have completed his first *decade* in business; he opened his shop nine years ago.

   decade means _____

8. The blade slipped and cut my hand. Two *sutures* were needed to close the wound.

   sutures means _____

9. When the bald-headed fellow pretended he was the rightful King of France, Huck and Jim believed him. They were quite *gullible*.

   gullible means _____

10. While *confined* here in the Birmingham city jail, I came across your recent statement calling my present activities "unwise and untimely."—Martin Luther King, Jr.

    confined means _____

11. A *probe* into the suspect's financial dealings disclosed evidence of large-scale fraud.

    probe means _____

12. The dealer asked $190 for the radio, and I gave him his price; we did not *haggle*.

    haggle means _____

13. I know you asked for coleslaw, but I forgot to order it. I am sorry for the *lapse*.

    lapse means _____

14. We moved into first place, but our glory was *ephemeral*. The next day we lost a doubleheader and dropped to third.

    ephemeral means _____

15. It was not that he felt any emotion akin to love for Irene Adler. All emotions, and that one particularly, were *abhorrent* to his cold, precise but admirably balanced mind.—Arthur Conan Doyle

    abhorrent means _____

16. Jean greeted everyone, but when I said, "Hello," she walked past me as if I did not exist. The *snub* bothered me the rest of the day.

    snub means _____

17. As I was leaving the meeting, I realized that I had *unwittingly* taken someone else's coat. Embarrassed, I ran back and apologized.

    unwittingly means _____

18. If the bomb had *detonated*, the consequences would have been frightful.

    detonated means _____

19. I *immersed* my hands in warm soapy water to loosen the dirt.

    immersed means _____

20. Perhaps in heaven, but certainly not until then, shall I ever taste anything so *ambrosial* as that fried chicken and coffee ice cream!—Dorothy Canfield Fisher

    ambrosial means _____

Study Your New Words, *Group 3*

You have just attempted to learn the meanings of twenty words from "commonsense" clues in their contexts. Now, for a firmer grasp of these words, study the following:

WORD	MEANING	TYPICAL USE
abhorrent (*adj.*) ab-'hȯr-ənt	(followed by *to*) in conflict; utterly opposed; loathsome; repugnant (*ant.* **admirable**)	Please do not ask me to tell an untruth; lying is *abhorrent* to me.
abhor (*v.*) əb-'hȯr	utterly detest; loathe; hate	
admonish (*v.*) ad-'män-ish	reprove gently but seriously; warn of a fault; caution (*ant.* **commend**)	The teacher *commended* me on my improvement in writing, but *admonished* me for my lateness to class.
admonition (*n.*) ˌad-mə-'nish-ən	gentle warning; friendly reproof	
ambrosial (*adj.*) am-'brō-zhəl	extremely pleasing to taste or smell; delicious; like *ambrosia* (the food of the gods)	Taste this ripe pineapple; it has an *ambrosial* flavor.
confine (*v.*) kən-'fīn	shut up; imprison; keep in narrow, cramped quarters (*ant.* **free**)	On July 14, 1789, a Paris mob freed the prisoners *confined* in the Bastille.
confinement (*n.*) kən-'fīn-mənt	imprisonment	
decade (*n.*) 'dek-ˌād	period of ten years	In the United States, the 1930's were the *decade* of the Great Depression.

detonate (v.)
'det-ə-ˌnāt
explode with suddenness and violence; cause (something) to explode
Fallout showed that a nuclear device had probably been *detonated*.

detonation (n.)
ˌdet-ᵊn-'ā-shən
explosion

ephemeral (adj.)
i-'fem-ə-rəl
lasting one day only; fleeting; transitory; short-lived
(*ant.* **permanent**)
Day-lily blossoms are *ephemeral*; they last only for a day.

gullible (adj.)
'gəl-ə-bəl
easily deceived or cheated; credulous
(*ant.* **astute**)
A few investors were *gullible* enough to buy the worthless stock, but most were too *astute* to be deceived.

gull (v.)
'gəl
deceive; cheat

haggle (v.)
'hag-əl
dispute or argue over a price in a petty way; bargain; wrangle
Have they agreed on a price yet, or are they still *haggling*?

immerse (v.)
im-'ərs
1. plunge or place into a liquid; dip; duck
I filled a basin with lukewarm water and *immersed* my foot in it.

2. engross; absorb
She is *immersed* in her book.

immersion (n.)
im-'ər-zhən
state of being deeply engrossed; absorption

insomnia (n.)
in-'säm-nē-ə
inability to sleep; abnormal wakefulness; sleeplessness
The former hostages now get a normal amount of sleep; during their imprisonment they suffered from *insomnia*.

insomniac (n.)
in-'säm-nē-ˌak
person suffering from insomnia

lapse (n.)
'laps
1. slip; error; accidental mistake; trivial fault
I wrote your name with one *t*, instead of two. Please forgive the *lapse*.

2. interval
He returned after a *lapse* of ten years.

lapse (v.)
'laps
cease being in force; become invalid

probe (n.)
'prōb
critical inquiry into suspected illegal activity; investigation
A *probe* is being conducted to learn what happened to the missing funds.

prober (n.)
'prōb-ər
investigator

render (v.)
'ren-dər
hand down officially; deliver (as a verdict); give
Tension was high in the courtroom as the jury filed in to *render* its verdict.

rendering (n.)
'ren-dər-iŋ
presentation; interpretation

repast (*n.*) ri-'past	food for one occasion of eating; meal	She eats little; her lunch would hardly make a *repast* for a sparrow.
replenish (*v.*) ri-'plen-ish	bring back to condition of being full; refill	Every 200 miles we stopped at a service station to *replenish* the gas tank.
score (*n.*) 'skȯ(ə)r	group or set of twenty; twenty	We have nineteen signatures already, and if we get one more, we'll have an even *score*.
snub (*n.*) 'snəb	act or instance of *snubbing* (treating with contempt); rebuff; slight; insult	Why did Sharon invite everyone but me? Was it just an oversight, or a deliberate *snub*?
snub (*v.*) 'snəb	treat with disdain or contempt; slight	
suture (*n.*) 'sü-chər	strand or fiber used to sew parts of the living body; also, stitch made with such material	A few days after the cut finger was sewn together, the patient returned for the removal of the *sutures*.
unwittingly (*adv.*) ən-'wit-iŋ-lē	unintentionally; by accident; inadvertently (*ant.* **intentionally**)	I *unwittingly* opened a letter addressed to you. Please forgive me.

Apply What You Have Learned

EXERCISE 2.13: SENTENCE COMPLETION

Which choice, A or B, makes the sentence correct? Write the *letter* of your answer in the space provided.

1. When you _____, your body is totally immersed.

   (A) take a shower   (B) swim underwater

2. A probe of the corporation is under way; several of its top officers have been _____.

   (A) questioned   (B) promoted

3. Dawson entered the House in _____ and served for a score of years until his defeat in 1991.

   (A) 1971   (B) 1961

4. The guests _____ about the ambrosial food.

   (A) raved   (B) complained

5. Shoppers will find the selection _____ because the shelves have been replenished.

   (A) poor   (B) excellent

6. If you regularly watch TV at 3 _____, you may be an insomniac.

   (A) A.M.   (B) P.M.

7. I offered my hand, and _____. I cannot forgive the snub.

   (A) we walked off the field together   (B) he didn't take it

8. Did you _____ by yourself, or did someone join you in your repast?

   (A) study   (B) dine

9. For the first decade of her life, she lived on a farm. When she was _____, her family moved to the city.

   (A) ten   (B) eleven

10. They haggled. Joan wanted ten dollars for the used book, and Audrey thought that was _____.

    (A) too high   (B) a fair price

EXERCISE 2.14: CONCISE WRITING

Express the thought of each sentence below in no more than four words.

1. The fame that they achieved lasted only for a very short time.

   _____

2. She stays awake most of the night because she has a great deal of trouble falling asleep.

   _____

3. Some shoppers enjoy arguing over a price in a petty way.

   _____

4. Were the stitches that were used to sew up the wound removed?

   _____

5. No one who is serving a prison term likes being kept in narrow, confined quarters.

   _____

6. It is hard to believe how easy it is for others to cheat him.

   _____

7. Without realizing what I was doing, I treated you with contempt.

   _____

8. We utterly detest the way they have been behaving themselves.

   _____

9. Has the policy that you own ceased to be in force?

   _____

10. The people who had committed the offenses were reproved in a gentle but firm manner.

EXERCISE 2.15: SYNONYMS AND ANTONYMS

A. In the blank space, insert a SYNONYM from pages 25–27 for the italicized word.

_____ **1.** We *bargained* for more than ten minutes.

_____ **2.** She took it as an *insult*.

_____ **3.** Has your glass been *refilled*?

_____ **4.** What causes *sleeplessness*?

_____ **5.** A mental *slip* prevented me from recalling your name.

B. In the blank space, insert an ANTONYM from pages 25–27 for the italicized word.

_____ **6.** It was a *permanent* friendship.

_____ **7.** Your opponent was quite *astute*.

_____ **8.** Did she step on your foot *intentionally*?

_____ **9.** The chief *commended* us.

_____ **10.** On what grounds can the suspect be *freed*?

EXERCISE 2.16: CLOSE READING

Carefully read the statements below and answer the questions.

STATEMENTS

As a child, Roy believed that there were lions, tigers, and fire-breathing dragons in the woods near his home, as well as buried pirate treasure.

Andy consumed a seven-course dinner, but Margie had only a thin slice of cantaloupe.

Louise did not reach her cousin in her first try because she dialed 384-8439, instead of 384-8349.

The florist did exceptionally well on opening day, but after that there were so few customers that he had to go out of business.

Rivers favored an investigation, but Thompson said it would be a waste of time and money.

When Gail was gently reminded that it was getting late and that the bus would soon arrive, she said, ''Mom, I'll be right down.''

Olga had to invent an excuse for her friend, though it was something that she loathed doing.

The payroll clerk was given an office that was scarcely larger than a closet.

While Chuck and Jim were hesitating, wondering about the water temperature, Estelle dived in and swam two laps.

Evan sold forty-two tickets, Stella twenty-nine, and Terry nineteen.

QUESTIONS

1. Who enjoyed ephemeral success? _____

2. Who must have felt confined? _____

3. Who admonished someone? _____

4. Who had an abhorrent experience? _____

5. Who was gullible? _____

6. Who opposed a probe? _____

7. Who had a meager repast? _____

8. Who was short of a score? _____

9. Who was immersed? _____

10. Who committed a lapse? _____

EXERCISE 2.17: COMPOSITION

Answer in a sentence or two.

1. Should employees be required to reach the age of threescore and ten before becoming eligible to retire? Why, or why not?

_____

_____

_____

2. Which could you more readily forgive, a snub or a lapse? Why?

_____

_____

_____

3. Why is a gullible customer not likely to haggle?

_____

_____

_____

4. Should someone who detonates firecrackers on the Fourth of July be admonished? Explain.

_____

_____

_____

5. Describe one of the most ambrosial repasts you ever had.

_____

_____

_____

EXERCISE 2.18: BRAINTEASERS

Fill in the missing letters.

1. We respected them, but they treated us with __ __ __ **t e m p t.**

2. If yellow is __ **o a t h** __ __ __ __ to you, choose another color.

3. Many windows were shattered by the __ __ **t o n** __ __ __ __ __.

4. Liz read the poem beautifully, but your __ **e n d** __ __ __ __ __ was even better.

5. Gregg was so __ __ **g r o s s** __ __ in his book that he didn't see us enter.

6. A team of experienced __ **r o b** __ __ __ is investigating the crash.

7. If you are king or queen for a day, your glory will be __ __ **h e m** __ __ __ __.

8. Most authors are soon forgotten, but a few achieve __ __ __ **m a n** __ __ __ fame.

9. The rebellious inmate was put into solitary __ __ __ **f i n** __ __ __ __ __.

10. It was his first warning. Never before had he been __ __ __ __ __ __ **s h e d.**

Part 4.
Mixed Contexts

This is a review section. It contains contexts of all the types we have met up to now—those with a contrasting word, or a similar word, or a commonsense clue. By this time, you should be able to deal with any of these contexts.

Pretest 4

Try to discover the meaning of the italicized word, and write its meaning in the space provided.

1. . . . then we examined the house itself. We divided its entire surface into compartments, which we numbered, so that none might be missed; then we *scrutinized* each individual square inch throughout the premises, including the two houses immediately adjoining, with the microscope, as before.

    —Edgar Allan Poe

    scrutinized means _____

2. "The two houses adjoining!" I exclaimed. "You must have had a great deal of trouble." "We had; but the reward offered is *prodigious*."

    —Edgar Allan Poe

    prodigious means _____

3. They meant to be of help, but they *hampered* us by getting in our way.

    hampered means _____

4. The vacation *rejuvenated* her. She returned looking years younger.

    rejuvenated means _____

5. If *acquitted*, the accused will walk out of the courtroom a free person.

    acquitted means _____

6. . . . I have known since childhood that faced with a certain kind of simple problem I have sometimes made it so *complex* that there is no way out.—Lillian Hellman

    complex means _____

7. Most of the merchandise was sold early in the season at regular prices. The *residue* is being marked down 50% for clearance.

    residue means _____

8. Each of us carried a small cylinder of oxygen in his pack, but we used it only in emergencies and found that, while its immediate effect was *salutary*, it left us later even worse off than before.
—James Ramsey Ullman

salutary means _____

9. In the twentieth century the automobile *superseded* the horse-drawn vehicle as a means of transportation.

superseded means _____

10. I would never have had the *effrontery* to do what they did. What nerve they had!

effrontery means _____

11. When he *withdrew* his hands from his gloves, the cold wind seemed to leap forward and grasp his unprotected fingers in an iron grip.—Edward A. Herron

withdrew means _____

12. There is great hardship in times of inflation and unemployment; they are *nettlesome* problems.

nettlesome means _____

13. I was about to leave for the beach, *oblivious* of my appointment with the dentist, when Mother reminded me.

oblivious means _____

14. They do some *zany* things. For example, in one scene, having lost their employer's shopping money, they try to steal a chunk of meat from the cage of a hungry lion at the zoo.

zany means _____

15. When the neighbor mainland would be *sweltering*, day and night alike, under a breathless heat, out here on the island there was always a cool wind blowing.—Sir Charles G. D. Roberts

sweltering means _____

16. It was an *excruciating* headache. I had to stay in bed.

excruciating means _____

17. The package was so *unwieldy* that it was hard to get a grip on it, and I dreaded taking it on the bus.

unwieldy means _____

18. We have not complained up to now; but our *forbearance* is coming to an end.

forbearance means _____

19. I thought you would be nervous when you were unexpectedly asked to give the first talk, but you were *unruffled*.

unruffled means _____

20. It was even whispered that Whymper and the Taugwalders had deliberately cut the rope, *consigning* their companions to death to save their own skins.—James Ramsey Ullman

consigning means _____

Study Your New Words, *Group 4*

WORD	MEANING	TYPICAL USE
acquit (*v.*) ə-'kwit	relieve from an accusation; pronounce not guilty; discharge; exculpate (*ant.* **convict**)	Two of the defendants were *convicted* of first-degree murder; the third was *acquitted*.
acquittal (*n.*) ə-'kwit-ᵊl	exculpation; discharge (*ant.* **conviction**)	
complex (*adj.*) käm-'pleks	having varied interrelated parts, and therefore hard to understand; complicated; intricate (*ant.* **simple**)	I would never try to repair a mechanism so *complex* as a wristwatch, but I can easily replace a watchband.
complexity (*n.*) kəm-'plek-sət-ē	difficulty; intricacy (*ant.* **simplicity**)	
consign (*v.*) kən-'sīn	give, transfer, or deliver, as if by signing over; hand over; commit	After they were sentenced, the two convicts were *consigned* to prison.
consignee (*n.*) ˌkän-sə-'nē	person to whom something is shipped	
effrontery (*n.*) i-'frənt-ə-rē	shameless boldness; insolence; gall; temerity	Her cousin had the *effrontery* to come to the party even though he had not been invited.
excruciating (*adj.*) ik-'skrü-shē-ˌāt-iŋ	causing great pain or anguish; agonizing; unbearably painful	I had feared that the drilling of the tooth would be *excruciating*, but I barely felt any pain.
forbearance (*n.*) fȯr-'ber-əns	act of forbearing (refraining); abstaining; leniency; patience (*ant.* **anger**)	If you stepped on my foot by accident, I would show *forbearance*. But if you tripped me on purpose, I would not be able to repress my *anger*.
hamper (*v.*) 'ham-pər	interfere with; hinder; impede (*ant.* **aid**)	We tried to leave the stadium quickly, but the dense crowd *hampered* our progress.
nettlesome (*adj.*) 'net-ᵊl-səm	literally, full of *nettles* (plants with stinging hairs); irritating; causing annoyance or vexation	How can we safely dispose of nuclear wastes? So far, no satisfactory answer has been found to this *nettlesome* question.
oblivious (*adj.*) ə-'bli-vē-əs	(usually followed by *of*) forgetful; unmindful; not aware	She had promised to wait, but she walked off without me, *oblivious* of her promise.
oblivion (*n.*) ə-'bliv-ē-ən	condition of being forgotten or unknown	

prodigious (*adj.*) prə-'dij-əs	extraordinary in amount or size; enormous; gigantic (*ant.* **tiny**)	In one year, there was a *prodigious* increase in the cost of oil; prices nearly tripled.
prodigy (*n.*) 'präd-ə-jē	person of extraordinary talent or ability; wonder	
rejuvenate (*v.*) ri-'jü-və-ˌnāt	make young or youthful again; give new vigor to; reinvigorate; refresh	A good night's sleep will *rejuvenate* you, and you will wake up feeling refreshed.
residue (*n.*) 'rez-ə-ˌd(y)ü	whatever is left after a part is taken, disposed of, or gone; remainder; rest	The floodwater receded, leaving a *residue* of mud in the streets.
residual (*adj.*) ri-'zij-ə-wəl	remaining after a part is used or taken	
salutary (*adj.*) 'sal-yə-ˌter-ē	favorable to health; healthful; curative; beneficial (*ant.* **deleterious**)	A winter in the South had a *salutary* effect on Manny; his cough disappeared. The icy Northern climate would have been *deleterious* to his health.
scrutinize (*v.*) 'skrüt-ᵊn-ˌīz	examine very closely; inspect	After *scrutinizing* my driver's license to see if there were any prior violations, the officer returned it to me.
scrutiny (*n.*) 'scrüt-ᵊn-ē	examination; inspection; review	
supersede (*v.*) ˌsü-pər-'sēd	force out of use; displace; supplant; replace	In many businesses, paper wrapping has been *superseded* by plastic.
sweltering (*adj.*) 'swel-tə-riŋ	oppressively hot; torrid (*ant.* **frigid**)	It was a *sweltering* day; everyone was perspiring.
swelter (*v.*) 'swel-tər	suffer from oppressive heat	
unruffled (*adj.*) ən-'rəf-əld	not upset or agitated; calm; cool; unflustered (*ant.* **discomposed**)	Most of us were *discomposed* by the new developments, but Elinor remained *unruffled*.
unwieldy (*adj.*) ən-'wēl-dē	hard to *wield* (handle) because of size or weight; unmanageable; bulky; cumbersome	Will you please help me dispose of the empty refrigerator carton? It is too *unwieldy* for one person to carry out.
unwieldiness (*n.*) ˌən-'wēl-dē-nəs	bulkiness	
withdraw (*v.*) with-'drȯ	1. take back; remove (*ant.* **deposit**) 2. draw back; go away; retreat; leave (*ant.* **advance**)	I *deposited* a check for $87.50 and *withdrew* $50 in cash. As the officers *advanced* toward the scene, the mob *withdrew*.

withdrawal (*n.*)   departure (*ant.* **approach**)
with- 'drȯ-əl

zany (*adj.*) 'zā-nē	having the characteristics of a clown; mildly insane; crazy; clownish	Warren would squirt you with a water pistol for a laugh; he has a *zany* sense of humor.
zany (*n.*) 'zā-nē	clown; buffoon	

Apply What You Have Learned

EXERCISE 2.19: SENTENCE COMPLETION

Which choice, A or B, makes the sentence correct? Write the *letter* of your answer in the space provided.

1. Your zany brother came to the meeting _____.

   (A) with a list of complaints   (B) in a gorilla costume

2. The treatments were salutary; the patient's condition _____.

   (A) improved   (B) worsened

3. Someone in the sweltering auditorium suggested that we turn off the _____.

   (A) air conditioning   (B) heat

4. After saying the pie you baked was not so delicious, Marge had the effrontery to _____.

   (A) apologize for her remark   (B) ask for a second helping

5. They thought that when they found _____, they would become rejuvenated.

   (A) Captain Kidd's treasure   (B) the Fountain of Youth

6. A superseded regulation _____.

   (A) is still in effect   (B) should be disregarded

7. In the imaginary country of Lilliput, where people were no more than six _____ tall, an ordinary human like Gulliver must have seemed prodigious.

   (A) inches   (B) feet

8. After his acquittal, the suspect _____.

   (A) requested a new trial   (B) thanked the jury

9. When your sister is criticized, she shows forbearance; she _____.

   (A) becomes enraged   (B) listens patiently

10. Oblivious of the sudden drop in temperature, I left the house _____.

    (A) without taking a sweater   (B) thinking it would snow

EXERCISE 2.20: CONCISE WRITING

Express the thought of each sentence below in no more than four words.

1. The instructions that you have drawn up are not easy to understand.

   _____

2. Who is the person to whom the goods are to be shipped?

   _____

3. What are the reasons for their being found not guilty?

   _____

4. She examined very closely the application that you sent in.

   _____

5. Some packages are hard to handle because they are too big or too heavy.

   _____

6. The pain that he had was so agonizing that he could not bear it.

   _____

7. The forces that have invaded the country must draw back.

   _____

8. She has problems that are causing her a great deal of vexation.

   _____

9. The part that is left is not of much importance.

   _____

10. Everyone looks with contempt on the shamelessly bold manner in which they behave themselves.

   _____

EXERCISE 2.21: SYNONYMS AND ANTONYMS

A. In the blank space, insert a SYNONYM from pages 34–36 for the italicized word.

_____ 1. They remained *cool* throughout the crisis.

_____ 2. She chose wallpaper with an *intricate* pattern.

_____ 3. The situation is rapidly becoming *unmanageable*.

_____ 4. Would you have had the *temerity* to open someone else's mail?

_____ **5.** He ordered the most expensive dinner, *unmindful* of the cost.

B. In the blank space, insert an ANTONYM from pages 34–36 for the italicized word.

_____ **6.** The company ended the year with a *tiny* profit.

_____ **7.** Why should the suspect have been *convicted*?

_____ **8.** The suggested remedy may have *deleterious* effects.

_____ **9.** We cannot remain in this *frigid* room.

_____ **10.** The security staff *aided* our efforts to gain admission.

EXERCISE 2.22: CLOSE READING

Carefully read the statements below and answer the questions.

STATEMENTS

When Martin asked permission to look through the files for the missing information, Muriel said, "Not now. Come back next week."

My aunt is more relaxed now that she has given up smoking, and her health has improved.

The recreation supervisor was able to find a way to stop the almost daily bitter fights we were having over the use of the tennis courts.

Though Simpson is still on the payroll, someone else has been put in charge.

Paul had been on the committee for a year, and we wanted him to stay, but he left.

When Jason's father died, Medea, an enchantress, brought him back to life and made him young again.

Humming the "Blue Danube Waltz," Tony danced around the room with a mopstick for a partner.

When the carpenter had finished, his helper swept up the sawdust and tossed it into the fireplace.

Valerie has not paid back the money she borrowed from Eva last month, but so far Eva has said nothing.

In his poem about the outlaw Jesse James, William Rose Benét wrote, "He was ten foot tall when he stood in his boots."

QUESTIONS

1. Who was superseded? _____

2. Who withdrew? _____

3. Who disposed of a residue? _____

4. Who was alleged to be of prodigious stature? _____

5. Who hampered someone? _____

6. Who resolved a nettlesome problem? _____

7. Who was rejuvenated? _____

8. Who acted like a zany? _____

9. Who showed forbearance? _____

10. Who made a salutary move? _____

EXERCISE 2.23: COMPOSITION

Answer in a sentence or two.

1. How much forbearance should we have with a zany driver? Explain.

_____

_____

_____

2. May we conclude that a person who seems unruffled has no nettlesome problems? Explain.

_____

_____

_____

3. Is it salutary to sunbathe for hours under a sweltering sun? Why, or why not?

_____

_____

_____

4. Should an official who hampers an investigation be superseded? Explain.

_____

_____

_____

5. Would you be joking or serious if you said that a friend who is oblivious of faces, names, and appointments has a prodigious memory? Why?

_____

_____

_____

EXERCISE 2.24: BRAINTEASERS

Fill in the missing letters.

1. Greasy foods leave a(n) __ __ __ __ **d u a l** film on dishes and silverware.

2. While we are sweltering here, people are shivering in __ **r i g** __ __ temperatures up north.

3. There is still plenty of life left in the old car. It is much too early to __ __ __ **s i g n** it to the scrap heap.

4. We cannot get Olly to stop clowning. He enjoys making a **b u f f** __ __ __ of himself.

5. Our national debt has reached __ __ __ **d i g** __ __ __ __ proportions, and it is still soaring.

6. Since the jury found no evidence against the defendants, it voted to __ __ __ __ __ **p a t** __ them of all charges.

7. After spurning our offers of assistance, the members of the committee had the __ __ **m e r i t** __ to say that we had never offered to help them.

8. Some of the concepts in advanced physics may be hard to understand at first because of their

    __ __ __ __ __ **e x i t** __.

9. One way to find a lost needle in a pile rug is to __ __ **r u t** __ __ __ __ __ the area where it was dropped.

10. Her brother was **d i s c o** __ __ __ __ __ __. Obviously, something had upset him.

CHAPTER 3

Building Vocabulary Through Central Ideas

One way to expand your vocabulary is to study words related to a central idea. For example, you can learn **bliss, delectable, ecstasy, elation,** and **jubilation** as "joy" words, and **chagrin, compunction, dejected, disconsolate,** and **lamentable** as "sorrow" words. Grouping lesson words in this way may make vocabulary study easier and more interesting.

Here are a few suggestions for getting the most out of this chapter.

1. Pay careful attention to each illustrative sentence. Then construct, at least in your mind, a similar sentence of your own.

2. Do the drill exercises thoughtfully, not mechanically. Review the words you miss.

3. Deliberately *use* your new vocabulary as soon as possible in appropriate situations—in chats with friends, class discussions, letters, and compositions. Only by *exercising* new words will you succeed in making them part of your active vocabulary.

1. Joy, Pleasure

WORD	MEANING	TYPICAL USE
bliss (*n.*) 'blis	perfect happiness	The young movie star could conceive of no greater *bliss* than winning an "Oscar."
blissful (*adj.*) 'blis-fəl	very happy	The soldiers' reunion with their families was a *blissful* occasion.
blithe (*adj.*) 'blīth	1. merry; joyous 2. heedless	He was so enraptured with the scenery that he drove right through the intersection in *blithe* disregard of the "Full Stop" sign.
buoy (*v.*) 'bü-ē	keep afloat; raise the spirits of; encourage	Your encouragement *buoyed* us and gave us hope.
buoyant (*adj.*) 'bȯi-ənt	1. cheerful 2. able to float	We need your *buoyant* companionship to lift us from boredom. The raft is sinking; it is not *buoyant*.

complacency (*n.*)
kəm-'plās-ᵊn-sē

self-satisfaction; smugness

Don't be too pleased with yourself; *complacency* is dangerous.

complacent (*adj.*)
kəm-'plās-ᵊnt

too pleased with oneself—often without awareness of possible dangers or defects; self-satisfied; smug

We should not be *complacent* about our security; we must be alert to potential threats.

convivial (*adj.*)
kən-'viv-ē-əl

1. fond of eating and drinking with friends
2. sociable

Our *convivial* host hates to dine alone.

conviviality (*n.*)
ˌkən-ˌviv-'ē-al-ə-tē

sociability

We enjoy the *conviviality* of holiday get-togethers.

delectable (*adj.*)
di-'lek-tə-bəl

very pleasing; delightful

The food was *delectable*; we enjoyed every morsel.

ecstasy (*n.*)
'ek-stə-sē

state of overwhelming joy; rapture

If we win tomorrow, there will be *ecstasy*; if we lose, gloom.

ecstatic (*adj.*)
ek-'stat-ik

in ecstasy; enraptured

The victors were *ecstatic*.

elated (*adj.*)
i-'lāt-əd

in high spirits; joyful

Except for my sister, who misses the old neighborhood, the family is *elated* with our new living quarters.

elation (*n.*)
i-'lā-shən

state of being elated; euphoria

Unfortunately, our *elation* was short-lived.

frolic (*v.*)
'fräl-ik

play and run about happily; have fun; romp

Very young children need a safe place to *frolic*.

frolicsome (*adj.*)
'fräl-ik-səm

full of merriment; playful

The clown's *frolicsome* antics amused the children.

gala (*adj.*)
'gā-lə

characterized by festivity

The annual Mardi Gras in New Orleans is a *gala* carnival of parades and merriment.

jocund (*adj.*)
'jäk-ənd

merry; cheerful

Our neighbor is a *jocund* fellow who tells amusing anecdotes.

jubilant (*adj.*)
'jü-bə-lənt

showing great joy; rejoicing; exultant

The defendant's friends are *jubilant* over her acquittal.

jubilation (*n.*)
ˌjü-bə-'lā-shən

rejoicing; exultation

On election night there usually is *jubilation* at the campaign headquarters of the victorious party.

2. Sadness

ascetic (*adj.*) ə-'set-ik	shunning pleasures; self-denying	The *ascetic* Puritans rigidly suppressed many forms of recreation.
ascetic (*n.*) ə-'set-ik	person who shuns pleasures and lives simply	Carl never goes to the movies, plays, or parties. He must be an *ascetic*.
chagrin (*n.*) shə-'grin	embarrassment; mortification; disappointment	Imagine my *chagrin* when I learned that I had not been invited to the party!
chagrined (*adj.*) shə-'grind	ashamed; mortified	When my blunder was pointed out to me, I was deeply *chagrined*.
compunction (*n.*) kəm-'pəŋ(k)-shən	regret; remorse; misgiving; qualm	We had no *compunction* about turning in the old car because it had become undependable.
contrite (*adj.*) kən-'trīt	showing deep regret and sorrow for wrongdoing; deeply penitent; repentant	Believing the young offender to be *contrite*, the dean decided to give him another chance.
contrition (*n.*) kən-'trish-ən	repentance	The ringleader showed no *contrition*, but his accomplices have expressed sorrow for their misdeeds.
dejected (*adj.*) di-'jek-təd	sad; in low spirits; depressed	We are elated when our team wins, but *dejected* when it loses.
dejection (*n.*) di-'jek-shən	lowness of spirits; sadness; depression	Cheer up. There is no reason for *dejection*.
disconsolate (*adj.*) dis-'kän-sə-lət	cheerless; inconsolable	The mother could not stop her *disconsolate* son from sobbing over the loss of his dog.
disgruntled (*adj.*) dis-'grənt-ᵊld	in bad humor; displeased; discontented	From her *disgruntled* expression I could tell she was not satisfied with my explanation.
doleful (*adj.*) 'dōl-fəl	causing grief or sadness; mournful; dolorous	The refugee told a *doleful* tale of hunger and persecution.
glum (*adj.*) 'gləm	moody; gloomy; dour	As they emerged from the conference, both the Mayor and the Governor were *glum* and refused to talk to reporters.
lament (*v.*) lə-'ment	mourn; deplore	We *lament* the loss of life, and we sympathize with the victims' families.

lamentable (*adj.*)
'lam-ən-tə-bəl

pitiable; rueful

He described the *lamentable* hardships of the three miners trapped in the underground chamber.

maudlin (*adj.*)
'mȯd-lən

weakly sentimental and tearful

After singing a couple of *maudlin* numbers, the quartet was asked for something more cheerful.

nostalgia (*n.*)
nə-'stal-jə

1. homesickness

2. yearning for the past

Toward the end of a vacation away from home, we usually experience a feeling of *nostalgia*.
In moments of *nostalgia*, I long for the good old days.

nostalgic (*adj.*)
nä-'stal-jik

homesick

When away from home for too long, we tend to become *nostalgic*.

pathetic (*adj.*)
pə-'thet-ik

arousing pity

Despite his *pathetic* condition, the released hostage had a ready smile.

pathos (*n.*)
'pā-thäs

quality in events or in art (literature, music, etc.) that arouses our pity

The young seamstress who precedes Sydney Carton to the guillotine adds to the *pathos* of A TALE OF TWO CITIES.

pensive (*adj.*)
'pen-siv

thoughtful in a sad way; melancholy

Unlike her cheerful, outgoing sister, Elizabeth was *pensive* and shy.

plight (*n.*)
'plīt

unfortunate state; predicament

Numerous offers of assistance were received after the *plight* of the distressed family was publicized.

poignant (*adj.*)
'pȯi-nyənt

painfully touching; piercing

One of the most *poignant* scenes in MACBETH occurs when Macduff learns that his wife and children have been slaughtered.

sullen (*adj.*)
'səl-ən

resentfully silent; glum; morose; gloomy

The *sullen* suspect refused to give his name and address.

throes (*n. pl.*)
'thrōz

anguish; pangs

Fortunate are those who have never experienced the *throes* of separation from a loved one.

tribulation (*n.*)
,trib-yə-'lā-shən

suffering; distress

The 1845 potato famine was a time of great *tribulation* in Ireland.

3. Stoutness

burly (*adj.*)
'bər-lē
strongly and heavily built; husky
(*ant.* **lank**)
Extra-large football uniforms were ordered to outfit our *burly* linemen.

buxom (*adj.*)
'bək-səm
plump and attractive
By the side of her skinny city cousin, the farm girl looked radiant and *buxom*.

cherubic (*adj.*)
chə-'rü-bik
chubby and innocent-looking; like a *cherub* (angel in the form of a child)
Your well-nourished nephew, despite his *cherubic* face, can be quite mischievous.

obese (*adj.*)
ō-'bēs
extremely overweight; corpulent; portly
(*ant.* **skinny**)
For a long, healthy life, one should give up smoking and avoid becoming *obese*.

obesity (*n.*)
o-'bē-sət-ē
excessive body weight; corpulence
Dieting under professional guidance may help reduce *obesity*.

pudgy (*adj.*)
'pəj-ē
short and plump; chubby
This ring is too small for a *pudgy* finger.

4. Thinness

attenuate (*v.*)
ə-'ten-yə-ˌwāt
make thin; weaken
Photographs of President Lincoln reveal how rapidly the cares of leadership aged and *attenuated* him.

emaciated (*adj.*)
i-'mā-shē-ˌāt-əd
made unnaturally thin; abnormally lean because of starvation or illness
(*ant.* **fleshy**)
Emaciated by his illness, the patient found, on his recovery, that his clothes were too big.

haggard (*adj.*)
'hag-ərd
careworn; gaunt
Haggard from their long ordeal, the rescued miners were rushed to the hospital for treatment and rest.

lank (*adj.*)
'laŋk
lean; ungracefully tall; lanky
(*ant.* **burly**)
Every basketball team longs for a *lank*, agile center who can control the boards.

svelte (*adj.*)
'svelt
slender; lithe
Ballet dancers observe a strict diet to maintain their *svelte* figures.

5. Flattery

adulation (*n.*)
ˌad-yə-'lā-shən

excessive praise; flattery

True leaders can distinguish sincere praise from blind *adulation.*

blandishment (*n.*)
'blan-dish-mənt

word or deed of mild flattery; allurement; enticement

Suitors often use terms of endearment, flowers, and similar *blandishments.*

cajole (*v.*)
kə-'jōl

persuade by pleasant words; wheedle; coax

My sister *cajoled* Dad into raising her allowance.

cajolery (*n.*)
kə-'jōl-ə-rē

persuasion by flattery; wheedling; coaxing

The sly fox used *cajolery* to gain his ends.

curry (*v.*) **favor** (*n.*)
'kər-ē 'fā-və(r)

seek to gain favor by flattery

The candidate tried to *curry favor* with the voters by praising their intelligence and patriotism.

fulsome (*adj.*)
'fúl-səm

offensive because of insincerity; repulsive; disgusting

How can you endure the *fulsome* praises of your subordinate who lauds your every decision, right or wrong?

ingratiate (*v.*)
in-'grā-shē-ˌāt

work (oneself) into favor

By trying to respond to every question, the new pupil tried to *ingratiate* herself with the teacher.

lackey (*n.*)
'lak-ē

follower who carries out another's wishes like a servant; toady

The queen could never get a frank opinion from the *lackeys* surrounding her, for they would always agree with her.

obsequious (*adj.*)
əb-'sē-kwē-əs

showing excessive willingness to serve; subservient; fawning

The *obsequious* subordinates vied with one another in politeness and obedience, each hoping to win the director's favor.

sycophant (*n.*)
'sik-ə-fənt

parasitic flatterer; truckler

Sycophants live at the expense of vain persons who enjoy flattery.

truckle (*v.*)
'trək-əl

submit in a subservient manner to a superior; fawn; make a doormat of oneself

Some employees, unfortunately, gain promotion by *truckling* to their supervisors.

Apply What You Have Learned

EXERCISE 3.1: SYNONYMS

In the space before each word or expression in column I, write the *letter* of its correct synonym from column II.

	COLUMN I		COLUMN II
_____	1. delightful	(A)	predicament
_____	2. arousing pity	(B)	attenuated
_____	3. plight	(C)	nostalgia
_____	4. mild flattery	(D)	haggard
_____	5. careworn	(E)	delectable
_____	6. self-denying	(F)	bliss
_____	7. perfect happiness	(G)	lackey
_____	8. weakened	(H)	blandishment
_____	9. subservient follower	(I)	pathetic
_____	10. homesickness	(J)	ascetic

EXERCISE 3.2: UNRELATED WORDS

Write the *letter* of the word unrelated in meaning to the other words on the line.

1. (A) ecstatic	(B) jubilant	(C) rapturous	(D) pensive	_____
2. (A) svelte	(B) slender	(C) slippery	(D) lithe	_____
3. (A) comedian	(B) lackey	(C) flatterer	(D) sycophant	_____
4. (A) tribulation	(B) insincerity	(C) suffering	(D) pangs	_____
5. (A) cajolery	(B) gloominess	(C) dejection	(D) melancholy	_____
6. (A) elation	(B) frolicsomeness	(C) euphoria	(D) adulation	_____
7. (A) wheedle	(B) attenuate	(C) ingratiate	(D) fawn	_____
8. (A) pathos	(B) pity	(C) complacency	(D) compassion	_____
9. (A) portly	(B) burly	(C) buxom	(D) contrite	_____
10. (A) jovial	(B) jocund	(C) blithe	(D) disconsolate	_____

EXERCISE 3.3: CONCISE WRITING

Express the thought of each sentence below in no more than four words. The first sentence has been rewritten as a sample.

1. What is the reason for your being in bad humor?

   <u>**Why are you disgruntled?**</u>

2. I was deeply regretful and full of sorrow for what I had done.

   _____

3. We look down on praise that is offered without sincerity.

   _____

4. Mom excels in the art of using pleasant words to persuade others.

   _____

5. They are altogether too willing to serve and obey their superiors.

   _____

6. The one who does the carpentry work is strongly and sturdily built.

   _____

7. Those who survived were little more than skin and bones.

   _____

8. The encouragement that we received from you brought our spirits up high.

   _____

9. A large number refused to take notice of the unfortunate situation that they saw we were in.

   _____

10. It is dangerous to be in a state of mind in which one is too satisfied with oneself.

   _____

EXERCISE 3.4: BRAINTEASERS

Fill in the missing letters.

1. The workers are __ __ __ __ __ __ **t e n t** __ __ because they did not get a raise.

2. No one smiled. It was a(n) __ __ __ __ __ __ __ **h o l y** occasion.

3. Whenever they try to __ __ __ **r a t** __ __ __ __ themselves with us, we suspect they are looking for a favor.

4. I was __ __ __ **g r i n** __ __, when I went to pay for my lunch, to find that I had left my money
at home.

5. We have no __ __ __ **p u n** __ __ __ __ __ about not waiting for Sally because she has never
waited for us.

6. The stolen car was in such **l a m e** __ __ __ __ __ __ condition when it was recovered that its
owner was moved to tears.

7. Anyone who enjoys adulation is an easy prey for __ __ __ __ __ __ **a n t s.**

8. Don't expect them to cater to your wishes like servants. They are not your __ __ __ **k e y s.**

9. This shop specializes in clothes for the tall and the __ **o r** __ __ __.

10. It is unwise to adopt a(n) __ __ __ __ **t i c** lifestyle of "all work and no play."

EXERCISE 3.5: SENTENCE COMPLETION

Fill each blank with the most appropriate word from the vocabulary list below.

VOCABULARY LIST

poignant	cajole	tribulation
buxom	burly	emaciated
throes	pathos	gala
fulsome	jubilation	elated
obesity	remorse	glum

1. The _____ movers lifted the piano with surprising ease.

2. After the game, there was wild _____ as supporters rushed onto the field
to congratulate their heroes.

3. The President looked _____ as he announced the disappointing news.

4. To a young child, a birthday is certainly a(n) _____ occasion.

5. Newspapers reported the _____ details of the futile rescue attempt.

6. The new supervisor was repelled by the _____ compliments of some of her
subordinates.

7. When Mr. Norwood was stopped for a traffic violation, he tried to _____
the officer into not writing a ticket.

8. The _____ appearance of the liberated prisoners shocked the world.

9. At the trial one of the suspects wept repeatedly, but the other showed no _____.

10. Many people watch their diets and exercise regularly to avoid _____.

EXERCISE 3.6: COMPOSITION

Answer in a sentence or two.

1. Who is more likely to do well in a marathon, a lank runner or a burly one? Why?

_____

_____

_____

_____

2. Give an example of something that can be done to buoy the spirits of a dejected friend.

_____

_____

_____

_____

3. Name two delectable foods that may have to be given up for a svelte waistline, and suggest substitutes for those foods.

_____

_____

_____

_____

4. If you accidentally hurt someone, would you be complacent or contrite? Explain.

_____

_____

_____

_____

5. Would you enjoy working for a company where some of the employees are obsequious and truckle to the boss? Explain.

_____

_____

_____

_____

EXERCISE 3.7: ANALOGIES

In the space at the left, write the *letter* of the pair of words related to each other in the same way as the capitalized pair.

Sample

___d___ ECSTASY : JOY

        a. thrift : wealth   *d.* terror : fear
        b. certainty : doubt   *e.* frigid : cold
        c. fondness : adoration

Solution

The first step is to find the relationship in the capitalized pair. Obviously ECSTASY is a state of overwhelming JOY. If we designate ECSTASY by the letter X, and JOY by the letter Y, we can express the ECSTASY : JOY relationship by saying, "X is a state of overwhelming Y."

a. Thrift : Wealth

> *Thrift* is a means by which one may acquire *wealth*. *Thrift* is NOT a state of overwhelming *wealth*.

b. Certainty : Doubt

> *Certainty* is the opposite of *doubt*. It is definitely NOT a state of overwhelming *doubt*.

c. Fondness : Adoration

> *Fondness* is a much milder expression of liking than *adoration*. Note that the trouble with this pair is the order. If it were reversed (ADORATION : FONDNESS), this pair would be a correct answer because *adoration* is a state of overwhelming *fondness*.

d. Terror : Fear

> *Terror* is a state of overwhelming *fear*. This choice looks very good, but let us also check the final pair.

e. Frigid : Cold

> *Frigid* is overwhelmingly *cold*. The relationship is correct. However, *frigid* and *cold* are adjectives, whereas the capitalized pair, ECSTASY : JOY, are nouns. If choice *e* were changed to FRIGIDITY : COLD (*nouns*), it would be acceptable.

Note that *terror* and *fear* in choice *d* are both nouns. This, plus the fact that *terror* is a state of overwhelming *fear*, makes *d* the correct choice.

_____ **1.** NOSTALGIA : PAST

        a. regret : deed   *d.* absence : presence
        b. yearning : eternity   *e.* memory : forgetfulness
        c. anticipation : future

_____ **2.** SYCOPHANT : SINCERITY

        a. thief : cleverness   *d.* friend : loyalty
        b. deceiver : truth   *e.* hero : courage
        c. coward : fear

_____ 3. ASCETIC : PLEASURE

      a. politician : votes   *d.* root : water
      b. plant : light   *e.* hermit : society
      c. scientist : truth

_____ 4. FOOD : OBESITY

      a. slip : fall   *d.* rainfall : flood
      b. spark : explosion   *e.* landslide : earthquake
      c. fatigue : work

_____ 5. DISCONSOLATE : CHEER

      a. intrepid : fear   *d.* frolicsome : merriment
      b. compassionate : sympathy *e.* plaintive : sorrow
      c. repentant : regret

Going Over the Answers

Since this is our first exercise in analogies, check your answers with the following, paying careful attention to the reasoning involved.

QUESTION	RELATIONSHIP OF X AND Y	ANSWER AND EXPLANATION
1.	*Nostalgia* is a yearning for the *past*.	*c.* *Anticipation* is a yearning for the *future*.
2.	A *sycophant* makes a pretense of *sincerity*.	*b.* A *deceiver* makes a pretense of *truth*.
3.	An *ascetic* shuns *pleasure*.	*e.* A *hermit* shuns *society*.
4.	Excessive *food* intake may cause *obesity*.	*d.* Excessive *rainfall* may cause a *flood*.
5.	A *disconsolate* person is without *cheer*.	*a.* An *intrepid* person is without *fear*.

6. Animal

WORD	MEANING	TYPICAL USE
apiary (*n.*) ′ā-pē-,er-ē	place where bees are kept	A beekeeper maintains an *apiary*.
aviary (*n.*) ′ā-vē-,er-ē	place where birds are kept	Some interesting birds of prey are confined in an *aviary* on the zoo grounds.
badger (*v.*) ′baj-ə(r)	tease; annoy; nag (originally to harass a trapped badger)	*Badgered* by the children's persistent pleas, their parents finally relented and allowed them to go to the movies.
halcyon (*adj.*) ′hal-sē-ən	calm; peaceful (from *halcyon*, a bird thought to calm the waves)	Most adults nostalgically recall the *halcyon* days of their youth.
lionize (*v.*) ′lī-ə-,nīz	treat as highly important	With the first publication of his poems, Robert Burns gained immediate fame and was *lionized* by Edinburgh society.
menagerie (*n.*) mə-′naj-ə-rē	place where animals are kept and trained; collection of wild animals	P. T. Barnum called his traveling circus, museum, and *menagerie* ''the greatest show on earth.''
molt (*v.*) ′mōlt	shed feathers, skin, hair, etc.	Birds, mammals, and snakes *molt* periodically.
ornithology (*n.*) ,ȯr-nə-′thäl-ə-jē	study of birds	Ellen developed an interest in *ornithology* after reading John Burroughs' writings on birds.
parasite (*n.*) ′par-ə-,sīt	animal, plant, or person living on others	Instead of seeking employment, he preferred to live as a *parasite* on his brother.
parasitic (*adj.*) ,par-ə-′sit-ik	living at the expense of another; sponging	Fleas are *parasitic* insects.
parrot (*v.*) ′par-ət	repeat mechanically, like a *parrot* (tropical bird that imitates human speech)	Does he really understand what he is saying, or is he merely *parroting* his teacher?
scavenger (*n.*) ′skav-ən-jə(r)	animal or person removing refuse, decay, etc.	Sea gulls are useful harbor *scavengers*, since they feed on garbage.

7. Health, Medicine

antidote (*n.*)
'ant-i-ˌdōt

remedy for a poison or evil

A bottle containing poison must have the *antidote* specified on the label.

astringent (*n.*)
ə-'strin-jənt

substance that shrinks tissues and checks flow of blood

According to its label, this after-shave lotion acts as an *astringent* by helping to check the bleeding of nicks and scrapes.

astringent (*adj.*)
ə-'strin-jənt

1. severe; stern
2. causing contraction

Instead of mild criticism, I got an *astringent* rebuke.

benign (*adj.*)
bi-'nīn

1. not dangerous (*ant.* **malignant**)

2. gentle; kindly

The patient was relieved to learn that his tumor was *benign*, not *malignant*.
The doorman is a kind, elderly man with a *benign* smile.

convalesce (*v.*)
ˌkän-və-'les

recover health after illness; recuperate

After the appendectomy you will have to *convalesce* for about a week before returning to school.

convalescent (*n.*)
ˌkän-və-'les-ᵊnt

person recovering from sickness

A *convalescent* should not be taxed with chores.

fester (*v.*)
'fes-tə(r)

form pus; rankle; rot; putrefy

When a wound *festers*, it becomes inflamed, swollen, and painful.

hypochondriac (*n.*)
ˌhī-pə-'kän-drē-ˌak

one who is morbidly anxious about personal health, or suffering from imagined illness

The *hypochondriac* often interprets a normal condition as a symptom of serious illness.

immunity (*n.*)
im-'yü-nət-ē

1. resistance (to a disease)

2. freedom (from an obligation)

Most people acquire life-long *immunity* to German measles once they have had that disease.
Federal and state properties within the city limits enjoy *immunity* from taxation.

immunize (*v.*)
'im-yə-ˌnīz

make *immune* (resistant to a disease)

Infants receive a series of injections to *immunize* them against serious childhood diseases.

lesion (*n.*)
'lē-zhən

injury; hurt

The slightest *lesion* on a tree's bark, if left untended, may kill the tree.

malignant (*adj.*)
mə-'lig-nənt

1. threatening to cause death (*ant.* **benign**)

An emergency operation was scheduled to remove the *malignant* tissues.

	2. very evil	The brothers came under the *malignant* influence of a neighborhood criminal who taught them to steal.
morbid (*adj.*) 'mȯr-bəd	1. gruesome	In describing his illness, he discreetly omitted the *morbid* details.
	2. having to do with disease	One sign of Lady Macbeth's *morbid* condition is that she was troubled by hallucinations and fantasies.
pestilential (*adj.*) ˌpes-tə-'len-shəl	1. morally harmful	Parents, teachers, and spiritual leaders have attacked certain TV programs as *pestilential*.
	2. pertaining to a *pestilence* (plague)	The flu is a *pestilential* disease.
regimen (*n.*) 'rej-ə-mən	set of rules, esp. to improve health	After the operation I had to follow a *regimen* of diet and exercise prescribed by my physician.
salubrious (*adj.*) sə-'lü-brē-əs	healthful	Southern Florida's *salubrious* climate attracts many convalescents.
sebaceous (*adj.*) si-'bā-shəs	greasy; secreting *sebum* (fatty matter secreted by the glands of the skin)	The *sebaceous* glands in the skin secrete an oily substance essential for skin health.
therapeutic (*adj.*) ˌther-ə-'pyüt-ik	curative	The "get-well" cards have had a *therapeutic* effect on the hospitalized patient.
toxic (*adj.*) 'täk-sik	poisonous	Operating a gasoline engine in a closed garage may cause death, as the exhaust fumes are dangerously *toxic*.
unguent (*n.*) 'əŋ-gwənt	salve; ointment	Flora's skin irritation was relieved after she applied the *unguent* prescribed by her physician.
virulent (*adj.*) 'vir-(y)ə-lənt	1. extremely poisonous; deadly; venomous 2. very bitter	Some insecticides and weed killers contain arsenic, a *virulent* substance. The rebels show a *virulent* antagonism to the present ruler.
viral (*adj.*) 'vī-rəl	caused by a *virus*	The flu is a *viral* disease.
virus (*n.*) 'vī-rəs	1. disease-causing substance too small to be seen through a microscope 2. corruptive force	Diseases like AIDS, rabies, smallpox, and polio are caused by a *virus*. What further measures are needed to combat the *virus* of prejudice?

8. Praise

acclaim (*v.*)
ə-'klām
welcome with approval; applaud loudly
I did not enjoy that novel although it was *acclaimed* by several leading reviewers.

encomium (*n.*)
en-'kō-mē-əm
speech or writing of high praise; tribute; eulogy
Lincoln's "Gettysburg Address" is, in part, an *encomium* of those who fought at the Battle of Gettysburg.

eulogize (*v.*)
'yü-lə-ˌjīz
praise; extol; laud; glorify
(*ant.* **vilify**)
The late composer was *eulogized* for his contributions to American music.

laudable (*adj.*)
'lòd-ə-bəl
praiseworthy; commendable
The bus driver's *laudable* safety record evoked high praise from her superiors.

laudatory (*adj.*)
'lòd-ə-ˌtòr-ē
expressing praise, eulogistic
Most of the critics wrote *laudatory* reviews of the new film; only one found fault with it.

plaudit (*n.*)
'plòd-ət
(used mainly in the plural) applause; enthusiastic praise
Responding to the *plaudits* of their admirers, the singers reappeared for an encore.

9. Defamation

calumnious (*adj.*)
kə-'ləm-nē-əs
falsely and maliciously accusing; defamatory; slanderous
Witnesses who heard the *calumnious* attack offered to testify in behalf of the slandered person.

derogatory (*adj.*)
di-'räg-ə-ˌtòr-ē
expressing low esteem; belittling; disparaging
(*ant.* **complimentary**)
Despite *derogatory* comments by some reviewers, the film is a box-office success.

imputation (*n.*)
ˌim-pyə-'tā-shən
charge, esp. an unjust or false charge; insinuation; accusation
My rival has tried to besmirch my character with the cowardly *imputation* that I am untrustworthy.

libel (*n.*)
'lī-bəl
false and defamatory printed (or written) statement
We shall certainly sue the newspaper that printed this *libel* against our company.

libelous (*adj.*)
'lī-bə-ləs
injurious to reputation; defamatory; calumnious

malign (*v.*) mə-'līn	speak evil of; vilify; traduce	I cannot bear to hear you *malign* so good a man.
slander (*n.*) 'slan-də(r)	false and defamatory spoken statement; calumny	The rumor that she was discharged is a vicious *slander*; the fact is that she resigned.
stigma (*n.*) 'stig-mə	mark of disgrace	With the *stigma* of a prison record, the ex-convict had difficulty in finding employment.
stigmatize (*v.*) 'stig-mə-ˌtīz	brand with a mark of disgrace	Surely no one would enjoy being *stigmatized* by a nickname like ''Dopey.''

10. Jest

banter (*n.*) 'bant-ə(r)	playful teasing; joking; raillery	The retiring employees were subjected to gentle *banter* about their coming life of ease.
caricature (*n.*) 'kar-i-kə-ˌchù(ə)r	drawing, imitation, or description that ridiculously exaggerates peculiarities or defects	The Class Night skit that drew the loudest plaudits was a *caricature* of the first day in high school.
droll (*adj.*) 'drōl	odd and laughter-provoking	''On Eating Crackers in Bed'' is surely a *droll* title for an essay.
facetious (*adj.*) fə-'sē-shəs	1. in the habit of joking 2. said in jest without serious intent	Our *facetious* club president has a way of turning almost every comment into a joke. When you are carrying a heavily loaded lunch tray, some joker may try to upset you with a *facetious* remark, like ''Hey, do you have a pen?''
flippant (*adj.*) 'flip-ənt	treating serious matters lightly	One should not be so *flippant* about the need for studying; it is a serious matter that may affect your graduation.
harlequin (*n.*) 'här-li-k(w)ən	buffoon; clown	The *harlequin's* clowning endeared him to all.
hilarious (*adj.*) hil-'ar-ē-əs	boisterously merry; very funny	The comedian was *hilarious*.
hilarity (*n.*) hil-'ar-ət-ē	noisy gaiety; mirth; jollity; glee	The laughter and shouting made passersby curious to learn what all the *hilarity* was about.

ironic or **ironical** (*adj.*) 'ī-'rän-ik 'ī-'rän-i-kəl	containing or expressing irony	It is *ironic* that a joyous event, like leaving for a vacation, should result in the tragic loss of life.
irony (*n.*) 'ī-rə-nē	1. species of humor whose intended meaning is the opposite of the words used	In *irony*, the basketball players nicknamed their 6'6" center "Shorty."
	2. state of affairs contrary to what would normally be expected	The breakdown occurred just after the car was inspected and found to be in perfect condition. What *irony*!
jocose (*adj.*) jō-'kōs	given to jesting; playfully humorous; jocular	Some columnists write in a *jocose* vein; others are inclined to be serious.
levity (*n.*) 'lev-ət-ē	lack of proper seriousness; trifling gaiety; frivolity	Some of us felt that George's giggling during the ceremony was an unforgivable *levity*.
ludicrous (*adj.*) 'lüd-ə-krəs	exciting laughter; ridiculous; farcical; absurd	Pie-throwing, falling down stairs, and similar *ludicrous* antics were common in early film comedies.
parody (*n.*) 'par-əd-ē	humorous imitation	The Washington press corps entertained the Chief Executive with a *parody* of a Presidential message to Congress.
sarcasm (*n.*) 'sär-ˌkaz-əm	sneering language intended to hurt a person's feelings	Instead of helping, he offered such *sarcasm* as "You have made your bed; now lie in it."
sarcastic (*adj.*) sär-'kas-tik	given to or expressing sarcasm	*Sarcastic* language can deeply hurt a person.
sardonic (*adj.*) sär-'dän-ik	bitterly sarcastic; mocking; sneering	Villains are often portrayed with a *sardonic* grin that suggests contempt for others.
satire (*n.*) 'sa-ˌtī(ə)r	language or writing that exposes follies or abuses by holding them up to ridicule	Jonathan Swift's GULLIVER'S TRAVELS is a brilliant *satire* on human follies.
satiric or **satirical** (*adj.*) sə-'tir-ik sə-'tir-i-kəl	given to or expressing satire	In *Catch-22*, a *satirical* novel, Joseph Heller ridicules the inflexibility of military bureaucrats.
travesty (*n.*) 'trav-ə-stē	imitation that makes a serious thing seem ridiculous; mockery	It is a *travesty* of justice that a notorious criminal should escape trial because of a technicality.

Apply What You Have Learned

EXERCISE 3.8: ANTONYMS

Each word or expression in column I has an ANTONYM (opposite) in column II. Insert the *letter* of the correct ANTONYM in the space provided.

COLUMN I	COLUMN II
_____1. mark of honor	(A) complimentary
_____2. susceptible	(B) poisonous
_____3. nontoxic	(C) halcyon
_____4. treat (someone) as unimportant	(D) doleful
_____5. hilarious	(E) levity
_____6. derogatory	(F) stigma
_____7. turbulent	(G) encomium
_____8. seriousness	(H) lionize
_____9. denunciation	(I) vilify
_____10. extol	(J) immune

EXERCISE 3.9: DEFINITIONS

In the space provided, write the *letter* of the word or expression that best defines the italicized word.

_____ 1. *Astringent* rebuke
(A) mild
(B) friendly
(C) undeserved
(D) stern

_____ 2. Effective *antidote*
(A) harlequin
(B) punishment
(C) remedy
(D) precaution

_____ 3. *Derogatory* comment
(A) unfair
(B) belittling
(C) congratulatory
(D) false

_____ 4. *Benign* ruler
(A) healthful
(B) aging
(C) kindly
(D) tyrannical

_____ 5. *Ironical* development
(A) contrary to expectation
(B) very sudden
(C) discouraging
(D) unfortunate

_____ 6. *Festering* slums
(A) decaying
(B) crime-ridden
(C) poverty-stricken
(D) spreading

_____ 7. Utterly *farcical*
(A) hopeless
(B) incompetent
(C) irresponsible
(D) absurd

	8. Prescribed *regimen*	(A) rules	(C) dose
		(B) medicine	(D) enforcement
	9. *Venomous* fangs	(A) vigorous	(C) dangerous
		(B) virulent	(D) pointed
	10. *Halcyon* atmosphere	(A) cloudy	(C) calm
		(B) noisy	(D) clear

EXERCISE 3.10: CONCISE WRITING

Express the thought of each sentence below in no more than four words. The first sentence has been rewritten as a sample.

1. We look down with contempt on those who live on others.

   We despise parasites.

2. Who is the person who wrote that false and defamatory statement?

3. He deliberately uses sneering language that can hurt people's feelings.

4. Those who suffer from imaginary illnesses are in urgent need of help.

5. They visited a place where animals are kept and trained.

6. At the present time, she is recovering from an illness.

7. He makes remarks that are meant as jokes and are not intended to be taken seriously.

8. The outcome was the opposite of what one would normally have expected.

9. Some tumors do not threaten the life of the patient.

10. At no time in the past did she speak evil of anyone.

EXERCISE 3.11: SENTENCE COMPLETION

Write the *letter* of the word (or set of words) that best completes the sentence.

1. Newspapers generally withhold the names of criminal offenders under sixteen so as not to

   _____ them.
   - (A) popularize
   - (B) libel
   - (C) stigmatize
   - (D) slander
   - (E) traduce

2. DON QUIXOTE, a _____ novel by Cervantes, ridicules exaggerated notions of chivalry.
   - (A) satirical
   - (B) sentimental
   - (C) historical
   - (D) realistic
   - (E) eulogistic

3. The _____ currently being exhibited in the _____ have attracted numerous students of ornithology.
   - (A) apes . . aviary
   - (B) parrots . . apiary
   - (C) bees . . menagerie
   - (D) monkeys . . apiary
   - (E) vultures . . aviary

4. The Olympic medal winner was _____ by the citizens of her hometown.
   - (A) badgered
   - (B) parodied
   - (C) maligned
   - (D) lionized
   - (E) caricatured

5. Winston Churchill _____ the heroes of the Battle of Britain in this memorable _____: "Never was so much owed by so many to so few."
   - (A) congratulated . . travesty
   - (B) defended . . encomium
   - (C) vilified . . plaudit
   - (D) acclaimed . . tribute
   - (E) extolled . . oration

EXERCISE 3.12: BRAINTEASERS

Fill in the missing letters.

1. At the dedication ceremony, the mayor will e _ l o g _ _ _ the scientist for whom the school is being named.

2. Fearing that failure to win a promotion might _ _ _ _ _ m a t _ _ _ her, Margaret did her best to succeed on the job.

3. It is i r o n _ _ _ _ that the severely paralyzed lad should have the name Hale, which means "healthy."

4. Swimming is believed to have _ _ _ _ _ a p e _ _ _ _ benefits for people who suffer from arthritis.

5. F a c e _ _ _ _ _ remarks on solemn occasions are entirely inappropriate.

6. The person who accidentally swallowed the poison was given a(n) _ _ _ _ d o t _ and rushed to the hospital.

7. Several newspaper editors commended the governor for his _ _ _ d a b _ _ efforts to prevent the strike.

8. Beneath the outer layer of the skin are the __ __ __ **a c e** __ __ __ glands, which secrete oil to lubricate the skin and the hair.

9. Many a life has been saved by the timely surgical removal of a(n) __ __ __ __ __ __ **a n t** growth.

10. Though responsible for the fatal collision, the envoy could not be arrested because of diplomatic __ __ __ **u n i t** __.

EXERCISE 3.13: COMPOSITION

Answer in a sentence or two.

1. Is badgering a convalescent forgivable? Explain.

_____

_____

_____

2. Would you feel maligned if someone called you a hypochondriac when you were not feeling well? Why, or why not?

_____

_____

_____

3. Is it a travesty for suspects who testify against fellow suspects to receive immunity from prosecution? Explain.

_____

_____

_____

4. Why is it derogatory to be called a "parasite"?

_____

_____

_____

5. Why would it be ironical for an ordinary high school tennis player to win a match from an acclaimed world champion?

_____

_____

_____

EXERCISE 3.14: ANALOGIES

Write the *letter* of the word that best completes the analogy.

Sample

Aviary is to *birds* as *apiary* is to ___e___ .
    a. flowers *b.* apes *c.* worms *d.* reptiles *e.* bees

Explanation

The first step is to find the relationship of *aviary* and *birds*. As you have learned, an *aviary* is a "place where birds are kept." Then say to yourself, an *apiary* is a "place in which what is kept?" The answer, of course, is *e*, bees.

1. *Invalid* is to *hypochondriac* as *real* is to _____ .

   a. sickly *b.* genuine *c.* healthful *d.* imagined *e.* impossible

2. *Birds* are to *ornithologist* as *poisons* are to _____ .

   a. bacteriologist *b.* pharmacist *c.* toxicologist *d.* physician *e.* coroner

3. *Waste* is to *scavenger* as *dirt* is to _____ .

   a. oil *b.* parasite *c.* cleanser *d.* ant *e.* weed

4. *Photograph* is to *caricature* as *fact* is to _____ .

   a. drawing *b.* exaggeration *c.* sketch *d.* truth *e.* description

5. *Ludicrous* is to *laugh* as *dolorous* is to _____ .

   a. weep *b.* laud *c.* exult *d.* condemn *e.* smile

11. Willingness—Unwillingness

WORD	MEANING	TYPICAL USE
alacrity (*n.*) ə-'lak-rət-ē	cheerful willingness; readiness; liveliness	Dr. Burke's class is one which pupils attend with *alacrity* and leave with reluctance.
aversion (*n.*) ə-'vər-zhən	strong dislike; repugnance; antipathy	Philip's *aversion* to work led to his dismissal.
involuntary (*adj.*) in-'väl-ən-ˌter-ē	not done of one's own free will; automatic; unintentional; spontaneous (*ant.* **voluntary**)	Sneezing is *involuntary*.
loath (*adj.*) 'lōth	unwilling; averse; disinclined; reluctant	We were *loath* to leave our friends, but my father's transfer to California left us no choice.

loathe (*v.*) 'lōth	have an intense aversion to; detest	We *loathe* liars.
volition (*n.*) vō-'lish-ən	will	Were you discharged or did you leave of your own *volition*?

---

12. Height

---

acclivity (*n.*) ə-'kliv-ət-ē	upward slope (*ant.* **declivity**)	The sharp *acclivity* compelled us to drive in low gear.
acme (*n.*) 'ak-mē	highest point; pinnacle; summit	Many believe that Shakespeare reached his *acme* as a playwright when he wrote *Hamlet*.
apogee (*n.*) 'ap-ə-jē	1. farthest point from the earth in the orbit of a heavenly body (*ant.* **perigee**) 2. highest point; culmination	At its *apogee*, the satellite was 560 miles (903 kilometers) from the earth, and at its perigee 150 miles (242 kilometers). The use of solar energy, though increasing, is still exceedingly far from its *apogee*.
climactic (*adj.*) klī-'mak-tik	arranged in order of increasing force and interest (*ant.* **anticlimactic**)	Notice the *climactic* order of ideas in this sentence: ''Swelled by heavy rains, brooks became creeks, creeks rivers, and rivers torrents.''
consummate (*adj.*) kən-'səm-ət	perfect, superb; carried to the highest degree	The pilot guided the plane onto the runway with *consummate* skill.
eminence (*n.*) 'em-ə-nəns	high rank	Raised suddenly to an *eminence* for which he was ill qualified, the executive could not get along with his new subordinates.
eminent (*adj.*) 'em-ə-nənt	standing out; notable; famous	Emily Dickinson was an *eminent* poet.
ethereal (*adj.*) i-'thir-ē-əl	of the heavens; celestial; airy; delicate; intangible	Charles was told by his employer, ''Get rid of your *ethereal* notions and come down to earth.''
exalt (*v.*) ig-'zȯlt	1. lift up with joy, pride, etc.; elate (*ant.* **humiliate**) 2. raise in rank, dignity, etc.; extol; glorify	My parents were *exalted* to learn that I had won a scholarship. Some films have *exalted* criminals to the level of heroes.

precipice (*n.*) 'pres-ə-pəs	very steep, overhanging place; cliff	The climbers had to make a lengthy detour around an insurmountable *precipice*.
precipitous (*adj.*) pri-'sip-ət-əs	1. steep as a precipice 2. hasty; rash	She descended from the summit in low gear, using her brakes all the way, since the road was so *precipitous*. Don't rush into a *precipitous* action that you may later regret. Take your time.
preeminent (*adj.*) prē-'em-ə-nənt	standing out above others; superior	As a violinmaker, Stradivarius remains *preeminent*.
sublimate (*v.*) 'səb-lə-ˌmāt	1. redirect the energy of a person's bad impulses into socially and morally higher channels 2. purify; refine	With the aid of dedicated social workers, energies that had once found release in gang fights were *sublimated* into wholesome club activities and sports. The alchemists failed in their efforts to *sublimate* baser metals, such as lead and copper, into gold.
sublime (*adj.*) sə-'blīm	elevated; noble; exalted; uplifting	Visitors to the Grand Canyon are uplifted and refreshed by its *sublime* scenery.
vertex (*n.*) 'vər-ˌteks	farthest point opposite the base, as in a triangle or pyramid; apex	The *vertex* of the largest Egyptian pyramid was originally 482 feet (147 meters) from the base.
zenith (*n.*) 'zē-nəth	1. highest point; culmination (*ant.* **nadir**) 2. point in the heavens directly overhead	Her election to the Senate marked the *zenith* of her long career in politics. At noon, the sun reaches the *zenith*.

13. Lowness, Depth

abject (*adj.*) 'ab-ˌjekt	deserving contempt; sunk to a low condition; wretched	For your *abject* submission to your tyrannical associate, we have the utmost contempt.
abysmal (*adj.*) ə-'biz-məl	deep; profound; immeasurably great	I was ashamed of my *abysmal* ignorance.
abyss (*n.*) ə-'bis	bottomless, immeasurably deep space	The sudden death of his closest friend threw Tennyson into an *abyss* of despair.

anticlimax (*n.*)
,ant-i-'klī-maks

abrupt decline from the dignified or important to the trivial or ludicrous; comedown; bathos
(*ant.* **climax**)

Sally used *anticlimax* when she said that my friend has a boundless appetite for classical music, Renaissance painting, and roasted peanuts.

chasm (*n.*)
'kaz-əm

deep breach; wide gap or rift

Prospects for a settlement became remote, as the *chasm* between the rival parties deepened.

declivity (*n.*)
di-'kliv-ət-ē

downward slope
(*ant.* **acclivity**)

The hill was ideal for beginning skiers because of its gentle *declivity*.

dregs (*n. pl.*)
'dregz

most worthless part; sediment at the bottom of a liquid

Thieves and hoodlums are among the *dregs* of society.

earthy (*adj.*)
'ər-thē

coarse; low

The contractor's helpers were excellent, though we did not exactly enjoy their *earthy* humor.

humble (*adj.*)
'həm-bəl

1. of low position or condition

Despite his *humble* origin, Lincoln rose to the highest office in the land.

2. not proud; unpretentious; modest; courteously respectful

Though Stella has done far more than anyone else, she has never boasted of her achievement; she is *humble*.

humiliate (*v.*)
hyü-'mil-ē-,āt

lower the pride, position, or dignity of; abase; degrade; mortify
(*ant.* **exalt**)

Ted feels that I *humiliated* him at the meeting when I said that his motion was unnecessary.

humility (*n.*)
hyü-'mil-ət-ē

freedom from pride; humbleness; lowliness; modesty

Boasters and braggarts need a lesson in *humility*.

menial (*adj.*)
'mē-nē-əl

low; mean; subservient; servile

Some might consider mowing lawns *menial* work, but Harvey loves it.

nadir (*n.*)
'nā-də(r)

lowest point
(*ant.* **zenith**)

Hopes of the American Revolutionary forces were at their *nadir* in the bitter winter of 1777–78 at Valley Forge.

plumb (*v.*)
'pləm

get to the bottom of; ascertain the depth of; fathom

Sherlock Holmes amazes readers by his ability to *plumb* the deepest mysteries.

profound (*adj.*)
prə-'faúnd

very deep; deeply felt; intellectually deep

Einstein's theories are understood by relatively few because they are so *profound*.

ravine (*n.*)
rə-'vēn

deep, narrow gorge worn by running water

Survivors of the plane that crashed in the mountain *ravine* were rescued by helicopter.

14. Relatives

filial (*adj.*)
'fil-ē-əl
of or like a son or daughter

Cordelia was the only one of King Lear's daughters that showed him *filial* affection.

fraternal (*adj.*)
frə-'tərn-ᵊl
of or like a brother

There was much *fraternal* affection between the brothers; they were devoted to one another.

genealogy (*n.*)
ˌjē-nē-'äl-ə-jē
a person's or family's descent; lineage; pedigree

Most people can trace their *genealogy* back to a grandparent, or a great-grandparent, but they know almost nothing about their earlier ancestors.

gentility (*n.*)
jen-'til-ət-ē
1. good manners

George Bernard Shaw's PYGMALION shows how a cockney flower girl quickly acquires the *gentility* necessary to pass as a duchess.

2. gentry; upper class

The duke scandalized some members of the *gentility* by marrying a commoner.

kith and kin (*n. pl.*)
'kith; 'kin
friends and relatives; kindred

Because he married in a distant state, the soldier had few of his *kith and kin* at the wedding.

maternal (*adj.*)
mə-'tərn-ᵊl
of or like a mother

The kindergarten teacher has a kindly, *maternal* concern for each pupil.

nepotism (*n.*)
'nep-ə-ˌtiz-əm
favoritism to relatives by those in power

Whenever a President appoints a relative to a government position, the cry of *nepotism* is raised by the opposition party.

paternal (*adj.*)
pə-'tərn-ᵊl
of or like a father

The molding of a child's character is an important maternal and *paternal* obligation.

progenitor (*n.*)
prō-'jen-ət-ə(r)
forefather

Adam is the Biblical *progenitor* of the human race.

progeny (*n.*)
'präj-ə-nē
offspring; children; descendants

Josiah Franklin's *progeny* numbered seventeen, the fifteenth being his son Benjamin.

sibling (*n.*)
'sib-liŋ
one of two or more children of a family

Eileen has three *siblings*—two younger brothers and an older sister.

15. Smell

aroma (*n.*) ə-'rō-mə	pleasant odor; bouquet	What a smoker may describe as a rich tobacco *aroma*, a nonsmoker may consider a disgusting stench.
aromatic (*adj.*) ˌar-ə-'mat-ik	sweet-scented; fragrant	Honeysuckle is *aromatic*.
fragrant (*adj.*) 'frā-grənt	having a pleasant odor; pleasantly odorous or odoriferous	A florist's shop is a *fragrant* place.
fusty (*adj.*) 'fəs-tē	1. stale-smelling; musty; moldy 2. old-fashioned	To rid the unused room of its *fusty* smell, we opened the windows and let the fresh air in. The *fusty* tenant refused to allow any modern appliance to be installed in the apartment.
incense (*n.*) 'in-ˌsens	substance yielding a pleasant odor when burned	Ancient Greek and Roman worshipers often burned *incense* to please their gods.
malodorous (*adj.*) mal-'ōd-ə-rəs	ill-smelling; stinking; fetid; unpleasantly odorous	The air was *malodorous*; someone nearby must have been burning garbage illegally.
noisome (*adj.*) 'nȯi-səm	1. offensive to smell; disgusting 2. harmful; noxious	The bus discharged *noisome* exhaust fumes that offended our nostrils. People were advised to remain indoors until the *noisome* fog was dispersed.
olfactory (*adj.*) äl-'fak-t(ə-)rē	pertaining to the sense of smell	Because of their superior *olfactory* sense, bloodhounds can pick up the trails of fleeing criminals.
pungent (*adj.*) 'pən-jənt	sharp in smell or taste; acrid; biting; stimulating	When you slice onions, the *pungent* fumes may cause your eyes to tear.
putrid (*adj.*) 'pyü-trəd	1. stinking from decay 2. extremely bad; corrupt	An occasional rinse with a soapy solution will keep garbage cans free of *putrid* odors. Any system that requires applicants for promotion to pay bribes is *putrid*.
rancid (*adj.*) 'ran-səd	unpleasant to smell or taste from being spoiled or stale	Butter or fish that has a *rancid* odor is unfit to eat.

rank (*adj.*) 'raŋk	1. having a strong, bad odor or taste; offensively gross or coarse 2. extreme	When threatened, a skunk protects itself effectively by emitting a *rank* odor. Many felt that the murderer's acquittal on the grounds of insanity was a *rank* injustice.
reek (*v.*) 'rēk	emit a strong, disagreeable smell; be permeated with	Even after the fire was extinguished and the tenants were allowed to return, the building *reeked* of smoke.
scent (*n.*) 'sent	smell; perfume	The room was fragrant with the *scent* of freshly cut lilacs.
scent (*v.*)	get a suspicion of	When I saw my two rivals putting their heads together in a whispered conference, I *scented* a plot.
unsavory (*adj.*) 'ən-'sāv(-ə)-rē	1. unpleasant to taste or smell 2. morally offensive	The *unsavory* odor was traced to a decaying onion in the vegetable bin. Opponents of the nominee alleged that he was an *unsavory* character with connections to the underworld.

Apply What You Have Learned

EXERCISE 3.15: SYNONYMS

In the space before each word or expression in column I, write the *letter* of its correct synonym from column II.

COLUMN I	COLUMN II
_____ 1. spicy	(A) abyss
_____ 2. most worthless part	(B) eminence
_____ 3. chasm	(C) humility
_____ 4. consummate	(D) precipitous
_____ 5. disinclined	(E) dregs
_____ 6. humiliated	(F) loath
_____ 7. descent	(G) pungent
_____ 8. high rank	(H) lineage
_____ 9. hasty	(I) humbled
_____ 10. freedom from pride	(J) perfect

EXERCISE 3.16: UNRELATED WORDS

Write the letter of the word unrelated in meaning to the other words on the line.

1. (A) contemptible (B) abject (C) reluctant (D) wretched (E) low _____

2. (A) putrid (B) unsavory (C) involuntary (D) fusty (E) malodorous _____

3. (A) children (B) offspring (C) scent (D) progeny (E) descendants _____

4. (A) vertex (B) apex (C) climax (D) acme (E) base _____

5. (A) rank (B) position (C) gross (D) offensive (E) coarse _____

6. (A) abyss (B) precipice (C) elevation (D) peak (E) cliff _____

7. (A) modesty (B) humility (C) unpretentiousness (D) pride (E) humbleness _____

8. (A) unwillingness (B) repugnance (C) antipathy (D) aversion (E) alacrity _____

9. (A) rift (B) acclivity (C) breach (D) ravine (E) gorge _____

10. (A) servile (B) paternal (C) obsequious (D) submissive (E) subservient _____

EXERCISE 3.17: SENTENCE COMPLETION

Fill each blank with the most appropriate word or expression from the vocabulary list below.

VOCABULARY LIST

maternal	progeny	exalted
rancid	bathos	kith and kin
attraction	aversion	chasm
gentility	delectable	humiliated
filial	climax	declivity

1. Janet's _____ to the water made her dread our swimming class.

2. It is only natural that we should be _____ by our successes.

3. Mother's Day gives children an opportunity to express their_____ love.

4. The gripping suspense at the_____ of the play held the audience breathless.

5. As we came down the steep _____, the speed of our car increased sharply.

6. The meal was wholesome and delicious except for the butter, which was _____ .

7. The youngsters received kinder treatment from total strangers than from their own _____ .

8. Coming as it did after three excellent skits, the rather dull final number produced an effect of _____ .

9. Your companion's earthy manner of speaking suggests that he has no _____ .

10. I felt _____ when I was notified that I had not passed the driving test.

EXERCISE 3.18: CONCISE WRITING

Express the thought of each sentence below in no more than four words. The first sentence has been rewritten as a sample.

1. Does the soap that you use have a pleasant odor?

   Is your soap fragrant? _____

2. This downward slope is as steep as a precipice.

   _____

3. The American people look down on favoritism to relatives by those in power.

   _____

4. Hell is an immeasurably deep place that has no bottom.

   _____

5. We saw no sediment at the bottom of the liquid.

   _____

6. Look at the point in the heavens directly over your head.

   _____

7. Their freedom from pride is something that is worthy of praise.

   _____

8. The record that she has compiled stands out above that of others.

   _____

9. This cheese is stale, and it has an unpleasant odor.

   _____

10. The yawning that I did was beyond the control of my will.

    _____

EXERCISE 3.19: BRAINTEASERS

Fill in the missing letters.

1. One whiff of that __ __ __ s o m e air made us hold our noses.

2. The eminent guitarist displayed her usual __ __ __ s u m __ __ __ __ control of her instrument.

3. After an occasional short trip to earth, the king of the gods would return to his

   __ __ h e r e __ __ palace.

4. By comparison to a mansion, a log cabin is a **h u m** __ __ __ dwelling.

5. We want no part of that deal! It is corrupt! It is __ __ __ **r i d** !

6. Destructive energy can be __ __ __ __ __ **m a t** __ __ towards constructive ends.

7. In a world torn by war and dissension, wouldn't you agree that peace and harmony would be

   __ __ __ **l i m e** ?

8. No one forced us to do it. We did it of our own __ __ **l i t** __ __ __ .

9. The __ __ **a s** __ between the opposing sides is widening.

10. For a scientist, the award of a Nobel Prize is the __ __ **m e** of fame.

EXERCISE 3.20: COMPOSITION

Answer in two or three sentences.

1. Describe a noisome situation to which you had a strong aversion.

   _____

   _____

   _____

2. Give an example of a necessary menial task that you were not loath to do.

   _____

   _____

   _____

3. Tell how a parent succeeded or failed to bridge a chasm between siblings.

   _____

   _____

   _____

4. Would you feel humiliated if someone said you were a student of consummate intelligence? Explain.

   _____

   _____

   _____

5. Is it humiliating to be called a consummate zany? Why, or why not?

   _____

   _____

EXERCISE 3.21: ANALOGIES

In the space at the left, write the *letter* of the pair of words that most nearly approaches the relationship between the capitalized words.

_____ 1. INFINITE : END

    a. wealthy : money
    b. blithe : happiness
    c. abysmal : bottom

    d. contrite : repentance
    e. delectable : delight

_____ 2. AUDITORY : HEARING

    a. keen : observing
    b. gustatory : touching
    c. tactile : tasting

    d. olfactory : smelling
    e. irritable : feeling

_____ 3. VERTEX : TRIANGLE

    a. peak : mountain
    b. summit : foot
    c. slope : base

    d. hill : ravine
    e. index : preface

_____ 4. PROGENY : PROGENITOR

    a. root : branch
    b. river : source
    c. genius : protector

    d. bricks : house
    e. orchestra : conductor

_____ 5. FETID : FRAGRANT

    a. imperfect : consummate
    b. humble : pretentious
    c. shallow : profound

    d. fresh : stale
    e. reeking : aromatic

---

16. Age

WORD	MEANING	TYPICAL USE
adolescent (*adj.*) ˌad-ᵊl-ʼes-ᵊnt	growing from childhood to adulthood; roughly, of the teenage period	Boys and girls undergo many changes in their *adolescent* years.
adolescent (*n.*)	teenager	As *adolescents* develop into adults, they tend to become more self-confident.
antediluvian (*adj.*) ˌant-i-də-ʼlü-vē-ən	antiquated; belonging to the time before the Biblical Flood (when all except Noah and his family perished)	Compared with today's supersonic jets, the plane the Wright brothers flew in 1903 seems *antediluvian*.
archaic (*adj.*) är-ʼkā-ik	no longer used, except in a special context; old-fashioned	An *archaic* meaning of the word "quick" is "living," as in the Biblical phrase "the quick and the dead."

callow (*adj.*)
'kal-ō

young and inexperienced; unfledged

A prudent executive cannot be expected to entrust the management of a company to a *callow* youth just out of college.

contemporary (*adj.*)
kən-'tem-pə-ˌrer-ē

of the same period or duration

The English Renaissance was not *contemporary* with the Italian Renaissance; it came two centuries later.

contemporary (*n.*)

person who lives at the same time as another

Benjamin Franklin was Thomas Jefferson's *contemporary*.

crone (*n.*)
'krōn

withered old woman

The use of the word *crone* is unfair to women because there is no corresponding word for a "withered old man."

decrepit (*adj.*)
di-'krep-ət

weakened by old age

Several *decrepit* inmates had to be carried to safety when the nursing home was evacuated during the fire.

defunct (*adj.*)
di-'fəŋ(k)t

dead; deceased; extinct

The Acme Lumber Company is still in business, but the Equity Appliance Corporation has long been *defunct*.

forebear (*n.*)
'fȯr-ˌbe(ə)r

forefather, ancestor

The world of our *forebears* centuries ago was much less polluted.

hoary (*adj.*)
'hȯr-ē

1. white or gray with age

Santa Claus is usually portrayed as an elderly, stout man with a *hoary* beard.

2. ancient

The plot of the novel is based on one of the *hoary* legends of Ancient Greece.

infantile (*adj.*)
'in-fən-ˌtīl

of or like an infant or infancy; childish

A child may revert to the *infantile* act of thumb-sucking when insecure.

inveterate (*adj.*)
in-'vet-ə-rət

1. firmly established by age; deep-rooted

From their ancestors, Americans have inherited an *inveterate* dislike of tyranny.

2. habitual

My cousin would like to give up cigarettes, but it will not be easy; she is an *inveterate* smoker.

juvenile (*adj.*)
'jü-və-ˌnīl

1. of or for youth; youthful

Books for grade-school children are usually located in the *juvenile* section of the library.

2. immature

Jody suggested we play hide-and-seek, but we told her not to be *juvenile*.

longevity (*n.*)
län-'jev-ət-ē

1. long life

Methuselah is renowned for his *longevity*; according to the Bible, he lived for 969 years.

2. length of life

Medical advances are prolonging the average person's *longevity*.

matriarch (*n.*)
'mā-trē-ˌärk

1. mother and ruler of a family

Mama, in *A Raisin in the Sun*, is the *matriarch* of the Younger family.

2. highly respected elderly lady

mature (*adj.*)
mə-'t(y)u̇(ə)r

1. full-grown; ripe

Rita, 23, was not appointed manager because the employer wanted a more *mature* person in that position.

2. carefully thought out

These are *mature* plans; they were not devised hastily.

nonage (*n.*)
'nän-ij

legal minority; period before maturity

On his twenty-first birthday, the heir assumed control of his estate from the trustees who had administered it during his *nonage*.

nonagenarian (*n.*)
ˌnō-nə-jə-'ner-ē-ən

person in his or her 90's
(Note also **octogenarian,** person in the 80's, and **septuagenarian,** person in the 70's.)

George Bernard Shaw, among his many other distinctions, was a *nonagenarian*, for he lived to be 94.

obsolescent (*adj.*)
ˌäb-sə-'les-ᵊnt

going out of use; becoming obsolete

The company will soon have to replace its *obsolescent* machinery if it is to compete successfully with rivals who have state-of-the-art equipment.

obsolete (*adj.*)
ˌäb-sə-'lēt

no longer in use; out-of-date

The calculator has made the slide rule *obsolete*.

patriarch (*n.*)
'pā-trē-ˌärk

1. venerable old man

Practically all of the *patriarch's* children, grandchildren, and great-grandchildren attended his eightieth birthday.

2. father and ruler of a family or tribe; founder

According to the Bible, the human family is descended from the *patriarch* Adam and his wife Eve.

posthumous (*adj.*)
'päs-chə-məs

1. published after the author's death

Only two of Emily Dickinson's poems were published before her death; the rest are *posthumous*.

2. occurring after death

Posthumous fame is of no use to an artist who struggles for a lifetime and dies unknown.

primeval (*adj.*)
prī-'mē-vəl

pertaining to the world's first ages; primitive

From the exposed rock strata in the Grand Canyon, scientists have learned much about *primeval* life on this planet.

primordial (*adj.*)
prī-'mȯrd-ē-əl

1. existing at the very beginning

Humanity's *primordial* conflict with the environment has continued to the present day.

2. elementary; primary; first in order

One of the *primordial* concepts of science is that light travels at the rate of 186,000 miles per second.

pristine (*adj.*)
'pris-ˌtēn

in original, long-ago state; uncorrupted

A diamond in its *pristine* state as it comes from the mine looks altogether different from the diamond in a ring.

puberty (*n.*)
'pyü-bərt-ē

physical beginning of manhood (at about age 14) or womanhood (at about age 12)

Among the changes in boys at *puberty* are a deepening of the voice and the growth of hair on the face.

puerile (*adj.*)
'pyü(-ə)r-əl

foolish for a grown person to say or do; childish

Some thought it was fun to throw snowballs at passing cars; others considered it *puerile*.

senile (*adj.*)
'sēn-ˌīl

showing the weakness of age

Grandfather no longer has the energy he used to have. He often forgets things. He is becoming *senile*.

superannuated (*adj.*)
ˌsü-pər-'an-yə-wāt-əd

retired on a pension; extremely old

Some *superannuated* citizens can be more productive than many still in the work force.

venerable (*adj.*)
'ven-ər-ə-bəl

worthy of respect because of advanced age, achievement, virtue, or historical importance

At family reunions, our *venerable* grandmother, now past 80, sits at the head of the table.

veteran (*n.*)
'vet-ə-rən

1. person experienced in some occupation, art, or profession

In her bid for reelection, the mayor—a *veteran* of twenty years in public service—cited her opponent's lack of experience.

2. ex-member of the armed forces

Many *veterans* of the Vietnam War found it hard to readjust to civilian life.

yore (*n.*)
'yȯ(ə)r

(always preceded by *of*) long ago

In days of *yore* there was trial by combat; today, we have trial by jury.

17. Sobriety—Intoxication

abstemious (*adj.*)
ab-'stē-mē-əs

sparing in eating and drinking; temperate; abstinent

Employers usually do not hire known alcoholics, preferring personnel who are *abstemious* in their habits.

carousal (*n.*)
kə-'raü-zəl

jovial feast; drinking party

While the enemy was celebrating Christmas Eve in a merry *carousal*, Washington and his troops—quite sober—crossed the Delaware and took them by surprise.

dipsomania (*n.*)
ˌdip-sə-'mā-nē-ə

abnormal, uncontrollable craving for alcohol; alcoholism

An organization that has helped many persons to overcome *dipsomania* is Alcoholics Anonymous.

inebriated (*adj.*)
in-'ē-brē-ˌāt-əd

drunk; intoxicated

Captain Billy Bones, *inebriated* from too much rum, terrorized the other patrons of the Admiral Benbow Inn.

sober (*adj.*)
'sō-bə(r)

1. not drunk; temperate
(*ant.* **drunk; intoxicated**)

The motorist's obligation to be *sober* must be emphasized in driver-training programs.

2. serious; free from excitement or exaggeration

My immediate thought was to leave but, after *sober* consideration, I decided not to.

sobriety (*n.*)
sə-'brī-ət-ē

temperance; abstinence

Sobriety is a virtue.

sot (*n.*)
'sät

person made foolish by excessive drinking; drunkard

Don't ask a *sot* for directions; consult someone whose mind is clear.

teetotaler (*n.*)
'tē-'tōt-ᵊl-ə(r)

person who totally abstains from intoxicating beverages
(*ant.* **dipsomaniac**)

Former dipsomaniacs who are now *teetotalers* deserve admiration for their courage and willpower.

---

18. Sea

---

bow (*n.*)
'baü

forward part of a ship; prow
(*ant.* **stern**)

A search from *bow* to *stern* before sailing disclosed that no stowaways were on board.

brine (*n.*)
'brīn

1. salty water

Brine can be converted to drinking water, but at high cost.

2. ocean; sea; the deep

Anything on deck that was not firmly secured would have been blown into the *brine*.

doldrums (*n. pl.*)
'dōl-drəmz

1. calm, windless part of the ocean near the equator

Becalmed in the *doldrums*, the sailing vessel was "As idle as a painted ship/ Upon a painted ocean."

2. listlessness

The rise in sales and employment showed that America was emerging from the economic *doldrums*.

flotsam (*n.*) 'flät-səm	wreckage of a ship or its cargo found floating on the sea; driftage	*Flotsam* from the sunken freighter littered the sea for miles around.
jetsam (*n.*) 'jet-səm	goods cast overboard to lighten a ship in distress	*Jetsam* washed ashore indicated that frantic efforts had been made to lighten the ship's cargo.
jettison (*v.*) 'jet-ə-sən	throw (goods) overboard to lighten a ship or plane; discard	The pilot of the distressed plane *jettisoned* surplus fuel before attempting an emergency landing.
leeward (*adj.*) 'lē-wərd	in the direction away from the wind (*ant.* **windward**)	To avoid the wind, we chose deck chairs on the *leeward* side of the ship.
marine (*adj.*) mə-'rēn	of the sea or shipping; nautical; maritime	If you are fascinated by undersea plants and animals, you may want to study *marine* biology.
mariner (*n.*) 'mar-ə-nər	sailor; seaman	Her uncle is an experienced *mariner*.
starboard (*adj.*) 'stär-bərd	pertaining to the right-hand side of a ship when you face the bow (forward) (*ant.* **port**)	When a ship follows a southerly course, sunrise is on the *port* side and sunset on the *starboard* side.

19. Cleanliness—Uncleanliness

carrion (*n.*) 'kar-ē-ən	decaying flesh of a carcass	Vultures fed for several days on the air-polluting *carrion* left by hunters.
contaminate (*v.*) kən-'tam-ə-ˌnāt	make impure by mixture; pollute (*ant.* **decontaminate**)	Many of our rivers have been *contaminated* by sewage.
dross (*n.*) 'dräs	waste; refuse	When you revise your composition, eliminate all meaningless expressions, repetitions, and similar *dross*.
expurgate (*v.*) 'ek-spər-ˌgāt	remove objectionable material from a book; bowdlerize; purify	In his FAMILY SHAKESPEARE (published 1818), Bowdler *expurgated* Shakespeare's works, removing words and expressions that he considered improper for reading aloud in a family.
immaculate (*adj.*) im-'ak-yə-lət	spotless; absolutely clean; pure; faultless	With some water, a cloth, and a little energy, a dirty windshield can be made *immaculate*.
offal (*n.*) 'ä-fəl	waste parts of a butchered animal; refuse; garbage	Sea gulls hovered about the wharf where fish was being sold, waiting to scoop up any *offal* cast into the water.

purge (*v.*) 'pərj	cleanse; purify; rid of undesired element or person	If elected, the candidate vowed he would *purge* the county administration of corruption and inefficiency.
slatternly (*adj.*) 'slat-ərn-lē	untidy; dirty from habitual neglect; slovenly	There were cobwebs on the walls, dust on the shelves, and dirty dishes in the sink; it was a *slatternly* kitchen.
sloven (*n.*) 'sləv-ən	person habitually untidy, dirty, or careless in dress, habits, etc.	It is difficult for an immaculate person to share a room with a *sloven*.
sordid (*adj.*) 'sȯrd-əd	filthy; vile	As soon as the athlete received the bribe offer, he informed his coach of the *sordid* affair.
squalid (*adj.*) 'skwäl-əd	filthy from neglect; dirty; degraded	If we had entered without removing our muddy boots, we would have made the house *squalid*.
squalor (*n.*) 'skwäl-ər	filth; degradation; sordidness	People do a great deal of washing, vacuuming, and mopping because they do not want to live in *squalor*.
sully (*v.*) 'səl-ē	tarnish; besmirch; defile	The celebrity felt that her name had been *sullied* by the publicity given her son's arrest for speeding.

20. Nearness

adjacent (*adj.*) ə-'jās-ᵊnt	lying near or next to; bordering; adjoining	Alaska is *adjacent* to northwestern Canada.
approximate (*adj.*) ə-'präk-sə-mət	nearly correct (*ant.* **exact; precise**)	The *approximate* length of a year is 365 days; its *exact* length is 365 days, 5 hours, 48 minutes, and 46 seconds.
contiguous (*adj.*) kən-'tig-yə-wəs	touching; adjoining	England and France are not *contiguous*; they are separated by the English Channel.
environs (*n. pl.*) in-'vī-rənz	districts surrounding a place; suburbs	Many of the city's former residents now live in its immediate *environs*.
juxtapose (*v.*) 'jək-stə-ˌpōz	put side by side; put close together	If you *juxtapose* the two cabinets, you will see that one is slightly taller than the other.
juxtaposition (*n.*) ˌjək-stə-pə-'zish-ən	close or side-by-side position	Soap should not be placed in *juxtaposition* with foods because it may impart its scent to them.

propinquity (*n.*)	1. kinship	Disregarding *propinquity*, the executive gave the post to a highly recommended stranger rather than to his own nephew.
prō-'piŋ-kwət-ē	2. nearness of place; proximity	There were large shrubs too close to the house, and their *propinquity* added to the dampness indoors.

Apply What You Have Learned

EXERCISE 3.22: ANTONYMS

Each word in column I has an *antonym* in column II. Insert the *letter* of that antonym in the space provided.

	COLUMN I		COLUMN II
_____	**1.** full-fledged	(A)	teetotaler
_____	**2.** sturdy	(B)	abstinent
_____	**3.** dipsomaniac	(C)	filthy
_____	**4.** right	(D)	callow
_____	**5.** intemperate	(E)	bow
_____	**6.** windward	(F)	approximate
_____	**7.** exact	(G)	intoxication
_____	**8.** immaculate	(H)	leeward
_____	**9.** stern	(I)	decrepit
_____	**10.** sobriety	(J)	port

EXERCISE 3.23: SYNONYMS

Select the *synonym* of the italicized word and enter its *letter* in the space provided.

_____ **1.** *Unexpurgated* edition

(A) abbreviated (C) purified
(B) unpurified   (D) bowdlerized

_____ **2.** Jefferson's *forebears*

(A) contemporaries (C) ancestors
(B) rivals   (D) followers

_____ **3.** *Defunct* princess

(A) dead   (C) intemperate
(B) infantile (D) slatternly

_____ **4.** *Inveterate* latecomer   (A) strange   (C) juvenile
                                   (B) extinct   (D) habitual

_____ **5.** *Sober* estimates   (A) approximate   (C) exaggerated
                                   (B) calm   (D) inaccurate

_____ **6.** Venerable *patriarch*   (A) founder   (C) monument
                                   (B) martyr   (D) philosopher

_____ **7.** *Jettisoned* cargo   (A) surplus   (C) discarded
                                   (B) wrecked   (D) loaded

_____ **8.** *Primordial rights*   (A) inherited   (C) elementary
                                   (B) secondary   (D) royal

_____ **9.** Surface *dross*   (A) waste   (C) dregs
                                   (B) flotsam   (D) polish

_____ **10.** *Contiguous* properties   (A) sordid   (C) noxious
                                   (B) contagious   (D) touching

EXERCISE 3.24: SENTENCE COMPLETION

Fill each blank with the most appropriate word from the vocabulary list below.

VOCABULARY LIST

juxtaposition	puberty	primeval
obsolescent	abstemious	dross
squalid	puerile	obsolete
senility	immaculate	nonage
longevity	jetsam	carrion

1. Aunt Matilda thinks it childish for grown-ups to yell and boo at ball games. She cannot understand their _____ behavior.

2. When individuals distinguished for their advanced age are interviewed by the press, they are usually asked for the secret of their _____ .

3. As a means of transportation, the horse-drawn carriage has long been _____ .

4. In the hospital, every room was spotless. The corridors, too, were _____ .

5. During his legal minority, the young monarch had heeded his advisers, but, once past his _____ , he took absolute personal control.

6. Most eighth-graders have reached the stage of development known as _____ .

7. The two troublemakers sat side by side. This _____ gave them ample opportunity to create disturbances.

8. Jackals feed on the decaying flesh of a carcass. Kites, hawks, and buzzards also subsist on

————————————————————— .

9. By studying fossils, scientists have learned a great deal about —————————————————
plants and animals.

10. When pedestrians track in mud from dirty streets, the custodial staff has to mop the halls and

stairways frequently to keep them from becoming ————————————————— .

EXERCISE 3.25: CONCISE WRITING

   Express the thought of each sentence below in no more than four words. The first sentence has
been rewritten as a sample.

1. Some former members of the armed forces are between eighty and eighty-nine years of age.
   Some veterans are octogenarians.———————————————————————————

2. Our uniforms are so clean that there is not a spot on them.

   —————————————————————————————————————

3. Was Shakespeare living at the time that Elizabeth was alive?

   —————————————————————————————————————

4. Most of the men and women in their seventies no longer go to work.

   —————————————————————————————————————

5. We know several men and women who totally abstain from alcohol.

   —————————————————————————————————————

6. The computer that we own is going out of use.

   —————————————————————————————————————

7. Was this play published after the death of its author?

   —————————————————————————————————————

8. Move those two tables so that one is right alongside the other.

   —————————————————————————————————————

9. She had a craving for intoxicating beverages that she could not control.

   —————————————————————————————————————

10. Wreckage from the ship and its cargo is drifting ashore.

   —————————————————————————————————————

EXERCISE 3.26: BRAINTEASERS

Fill in the missing letters.

1. The office staff consists of three newcomers and one _ _ _ _ **r a n**.

2. The guests helped themselves generously, except for a few dieters who were noticeably _ _ **s t e m** _ _ _ _.

3. What Mama says goes in this house. She is the _ _ _ _ _ **a r c h** of the family.

4. The city is congested, but its _ _ _ _ **i r o n** _ are sparsely populated.

5. Merchants are complaining that business has been in the _ **o l d** _ _ _ _.

6. Thanks to the cleanup sponsored by the Block Association, the vacant lot is now _ _ _ _ _ _ **l a t e.**

7. The edifice is still called the Price Corporation Building, even though that company has long been _ _ **f u n** _ _.

8. This must be the room of a(n) _ _ **o v e n**; it is so untidy!

9. She can play tennis almost every day because of the _ _ **o x** _ _ _ _ _ of her house to the courts.

10. The _ _ _ _ _ **t a l e** _ next to us didn't even taste his champagne.

EXERCISE 3.27: COMPOSITION

Answer in two or three sentences.

1. What can apartment house dwellers do to prevent an adjacent vacant lot from becoming squalid?

_____

_____

_____

2. Is it puerile for a mature person to play chess? Explain.

_____

_____

_____

3. If you were an employer, would you hire a former dipsomaniac? Why, or why not?

_____

_____

_____

4. Suggest one thing you can do to ease the plight of a grandparent who is becoming senile.

_____

_____

_____

5. How does the jettisoning of sludge by oil tankers affect marine plant and animal life?

_____

_____

_____

EXERCISE 3.28: ANALOGIES

Write the *letter* of the word that best completes the analogy.

1. *Drought* is to *rain* as *doldrums* is to _____.
   a. sea *b.* calm *c.* sails *d.* sunshine *e.* wind

2. *Refrigerator* is to *chill* as *brine* is to _____.
   a. moisten *b.* preserve *c.* spoil *d.* fill *e.* spill

3. *Employed* is to *salary* as *superannuated* is to _____.
   a. bonus *b.* wages *c.* pension *d.* royalties *e.* commission

4. *Banana* is to *peel* as *carcass* is to _____.
   a. offal *b.* meat *c.* game *d.* hunter *e.* carrion

5. *Front* is to *rear* as *bow* is to _____.
   a. leeward *b.* prow *c.* port *d.* stern *e.* starboard

21. Reasoning

WORD	MEANING	TYPICAL USE
analogy (*n.*) ə-'nal-ə-jē	likeness in some respects between things otherwise different; similarity; comparison	An *analogy* is frequently made between life and a candle, since each lasts a relatively short time, and each is capable of being snuffed out.
arbitrary (*adj.*) 'är-bə-ˌtrer-ē	autocratic; despotic; tyrannical; proceeding from a whim or fancy (*ant.* **legitimate**)	A promotion should depend on an employee's record rather than on some official's *arbitrary* decision.

arbitrate (*v.*)
'är-bə-ˌtrāt

1. decide a dispute, acting as an *arbiter* or *arbitrator* (judge)

2. submit a dispute to arbitration

When the opposing claimants asked me to *arbitrate*, it was understood they would abide by my decision.
Neither side has shown any eagerness to *arbitrate*.

axiom (*n.*)
'ak-sē-əm

self-evident truth; maxim

It is an *axiom* that practice makes perfect.

axiomatic (*adj.*)
ˌak-sē-ə-'mat-ik

self-evident; universally accepted as true

It is *axiomatic* that expenditures should not exceed income.

bias (*n.*)
'bī-əs

opinion formed before there are grounds for it; prejudice; predilection; partiality

Prospective jurors with a *bias* for or against the defendant were not picked for the jury.

bigoted (*adj.*)
'big-ət-əd

intolerant; narrow-minded

It is futile to argue with *bigoted* persons; they hold stubbornly to their prejudices.

bigotry (*n.*)
'big-ə-trē

views or behavior of a *bigot* (one intolerantly devoted to one's own beliefs and prejudices); narrow-mindedness; intolerance

On hearing the verdict, the defendant accused the judge and the jury of *bigotry*.

cogitate (*v.*)
'käj-ə-ˌtāt

think over; consider with care; ponder

Since the matter is important, I must have time to *cogitate* before announcing my decision.

criterion (*n.*)
krī-'tir-ē-ən

standard; rule or test for judging (*pl.* **criteria**)

Two of the *criteria* that experts consider in judging an automobile are fuel consumption and frequency of repair.

crux (*n.*)
'krəks

most important point; essential part

Skip over the minor points and get to the *crux* of the matter.

deduce (*v.*)
di-'d(y)üs

derive by reasoning; infer

From the fact that the victim's wallet and jewelry were not taken, we *deduced* that robbery had not been a motive for the murder.

dilemma (*n.*)
də-'lem-ə

situation requiring a choice between two equally bad alternatives; predicament

Trapped by the flames, the guests on the upper stories faced the *dilemma* of leaping or waiting for an uncertain rescue.

dogmatic (*adj.*)
dȯg-'mat-ik

asserting opinions as if they were facts; opinionated; asserted without proof

If, without offering any proof at all, you keep insisting that the plan will not work, you are being *dogmatic*.

eclectic (*adj.*)
e-'klek-tik

choosing (ideas, methods, etc.) from various sources

In some matters I follow the progressives and in others the conservatives; you may consider me *eclectic*.

fallacious (*adj.*)
fə-'lā-shəs

based on a *fallacy* (erroneous idea); misleading; deceptive
(*ant.* **sound; valid**)

For centuries people held the *fallacious* view that the sun revolves around the earth.

fallible (*adj.*)
'fal-ə-bəl

liable to be mistaken
(*ant.* **infallible**)

Umpires occasionally make mistakes; like other human beings, they too are *fallible*.

heterodox (*adj.*)
'het-ə-rə-ˌdäks

rejecting regularly accepted beliefs or doctrines; heretical; nonconformist
(*ant.* **orthodox**)

Political dissenters in dictatorships are often persecuted for their *heterodox* beliefs.

hypothetical (*adj.*)
ˌhī-pə-'thet-i-kəl

supposed; having the characteristics of a *hypothesis*, a supposition made as a basis for reasoning or research. (If supported by considerable evidence, a hypothesis becomes a *theory*, and eventually, if no exceptions are found, a *law*.)

The detective investigated each employee because of a *hypothetical* notion that the robber had received ''inside'' information.

illusion (*n.*)
il-'ü-zhən

misleading appearance; false impression; misconception

Barbara had thought that no college student could be dishonest, but the theft of her textbooks shattered that *illusion*.

indubitable (*adj.*)
in-'d(y)ü-bət-ə-bəl

certain; incontrovertible; indisputable
(*ant.* **questionable; doubtful**)

The defendant's confession, added to the witnesses' testimony, makes his guilt *indubitable*.

orthodox (*adj.*)
'òr-thə-ˌdäks

generally accepted, especially in religion; conventional; approved
(*ant.* **heterodox; unorthodox**)

At the dinner table, it is *orthodox* to use a knife and fork instead of your fingers.

paradoxical (*adj.*)
ˌpar-ə-'däk-si-kəl

having the characteristics of a *paradox* (a self-contradictory statement which may nevertheless be true)

It is *paradoxical* but true that teachers may be taught by their pupils.

plausible (*adj.*)
'plò-zə-bəl

superficially true or reasonable; apparently trustworthy

In the Middle Ages, the view that the earth is flat seemed *plausible*.

preposterous (*adj.*)
pri-'päs-t(ə-)rəs

senseless; absurd; irrational

The choice of Stella for the leading role is *preposterous*; she can't act.

rational (*adj.*)
'rash-ə-nᵊl

1. able to think clearly; intelligent; sensible (*ant.* **absurd; irrational**)
2. based on reason

Humans are *rational*; animals have little power of reason.
Mobs, as a rule, do not make *rational* decisions.

rationalize (*v.*)
'rash-ə-nᵊl-ˌīz

invent excuses for one's actions, desires, failures, etc.

The fox in the fable *rationalized* his failure to get at the grapes by claiming that they were sour.

sophistry (*n.*) 'säf-ə-strē	clever but deceptive reasoning	Imagine the *sophistry* of that child! He denied having a water pistol because, as he later explained, he had two.
specious (*adj.*) 'spē-shəs	apparently reasonable, but not really so	The contractor's claim that her employees have an average experience of five years is *specious*; one has had twenty years of experience, but the other three are beginners.
speculate (*v.*) 'spek-yə-ˌlāt	1. reflect; meditate; conjecture	Space exploration may solve a problem on which we have long *speculated*—whether or not human life exists elsewhere in the universe.
	2. buy or sell with the hope of profiting by price fluctuations	Aunt Susan never invests in risky stocks; she does not *speculate* .
tenable (*adj.*) 'ten-ə-bəl	capable of being maintained or defended (*ant.* **untenable**)	An argument supported by facts is more *tenable* than one based on hearsay.

---

22. Shape

---

amorphous (*adj.*) ə-'mȯr-fəs	shapeless; having no definite form; unorganized	At first my ideas for a term paper were *amorphous*, but now they are beginning to assume a definite shape.
concave (*adj.*) kän-'kāv	curved inward, creating a hollow space (*ant.* **convex**)	In its first and last quarters, the moon is crescent-shaped; its inner edge is *concave* and its outer *convex*.
contour (*n.*) 'kän-ˌtü(ə)r	outline of a figure	The *contour* of our Atlantic coast is much more irregular than that of our Pacific coast.
distort (*v.*) dis-'tȯrt	1. twist out of shape 2. change from the true meaning	My uncle suffered a minor stroke that temporarily *distorted* his face. A company that speaks of the ''average experience'' of its technicians may be *distorting* the truth, as some of them may have had no experience.
malleable (*adj.*) 'mal-yə-bəl	1. capable of being shaped by hammering, as a metal 2. adaptable	Copper is easily shaped into thin sheets because it is very *malleable*. Had they asked me, I would not have reduced the price, but they bargained with my partner, who is more *malleable*.

rotund (*adj.*) rō-'tənd	1. rounded out; plump	Santa Claus has a white beard and a *rotund* figure.
	2. full-toned	The announcer introduced each of the players in a clear, *rotund* voice.
sinuous (*adj.*) 'sin-yə-wəs	bending in and out; winding; serpentine	Signs that forewarn motorists of a *sinuous* stretch of road often indicate a safe speed for negotiating the curves.
symmetrical (*adj.*) sə-'me-tri-kəl	balanced in arrangement; capable of division by a central line into similar halves (*ant.* **asymmetrical**)	This badly misshapen bumper was perfectly *symmetrical* before the accident.
symmetry (*n.*) 'sim-ə-trē	balance; harmony	It is amazing how a flock of wild geese can maintain perfect *symmetry* in flight.

23. Importance—Unimportance

grave (*adj.*) 'grāv	deserving serious attention; weighty; momentous	The President summoned the cabinet into emergency session on receipt of the *grave* news.
nugatory (*adj.*) 'n(y)ü-gə-ˌtȯr-ē	of little or no value; trifling; worthless; useless	My last-minute cramming was *nugatory*; at the examination, I didn't remember a thing.
paltry (*adj.*) 'pȯl-trē	practically worthless; trashy; piddling; petty	I complain not because of the *paltry* few pennies I was overcharged but because of the principle involved.
paramount (*adj.*) 'par-ə-ˌmaȯnt	chief; above others; supreme	A *paramount* concern of the parents is the welfare of their children.
relevant (*adj.*) 'rel-ə-vənt	bearing upon the matter in hand; pertinent (*ant.* **irrelevant; extraneous**)	The prosecutor objected that the witness' testimony had nothing to do with the case, but the judge ruled that it was *relevant*.

24. Modesty

| **coy** (*adj.*) 'kȯi | pretending to be shy | Annabelle's shyness was just a pretense; she was being *coy*. |

demure (*adj.*) di-'myú(ə)r	1. falsely modest or serious; coy	The children giggled behind the teacher's back, but as soon as he turned around they looked *demure*.
	2. grave; prim	Who would have guessed that so *demure* a person as Mr. Lee was addicted to betting on horse races?
diffident (*adj.*) 'dif-əd-ənt	lacking self-confidence; unduly timid; shy (*ant.* **confident**)	Though Carlo's teachers were confident that he would succeed, he himself was *diffident*.
modest (*adj.*) 'mäd-əst	not thinking too highly of one's merits; unpretentious; humble (*ant.* **ambitious**)	Joe is the real hero, but he is too *modest* to talk about it.
modesty (*n.*) 'mäd-əs-tē	freedom from conceit or vanity; unpretentiousness; humility	*Modesty* prevents Donna from wearing any of the medals she has won.
staid (*adj.*) 'stād	of settled, quiet disposition; sedate	Shocking pink is much too loud; beige is more *staid*.

25. Vanity

brazen (*adj.*) 'brāz-ᵊn	1. shameless; impudent	Two persons in the audience were smoking in *brazen* defiance of the "No Smoking" sign.
	2. made of brass or bronze	We have a pair of *brazen* candlesticks.
egoism (*n.*) 'ē-gə-ˌwiz-əm	excessive concern for oneself; selfishness; conceit (*ant.* **altruism**)	By assuming full credit for our committee's hard work, the chairperson has disclosed her *egoism*.
ostentatious (*adj.*) ˌäs-tən-'tā-shəs	done to impress others; showy; pretentious	Parked next to our staid family car was an *ostentatious* red convertible.
overweening (*adj.*) ˌō-və(r)-'wē-niŋ	thinking too highly of oneself; arrogant; presumptuous	After his initial victories, the *overweening* pugilist boasted that he was invincible.
pert (*adj.*) 'pərt	too free in speech or action; bold; saucy; impertinent	Most of us addressed the speaker as "Dr. Bell," but one sophomore began a question with a *pert* "Doc."
vain (*adj.*) 'vān	1. conceited; excessively proud or concerned about one's personal appearance or achievements 2. empty; worthless 3. futile	Oscar boasts about his awards to everyone, even strangers. I have never seen such a *vain* person. We have had enough of your *vain* promises; you never keep your word. Anna made a valiant but *vain* effort to get her sister to stop smoking.

vainglorious (adj.) vān-'glōr-ē-əs	excessively proud or boastful; elated by vanity	*Vainglorious* Ozymandias had these words inscribed on the pedestal of his statue, now shattered: ''Look on my works, ye Mighty, and despair!''
vanity (n.) 'van-ə-tē	condition of being too vain about one's appearance or achievements; conceit (*ant.* **humility**)	If you are free of *vanity*, you will not be fooled by flatterers.

Apply What You Have Learned

EXERCISE 3.29: ANTONYMS

Each italicized word in column I has an *antonym* in column II. Insert the *letter* of that antonym in the space provided.

	COLUMN I		COLUMN II
1. _____	*confident* outlook	(A)	altruism
2. _____	*legitimate* ruling	(B)	fallacious
3. _____	shows *vanity*	(C)	diffident
4. _____	*questionable* evidence	(D)	arbitrary
5. _____	example of *egoism*	(E)	rational
6. _____	*sound* reasoning	(F)	indubitable
7. _____	*ambitious* expectations	(G)	concave
8. _____	*absurd* conclusion	(H)	humility
9. _____	*relevant* details	(I)	modest
10. _____	*convex* surface	(J)	extraneous

EXERCISE 3.30: UNRELATED WORDS

Write the letter of the word unrelated in meaning to the other words on the line.

1. (A) deceptive   (B) infallible   (C) erroneous   (D) fallacious   _____

2. (A) bold   (B) immodest   (C) pertinent   (D) impudent   _____

3. (A) intolerance   (B) prejudice   (C) impartiality   (D) bias   _____

4. (A) concave   (B) buxom   (C) rotund   (D) corpulent   _____

5. (A) unrelated   (B) impertinent   (C) rude   (D) irrelevant   _____

6. (A) petty   (B) piddling   (C) paltry   (D) prim   _____

7. (A) heretical   (B) paradox   (C) heterodox   (D) unorthodox   _____

8. (A) preposterous   (B) vain   (C) proud   (D) conceited   _____

9. (A) shy   (B) diffident   (C) arrogant   (D) coy   _____

10. (A) indisputable   (B) axiomatic   (C) incontrovertible   (D) hypothetical   _____

EXERCISE 3.31: SENTENCE COMPLETION

Fill each blank with the most appropriate word from the vocabulary list below.

VOCABULARY LIST

axiomatic	analogy	saucy
dilemma	staid	hypothesis
theory	paradox	dogmatic
paramount	illusion	speculating
sophistry	relevant	ostentatious

1. Scientific research usually begins with a(n) _____ .

2. Grandmother and Grandfather look dignified and _____ in their wedding picture.

3. Jack never wears any of his medals because he doesn't want to appear _____ .

4. On a sinking ship, saving the lives of the passengers is the _____ consideration.

5. When exasperated with my little brother, I call him a ''snake,'' but my parents do not like the

   _____ .

6. It is _____ that the shortest distance between any two points on a plane surface is a straight line.

7. As we were discussing tomorrow's picnic, Dinah interrupted with a(n) _____ question about the weather forecast.

8. The company faces the _____ of going into bankruptcy or seeing its debts mount further.

9. _____ always involves risk, as prices fluctuate.

10. What I had been reasonably certain was a ship approaching on the horizon turned out to be a

   mere _____ .

EXERCISE 3.32: CONCISE WRITING

Express the thought of each sentence below in no more than four words. The first sentence has been rewritten as a sample.

1. His weakness is that he is excessively concerned about his personal appearance.

   His weakness is vanity.

2. People dislike commands that proceed from someone's whim or fancy.

_____

3. We're in a situation in which we must make a choice between two equally bad alternatives.

_____

4. The reasons that he gave seemed reasonable, but they really were not.

_____

5. She sometimes expresses opinions without offering proof to support them.

_____

6. The questions you are asking have no bearing on the matter in hand.

_____

7. What is the supposition on which she is basing her research?

_____

8. Traders like to buy or sell with the expectation of making profits from price fluctuations.

_____

9. The thoughts that I had in my brain had no definite shape or form.

_____

10. What is the reason for your lack of confidence in yourself?

_____

EXERCISE 3.33: BRAINTEASERS

Fill in the missing letters.

1. The __ __ __ __ **o u r** of the distant peak grew more distinct in the sky.

2. Why must you insist that you are always right? Don't you know that everyone is

   __ **a l l** __ __ __ __?

3. These __ __ **t e n t** __ __ __ __ __ __ furnishings were meant to impress guests.

4. A deer's antlers are perfectly __ __ __ **m e t** __ __ __ __ __.

5. It is __ __ __ __ __ **m a t** __ __ that opposites attract.

6. The older settlers found it hard to adapt to the new circumstances; the younger ones were much

   more __ **a l l** __ __ __ __ __.

7. It is a maxim that a person with _ _ _ _ **w e e** _ _ _ _ ambitions is almost surely headed for a downfall.

8. The path was so **s i n** _ _ _ _ that we soon lost our sense of direction.

9. Most investors were dissatisfied with their _ _ _ **a t** _ _ _ gains.

10. Are you so wrapped up in your own _ **g o** _ _ _ that you give no thought to others?

EXERCISE 3.34: COMPOSITION

Answer in two or three sentences.

1. Why is it difficult for vain individuals to admit that they are fallible?

_____

_____

_____

2. Who is more likely to be popular—a modest champion, or an overweening one? Why?

_____

_____

_____

3. What would be your most important criterion in arbitrating a dispute between two members of your family? Explain.

_____

_____

_____

4. Would you regard it as nugatory if your opponent in an election distorted one of your statements? Why, or why not?

_____

_____

_____

5. Why is it preposterous for a person with a bias against consumers to be nominated to head a consumer protection agency?

_____

_____

_____

EXERCISE 3.35: ANALOGIES

In the space at the left, write the *letter* of the best choice.

_____ **1.** CONTOUR : STATUE

    a. shadow : body   *d.* area : surface
    b. coastline : island   *e.* original : imitation
    c. peak : mountain

_____ **2.** CRUX : ARGUMENT

    a. title : book   *d.* door : house
    b. bridge : river   *e.* costume : actor
    c. kernel : nut

_____ **3.** CONCAVE : CONVEX

    a. bowl : platter   *d.* cavity : swelling
    b. bulge : dent   *e.* building : dome
    c. cup : saucer

_____ **4.** HYPOTHESIS : TRUTH

    a. supposition : fact   *d.* folly : wisdom
    b. proof : conclusion   *e.* guess : blunder
    c. deceit : honesty

_____ **5.** RATIONALIZING : SELF-DECEPTION

    a. speculating : thrift   *d.* brazenness : courtesy
    b. egoism : shyness   *e.* boasting : vanity
    c. cogitating : brain

CHAPTER 4

Words Derived From Greek

A great revival of interest in ancient Greek and Latin civilizations took place in England during the years 1500–1650, a period known as the Renaissance. At that time numerous ancient Greek and Latin words and their derivatives were incorporated into our language. This pattern of language growth has continued to the present day. When modern scientists need to name a new idea, process, or object, they tend to avoid existing English words because these already may have several other meanings. Instead they prefer to construct a new English word out of one or more ancient Greek or Latin words. Ancient Greek has been especially preferred as a source of new words in the scientific and technical fields.

Here are twenty-five ancient Greek prefixes and roots that have enriched our language. Each one, as you can see, has produced a group of useful English words.

1. PHOBIA: "fear," "dislike," "aversion"

WORD	MEANING
acrophobia (*n.*) ˌak-rə-ˈfō-bē-ə	fear of being at a great height
agoraphobia (*n.*) ˌag-ə-rə-ˈfō-bē-ə	fear of open spaces
Anglophobia (*n.*) ˌaŋ-glə-ˈfō-bē-ə	dislike of England or the English (*ant.* **Anglophilia**)
claustrophobia (*n.*) ˌklȯ-strə-ˈfō-bē-ə	fear of enclosed or narrow spaces
Germanophobia (*n.*) jer-ˌman-ə-ˈfō-bē-ə	dislike of Germany or the Germans (*ant.* **Germanophilia**)
hydrophobia (*n.*) ˌhī-drə-ˈfō-bē-ə	1. morbid (abnormal) fear of water 2. rabies
monophobia (*n.*) ˌmä-nō-ˈfō-bē-ə	fear of being alone

phobia (*n.*) ˈfō-bē-ə	fear; dread; aversion
photophobia (*n.*) ˌfōt-ə-ˈfō-bē-ə	morbid aversion to light
xenophobia (*n.*) ˌzen-ə-ˈfō-bē-ə	aversion to foreigners

The form *phobe* at the end of a word means "one who fears or dislikes." For example:

Russophobe (*n.*) ˈrə-sə-ˌfōb	one who dislikes Russia or the Russians (*ant.* **Russophile**)

Also: **Francophobe, Anglophobe, Germanophobe,** etc.

EXERCISE 4.1

In each blank, insert the most appropriate word from group 1, *phobia*.

1. You would not expect a professional mountain climber to have _____.

2. As we grow up, we overcome our childhood _____ of the dark.

3. Passage of the Chinese Exclusion Act of 1882 proves that some degree of _____ existed in our nation at that time.

4. Youngsters who suffer from _____ do not make a habit of hiding in closets.

5. After many decades of _____, the French joined the West Germans in close economic ties following World War II.

2. PHIL (PHILO): "loving," "fond of"

philanthropist (*n.*) fə-ˈlan-thrə-pəst	lover of humanity; person active in promoting human welfare (*ant.* **misanthrope**)
philanthropy (*n.*) fə-ˈlan-thrə-pē	love of humanity, especially as shown in donations to charitable and socially useful causes (*ant.* **misanthropy**)
philatelist (*n.*) fə-ˈlat-ᵊl-əst	stamp collector
philately (*n.*) fə-ˈlat-ᵊl-ē	collection and study of stamps
philharmonic (*adj.*) ˌfil-ər-ˈmän-ik	pertaining to a musical organization, such as a symphony orchestra (originally, "loving music")

philhellenism (*n.*) fil-'hel-ə-ˌniz-əm	support of Greece or the Greeks
philogyny (*n.*) fə-'läj-ə-nē	love of women (*ant.* **misogyny**)
philology (*n.*) fə-'läl-ə-jē	study (love) of language and literature
philosopher (*n.*) fə-'läs-ə-fə(r)	lover of, or searcher for, wisdom or knowledge; person who regulates his or her life by the light of reason

The form *phile* at the end of a word means "one who loves or supports." For example:

Anglophile (*n.*) 'aŋ-glə-ˌfīl	supporter of England or the English (*ant.* **Anglophobe**)
audiophile (*n.*) 'ȯd-ē-ō-ˌfīl	one who is enthusiastic about high-fidelity sound reproduction on records and tapes
bibliophile (*n.*) 'bib-lē-ə-ˌfīl	lover of books (*ant.* **bibliophobe**)
Francophile (*n.*) 'fraŋ-kə-ˌfīl	supporter of France or the French (*ant.* **Francophobe**)

EXERCISE 4.2

In each blank, insert the most appropriate word from group 2, *phil* (*philo*).

1. Socrates, the great Athenian _____, devoted his life to seeking truth and exposing error.

2. The _____ was proud of his fine collection of beautifully bound volumes.

3. Do you collect stamps? I, too, was once interested in _____.

4. The _____s among the American colonists were opposed to the war with England.

5. In her will, the _____ bequeathed more than a million dollars to charity.

6. _____s are especially eager to listen to newly released recordings by outstanding artists.

3. MIS: "hate" (MIS means the opposite of PHIL.)

misandry (*n.*) 'mi-ˌsan-drē	hatred of males
misanthrope (*n.*) 'mis-ᵊn-ˌthrōp	hater of humanity (*ant.* **philanthropist**)

misanthropy (*n.*) mis-'an-thrə-pē	hatred of humanity (*ant.* **philanthropy**)
misogamy (*n.*) mə-'säg-ə-mē	hatred of marriage
misogyny (*n.*) mə-'säj-ə-nē	hatred of women (*ant.* **philogyny**)
misology (*n.*) mə-'säl-ə-jē	hatred of argument, reasoning, or discussion
misoneism (*n.*) ˌmis-ə-'nē-ˌiz-əm	hatred of anything new

EXERCISE 4.3

In each blank, insert the most appropriate word from group 3, *mis.*

1. Hamlet's _____ resulted from his mistaken conclusion that he had been betrayed by a woman—Ophelia.

2. When Gulliver returned from his travels, he could not endure the sight of fellow humans; he had become a _____ .

3. Surprisingly, the first of the fraternity members to marry was the one who had been the loudest advocate of _____ .

4. Isabel enjoys discussion and debate; she cannot be accused of _____ .

5. Some oppose innovation out of sheer _____ ; they do not want any change.

4. DYS: "bad," "ill," "difficult"

dysentery (*n.*) dis-ᵊn-ˌter-ē	inflammation of the large intestine
dysfunction (*n.*) dis-'fəŋk-shən	abnormal functioning, as of an organ of the body
dyslexia (*n.*) də-'slek-sē-ə	impairment of the ability to read
dyslogistic (*adj.*) ˌdis-lə-'jis-tik	expressing disapproval or censure; uncomplimentary (*ant.* **eulogistic**)
dyspepsia (*n.*) dis-'pep-shə	difficult digestion; indigestion (*ant.* **eupepsia**)
dysphagia (*n.*) dis-'fā-jə	difficulty in swallowing

dysphasia (*n.*) dis-'fā-zhə	speech difficulty resulting from brain injury
dysphoria (*n.*) dis-'fōr-ē-ə	sense of great unhappiness or dissatisfaction (*ant.* **euphoria**)
dystopia (*n.*) dis-'tō-pē-ə	imaginary place where living conditions are dreadful (*ant.* **utopia**)
dystrophy (*n.*) 'dis-trə-fē	faulty nutrition

EXERCISE 4.4

In each blank, insert the most appropriate word from group 4, *dys.*

1. To aid digestion, eat slowly; rapid eating may cause _____.

2. Those who ate the contaminated food became ill with _____.

3. Injury to the brain may result in _____, a complicated speech disorder.

4. Muscular _____ is a disease in which the muscles waste away.

5. When your throat is badly inflamed, you may experience some _____ at mealtime.

6. George Orwell's *Nineteen Eighty-Four* is about a totalitarian _____ where life is incredibly horrible.

---

5. EU: "good," "well," "advantageous" (EU means the opposite of DYS.)

---

eugenics (*n.*) yu̇-'jen-iks	science dealing with improving the hereditary qualities of the human race
eulogize (*v.*) 'yü-lə-ˌjīz	write or speak in praise of someone (*ant.* **vilify**)
eupepsia (*n.*) yu̇-'pep-shə	good digestion (*ant.* **dyspepsia**)
euphemism (*n.*) 'yü-fə-ˌmiz-əm	substitution of a "good" expression for an unpleasant one. Example: *sanitation* for *garbage collection.*
euphonious (*adj.*) yu̇-'fō-nē-əs	pleasing in sound (*ant.* **cacophonous**)
euphoria (*n.*) yu̇-'fȯr-ē-ə	sense of great happiness or well-being (*ant.* **dysphoria**)

| euthanasia (*n.*) ˌyü-thə-'nā-zhə | controversial practice of mercifully putting to death a person suffering from an incurable, painfully distressing disease (literally ''advantageous death'') |
| euthenics (*n.*) yu̇-'then-iks | science dealing with improving living conditions |

EXERCISE 4.5

In each blank, insert the most appropriate word from group 5, *eu.*

1. The audience liked the organist's _____ melodies.

2. Before conferring the award, the presiding officer will probably _____ the recipient.

3. The employee formerly called a ''janitor'' is now known by a _____ such as ''superintendent'' or ''custodian.''

4. Many believe that anyone who commits _____, regardless of the circumstances, is a murderer.

5. The _____ I felt when my teacher complimented my work this morning stayed with me for the rest of the day.

---

6. MACRO: ''large,'' ''long''
7. MICRO: ''small,'' ''minute''

---

macrocosm (*n.*) 'mak-rə-ˌkaz-əm	great world; universe (*ant.* **microcosm**)
macron (*n.*) 'māk-ˌrän	horizontal mark indicating that the vowel over which it is placed is long
macroscopic (*adj.*) ˌmak-rə-'skäp-ik	large enough to be visible to the naked eye (*ant.* **microscopic**)
microbe (*n.*) 'mī-ˌkrōb	microscopic living animal or plant; microorganism
microbicide (*n.*) mī-'krō-bə-ˌsīd	agent that destroys microbes
microdont (*adj.*) 'mī-krə-ˌdänt	having small teeth
microfilm (*n.*) 'mī-krə-ˌfilm	film of very small size

microgram (*n.*) 'mī-krə-ˌgram	millionth of a gram
micrometer (*n.*) 'mi-krō-ˌmēt-ər	millionth of a meter
microorganism (*n.*) ˌmī-krō-'òr-gə-ˌniz-əm	microscopic living animal or plant
microsecond (*n.*) 'mī-krə-ˌsek-ənd	millionth of a second
microsurgery (*n.*) ˌmī-krō-'serj-ə-rē	surgery with the aid of microscopes and minute instruments or laser beams
microvolt (*n.*) 'mī-krə-ˌvōlt	millionth of a volt
microwatt (*n.*) 'mī-krə-ˌwät	millionth of a watt
microwave (*n.*) 'mī-krə-wāv	1. very short electromagnetic wave 2. microwave oven (oven that cooks quickly by using microwaves)

EXERCISE 4.6

In each blank, insert the most appropriate word from groups 6 and 7, *macro* and *micro*.

1. Documents can be recorded in a minimum of space if photographed on _____.

2. Space exploration has made us more aware of the vastness of the _____.

3. A _____ enables us to measure very minute distances that cannot be measured accurately with a ruler.

4. An ant is visible to the naked eye, but an ameba is _____.

5. The dictionary uses a _____ to tell us that the *e* in *ēra* is a long vowel.

6. Thanks to the miracle of _____, the patient's detached retina was successfully reattached.

---

8. A (AN): "not," "without"

---

amoral (*adj.*) ā-'mòr-əl	not moral; without a sense of moral responsibility
amorphous (*adj.*) ə-'mòr-fəs	without (having no) definite form or shape
anarchy (*n.*) 'an-ər-kē	total absence of rule or government; confusion; disorder

anemia (*n.*) ə-'nē-mē-ə	lack of a normal number of red blood cells
anesthesia (*n.*) ‚an-əs-'thē-zhə	loss of feeling or sensation resulting from ether, chloroform, novocaine, etc.
anesthetic (*n.*) ‚an-əs-'thet-ik	drug that produces anesthesia
anhydrous (*adj.*) an-'hī-drəs	destitute of (without) water
anomaly (*n.*) ə-'näm-ə-lē	deviation from the common rule
anomalous (*adj.*) ə-'näm-ə-ləs	not normal; abnormal
anonymous (*adj.*) ə-'nän-ə-məs	nameless; of unknown or unnamed origin
anoxia (*n.*) a-'näk-sē-ə	deprivation of (state of being without) oxygen
apnea (*n.*) 'ap-nē-ə	temporary cessation of breathing
aseptic (*adj.*) ā-'sep-tik	free from disease-causing microorganisms
asymptomatic (*adj.*) ‚ā-‚sim-tə-'mat-ik	showing no symptoms of disease
atheism (*n.*) 'ā-thē-‚iz-əm	godlessness; denial of the existence of a Supreme Being
atrophy (*n.*) 'a-trə-fē	lack of growth from disuse or want of nourishment (*ant.* **hypertrophy**, hī-'pər-trə-fē, enlargement of a body part, as from excessive use)
atypical (*adj.*) ā-'tip-i-kəl	unlike the typical

EXERCISE 4.7

In each blank, insert the most appropriate word from group 8, *a(an)*.

1. The gift is _____. We have no idea who sent it.

2. In the tropics a snowstorm would be a(n) _____.

3. The administration of a(n) _____ prevents the patient from feeling pain during and immediately after an operation.

4. Wendy is _____ in one respect: she doesn't care for ice cream.

5. In _____ surgery, rigid precautions are taken to exclude disease-causing microorganisms.

6. Dan is cured. Medical tests show that he is _____.

9. MONO (MON): "one," "single," "alone"
10. POLY: "many"

monarchy (*n.*)
'män-ər-kē

rule by a single person
(*ant.* **polyarchy**)

monochromatic (*adj.*)
‚män-ə-krō-'mat-ik

of one color
(*ant.* **polychromatic**)

monocle (*n.*)
'män-i-kəl

eyeglass for one eye

monogamy (*n.*)
mə-'näg-ə-mē

marriage with one mate at a time
(*ant.* **polygamy**)

monogram (*n.*)
'män-ə-‚gram

two or more letters interwoven to represent a name

monograph (*n.*)
'män-ə-‚graf

written account of a single thing or class of things

monolith (*n.*)
'män-ᵊl-‚ith

single stone of large size

monolog(ue) (*n.*)
'män-ᵊl-‚og

long speech by one person in a group

monomania (*n.*)
‚män-ə-'mā-nē-ə

excessive concentration on one idea or subject

monomorphic (*adj.*)
‚män-ō-'mȯr-fik

having a single form
(*ant.* **polymorphic**)

monosyllabic (*adj.*)
‚män-ə-sə-'lab-ik

having one syllable
(*ant.* **polysyllabic**)

monotheism (*n.*)
'män-ə-thē-‚iz-əm

belief that there is one God
(*ant.* **polytheism**)

monotonous (*adj.*)
mə-'nät-ᵊn-əs

continuing in an unchanging tone; wearying

polyarchy (*n.*)
'pä-lē-‚är-kē

rule by many
(*ant.* **monarchy**)

polychromatic (*adj.*)
‚päl-i-krō-'mat-ik

having a variety of colors; multicolored
(*ant.* **monochromatic**)

polygamy (*n.*)
pə-'lig-ə-mē

marriage to several mates at the same time
(*ant.* **monogamy**)

polyglot (*adj.*) 'päl-i-ˌglät	speaking several languages
polyglot (*n.*)	person who speaks several languages
polygon (*n.*) 'päl-i-ˌgän	closed plane figure having, literally, "many angles" —and therefore many sides
polymorphic (*adj.*) ˌpäl-i-'mȯr-fik	having various forms (*ant.* **monomorphic**)
polyphonic (*adj.*) ˌpäl-i-'fän-ik	having many sounds or voices (*ant.* **homophonic**, having the same sound)
polysyllabic (*adj.*) ˌpäl-i-sə-'lab-ik	having more than three syllables (*ant.* **monosyllabic**)
polytechnic (*adj.*) ˌpäl-i-'tek-nik	dealing with many technical arts or sciences
polytheism (*n.*) 'päl-i-thē-ˌiz-əm	belief that there is a plurality of gods (*ant.* **monotheism**)

EXERCISE 4.8

In each blank, insert the most appropriate word from groups 9 and 10, *mono* and *poly*.

1. The idea of getting revenge on Moby Dick was never absent from Ahab's mind—it was his

   _____ .

2. Books for beginning readers contain relatively few _____ words.

3. The Romans obviously practiced _____, for they worshiped many gods.

4. A relative gave me a jacket embroidered with my own _____ .

5. A discussion in which you take part is practically a _____; you hardly give anyone else a chance to speak.

6. Our _____ neighbor speaks French, German, Russian, and English.

7. Professor Shaw's _____ on garden insecticides is being widely read.

8. A _____ institute offers instruction in many applied sciences and technical arts.

9. Repetitive work soon becomes _____ .

10. A huge _____, the 555-foot Washington Monument dominates the skyline of our nation's capital.

Review Exercises

REVIEW 1: GREEK PREFIXES AND ROOTS

In the space before each Greek prefix or root in column I, write the *letter* of its correct meaning from column II.

	COLUMN I		COLUMN II
_____	1. PHOBIA	*a.*	bad; ill; difficult
_____	2. MACRO	*b.*	small; minute
_____	3. PHIL (PHILO)	*c.*	not; without
_____	4. MONO (MON)	*d.*	one; single; alone
_____	5. A (AN)	*e.*	fear; dislike; aversion
_____	6. DYS	*f.*	one who loves or supports
_____	7. POLY	*g.*	many
_____	8. PHOBE	*h.*	loving; fond of
_____	9. MIS	*i.*	large; long
_____	10. MICRO	*j.*	good; well; advantageous
_____	11. EU	*k.*	hate
_____	12. PHILE	*l.*	one who fears or dislikes

REVIEW 2: OPPOSITES

In the blank space, write the word that means the OPPOSITE of the word defined. (The first answer has been filled in as an example.)

DEFINITION	WORD	OPPOSITE
1. belief in God	theism	atheism
2. supporter of Russia	Russophile	_____
3. conforming to a type	typical	_____
4. good digestion	eupepsia	_____
5. one who dislikes books	bibliophobe	_____
6. lover of humanity	philanthropist	_____
7. believing there is but one God	monotheistic	_____
8. harsh in sound	cacophonous	_____

9. showing a variety of colors   polychromatic   _____

10. infected   septic   _____

11. without a sense of moral responsibility   amoral   _____

12. married to several mates at the same time   polygamous   _____

13. invisible to the naked eye   microscopic   _____

14. enlargement, as from excessive use   hypertrophy   _____

15. rule by many   polyarchy   _____

16. sense of great happiness   euphoria   _____

17. expressing censure or disapproval   dyslogistic   _____

18. having but one syllable   monosyllabic   _____

19. the great world; universe   macrocosm   _____

20. having various forms   polymorphic   _____

REVIEW 3: SENTENCE COMPLETION

Fill each blank with the most appropriate word from the vocabulary list below.

VOCABULARY LIST

euphemistic	euphoria	dysentery
monogram	dysphagia	acrophobia
euthanasia	anesthesia	dystrophy
misanthropy	anomalous	philatelist
anonymous	monograph	xenophobia

1. There is a conflict in the minds of many between the commandment ''Thou shalt not kill'' and the practice of _____ .

2. A two-headed horse would be a(n) _____ sight.

3. The new regime dislikes foreigners; it exhibits a profound _____ .

4. Though the letter was _____, I was able to discover who had written it.

5. The term ''mortician'' is a(n) _____ term for ''undertaker.''

6. The drinking of contaminated water can cause _____, an inflammation of the large intestine.

7. A(n) _____ collects stamps.

8. I had no dread of heights, but my companion's _____ became more severe as we approached the summit.

9. So effective was the local _____ that the patient experienced practically no pain during the surgery.

10. The biology professor is the author of a(n) _____ on earthworms.

REVIEW 4: CONCISE WRITING

Express the thought of each sentence below in no more than four words. The first sentence has been rewritten as a sample.

1. Scrooge has nothing but hate and contempt for other human beings.

   Scrooge is a misanthrope.

2. That patient does not have the normal number of red blood cells.

   _____

3. It is impossible to see viruses with the naked eye.

   _____

4. Beret suffered from a fear of being in the midst of open spaces.

   _____

5. It is against the law for people to be married to several mates at the same time.

   _____

6. Clouds in the sky generally have no definite shape or form.

   _____

7. Carnegie used his millions to promote the welfare of his fellow human beings.

   _____

8. Many inhabitants had a disease characterized by an inflammation of the large intestine.

   _____

9. The fear of being at a great height is quite common.

   _____

10. Mama is an individual who lives her life by the light of reason.

    _____

REVIEW 5: BRAINTEASERS

Fill in the missing letters.

1. Stop using __ __ __ __ __ __ __ l a b __ __ words just to impress others.

2. Many __ __ __ l a t e __ __ __ __ __ own stamps from almost every nation.

3. The dog owner used a(n) __ __ __ h e m __ __ __ when he told us that his ailing poodle had been "put to sleep" by the veterinarian.

4. One would not expect a **b i b** __ __ __ __ __ __ __ __ to have a library card.

5. If we had no laws or government, there would be total __ __ **a r c** __ __.

6. Is there really a(n) __ **t o p** __ __, where living conditions are ideal?

7. Under favorable conditions, an accident victim's detached limb can be reattached through __ __ __ __ __ __ **u r g e** __ __.

8. My __ __ __ __ **h a g** __ __ has eased, but it is still hard for me to swallow.

9. The star was delighted when critics wrote __ __ **l o g** __ __ __ __ __ reviews about her new film.

10. In heated discussions, people may sometimes lose their heads, call each other names, and __ __ __ **i f** __ each other.

REVIEW 6: COMPOSITION

Answer in two or three sentences.

1. If you were a discussion leader, what could you do to prevent an audience from having to listen to a monotonous monologue?

_____

_____

2. How would an invasion by hundreds of cacophonous birds affect the euphoria of people living in the neighborhood?

_____

_____

3. Would it be an anomaly for a well-known Francophobe to choose to live permanently in France? Why, or why not?

_____

_____

4. In your opinion, has the ready availability of anesthesia affected the phobias that people have about surgery? Explain.

_____

_____

5. Is it atypical for an immigrant to encounter no xenophobia whatsoever? Explain.

_____

_____

REVIEW 7: ANALOGIES

Write the *letter* of the word that best completes the analogy.

1. *Anemia* is to *red blood cells* as *anoxia* is to _____.
   a. corpuscles   *b.* disease   *c.* oxygen   *d.* tissue   *e.* surgery

2. *Euthenics* is to *environment* as *eugenics* is to _____.
   a. surroundings   *b.* heredity   *c.* nutrition   *d.* health   *e.* education

3. *Dysphagia* is to *swallowing* as *dysphasia* is to _____.
   a. digestion   *b.* hearing   *c.* sight   *d.* speech   *e.* tasting

4. *Misanthropy* is to *humanity* as *misogamy* is to _____.
   a. women   *b.* novelty   *c.* marriage   *d.* argument   *e.* foreigners

5. *Polychromatic* is to *colors* as *polytechnic* is to _____.
   a. arts   *b.* sounds   *c.* forms   *d.* syllables   *e.* angles

11. LOGY: "science," "study," "account"

The study of Native American is a part of anthropology.

WORD	MEANING
anthropology (*n.*)	science dealing with the origin, races, customs, and beliefs of humankind
ˌan-thrə-ˈpäl-ə-jē	*Bacteriology requires the use of microscope.*
bacteriology (*n.*)	science dealing with the study of bacteria
bak-ˌtir-ē-ˈäl-ə-jē	*Mr. Krel teaches biology.*
biology (*n.*)	science dealing with the study of living organisms
bī-ˈäl-ə-jē	*Cardiology benefits those who have heart attack.*
cardiology (*n.*)	science dealing with the action and diseases of the heart
ˌkärd-ē-ˈäl-ə-jē	*Most police have to take criminology before starting duty.*
criminology (*n.*)	scientific study of crimes and criminals
ˌkrim-ə-ˈnäl-ə-jē	*My cousin takes dermatology at BU.*
dermatology (*n.*)	science dealing with the skin and its diseases
ˌdər-mə-ˈtäl-ə-jē	*Most environmentalist study ecology.*
ecology (*n.*)	science dealing with the relation of living things to their environment and to each other
i-ˈkäl-ə-jē	*Ethnology includes studying permative tribes.*
ethnology (*n.*)	branch of anthropology dealing with human races, their origin, distribution, culture, etc.
eth-ˈnäl-ə-jē	*Part of my family's genealogy derived from China.*
genealogy (*n.*)	account of the descent of a person or family from an ancestor
ˌjē-nē-ˈäl-ə-jē	*The study of rocks, stones are part of geology.*
geology (*n.*)	science dealing with the earth's history as recorded in rocks
jē-ˈäl-ə-jē	*Most weatherman on TV have degrees in meteorology.*
meteorology (*n.*)	science dealing with the atmosphere and weather
ˌmēt-ē-ə-ˈräl-ə-jē	*Human beings morphology are complex.*
morphology (*n.*)	1. scientific study of the forms and structures of plants and animals
mȯr-ˈfäl-ə-jē	2. form and structure of an organism or any of its parts
	Mythology is common in Egypt.
mythology (*n.*)	account or study of myths
mith-ˈäl-ə-jē	*The necrology in the newspaper was long.*
necrology (*n.*)	list of persons who have died recently
nə-ˈkräl-ə-jē	*The discovery of neuro-transmitters further the field of neurology.*
neurology (*n.*)	scientific study of the nervous system and its diseases
n(y)ů-ˈräl-ə-jē	
paleontology (*n.*)	science dealing with life in the remote past as recorded in fossils
ˌpā-lē-än-ˈtäl-ə-jē	*I found a fossil of a term, and get an A in paleontology.*
pathology (*n.*)	1. science dealing with the nature and causes of disease
pə-ˈthäl-ə-jē	2. something abnormal

Finding the cure of the flu is part of pathology.

petrology (*n.*) scientific study of rocks
pə-'träl-ə-jē

Doctors are concerned with physiology.

physiology (*n.*) science dealing with the functions of living things or their organs
ˌfiz-ē-'äl-ə-jē

psychology (*n.*) science of the mind
sī-'käl-ə-jē

I learn a lot about poverty in America in my sociology class.

sociology (*n.*) study of the evolution, development, and functioning of human society
ˌsō-sē-'äl-ə-jē

technology (*n.*) use of science to achieve a practical purpose; applied science
tek-'näl-ə-jē

theology (*n.*) study of religion and religious ideas
thē-'äl-ə-jē

EXERCISE 4.9

In each blank, insert the most appropriate word from group 11, *logy*.

1. Both ethnology and _____ deal with the origin and races of humankind.

2. The tale of Pyramus and Thisbe is one of the most appealing in Greek _____.

3. Advances in _____ have enabled industries to manufacture products at lower costs.

4. Sherlock Holmes is a fictional character who excels in _____.

5. Sufferers from skin disorders are often referred to a specialist in _____.

6. The good news is that the patient's medical tests show no evidence of _____.

12. BIO: "life"

abiogenesis (*n.*) spontaneous generation (development of life from lifeless matter)
ˌā-ˌbī-ō-'jen-ə-səs (*ant.* **biogenesis**)

amphibious (*adj.*) able to live both on land and in water
am-'fib-ē-əs

antibiotic (*n.*) antibacterial substance produced by a living organism
ˌant-i-bī-'ät-ik

autobiography (*n.*) story of a person's life written by that person
ˌȯt-ə-bī-'äg-rə-fē

biochemistry (*n.*) chemistry dealing with chemical compounds and processes in living plants
ˌbī-ō-'kem-ə-strē and animals

biocidal (*adj.*) ˌbī-ə-ˈsīd-ᵊl	destructive to life or living things
biodegradable (*adj.*) ˌbī-ō-di-ˈgrād-ə-bəl	capable of being readily decomposed into harmless substances by living microorganisms (*ant.* **nonbiodegradable**)
biogenesis (*n.*) ˌbī-ō-ˈjen-ə-səs	development of life from preexisting life (*ant.* **abiogenesis**)
biography (*n.*) bī-ˈäg-rə-fē	story of a person's life written by another person
biology (*n.*) bī-ˈäl-ə-jē	science dealing with the study of living organisms
biometry (*n.*) bī-ˈäm-ə-trē	statistical calculation of the probable duration of human life
or **biometrics** (*n.*) ˌbī-ō-ˈme-triks	statistical analysis of biologic data
biopsy (*n.*) ˈbī-ˌäp-sē	diagnostic examination of a piece of tissue from the living body
biota (*n.*) bī-ˈōt-ə	the living plants (flora) and living animals (fauna) of a region
microbe (*n.*) ˈmī-ˌkrōb	very minute living organism; microorganism; germ
symbiosis (*n.*) ˌsim-bī-ˈō-səs	the living together in mutually helpful association of two dissimilar organisms

EXERCISE 4.10

In each blank, insert the most appropriate word from group 12, *bio*.

1. Fish can live only in water, but frogs are _____.

2. One _____ widely used to arrest the growth of harmful bacteria is penicillin.

3. In his _____ AN AMERICAN DOCTOR'S ODYSSEY, Victor Heiser tells how he survived the Johnstown flood.

4. An example of _____ is provided by the fungus that lives in a mutually beneficial partnership with the roots of an oak tree.

5. A(n) _____ is a microscopic living organism.

6. The use of the pesticide DDT was discontinued when it was found to be too _____.

13. *TOMY (TOM): "cutting," "operation of incision"*

anatomy (*n.*) ə-'nat-ə-mē	1. dissection of plants, animals, or anything else for the purpose of studying their structure 2. structure of a plant or animal
appendectomy (*n.*) ˌap-ən-'dek-tə-mē	surgical removal of the appendix
atom (*n.*) 'at-əm	smallest particle of an element (literally, "not cut," "indivisible")
atomizer (*n.*) 'at-ə-ˌmī-zə(r)	device for converting a liquid to a fine spray
dichotomy (*n.*) dī-'kät-ə-mē	cutting or division into two; division
gastrectomy (*n.*) ga-'strek-tə-mē	surgical removal of part or all of the stomach
lobotomy (*n.*) lō-'bät-ə-mē	brain surgery for treatment of certain mental disorders
mastectomy (*n.*) ma-'stek-tə-mē	surgical removal of a breast
phlebotomy (*n.*) fli-'bät-ə-mē	opening of a vein to diminish the blood supply
tome (*n.*) 'tōm	one volume, or "cut," of a work of several volumes; scholarly book
tonsillectomy (*n.*) ˌtän-sə-'lek-tə-mē	surgical removal of the tonsils
tracheotomy (*n.*) ˌtrā-kē-'ät-ə-mē	surgical operation of cutting into the *trachea* (windpipe)

EXERCISE 4.11

In each blank insert the most appropriate word from group 13, *tomy (tom)*.

1. The sharp _____ between your promises and your deeds suggests that you are not reliable.

2. Even though I have had a number of colds and sore throats, my physician feels I do not need a(n) _____ .

3. In former times _____ (*bleeding*) was used indiscriminately as a treatment for practically all illnesses.

4. You will learn about the structure of the skeleton, the muscles, the heart, and other parts of the body when you study human _____ .

5. Only in certain cases of extremely serious mental illness is a(n) _____ to be considered.

---

14. POD: "foot"

---

antipodes (n. pl.) an-'tip-ə-,dēz	parts of the globe (or their inhabitants) diametrically opposite (literally, "with the feet opposite")
arthropod (n.) 'är-thrə-,päd	any invertebrate (animal having no backbone) with jointed legs. Example: insects.
chiropodist (n.) kə-'räp-əd-əst	one who treats ailments of the human foot
dipody (n.) 'dip-əd-ē	verse (line of poetry) consisting of two feet; a dimeter
podiatrist (n.) pə-'dī-ə-trəst	chiropodist
podium (n.) 'pōd-ē-əm	1. dais; raised platform 2. low wall serving as a foundation
pseudopod (n.) 'süd-ə-,päd or **pseudopodium** ,süd-ə-'pōd-ē-əm	(literally, "false foot") temporary extension of the protoplasm, as in the ameba, to enable the organism to move and take in food
tripod (n.) 'trī-,päd	utensil, stool, or caldron having three legs
unipod (n.) 'yü-nə-,päd	one-legged support

EXERCISE 4.12

In each blank, insert the most appropriate word from group 14, *pod*.

1. One who treats ailments of the feet is known as a chiropodist or a(n) _____ .

2. The English often call Australia and New Zealand the _____ , since these countries are almost diametrically opposite England on the globe.

3. As the guest conductor stepped onto the _____ , the audience burst into applause.

4. A crab is a(n) _____ ; so, too, are lobsters, bees, flies, spiders, and other invertebrates with segmented legs.

5. Joined at the top, the three poles supporting a tent form a(n) _____ .

15. HOMO: "one and the same," "like"
16. HETERO: "different"

homochromatic (*adj.*)   having the same color
ˌhō-mō-krə-'mat-ik

heterochromatic (*adj.*)   having different colors
ˌhet-ə-rō-krə-'mat-ik

homogeneous (*adj.*)   of the same kind; similar; uniform
ˌhō-mə-'jē-nē-əs

heterogeneous (*adj.*)   differing in kind; dissimilar; varied
ˌhet-ə-rə-'jē-nē-əs

homology (*n.*)   fundamental similarity of structure
hō-'mäl-ə-jē

heterology (*n.*)   lack of correspondence between parts
ˌhet-ə-'räl-ə-jē

homomorphic (*adj.*)   exhibiting similarity of form
ˌhō-mə-'mȯr-fik

heteromorphic (*adj.*)   exhibiting diversity of form
ˌhet-ə-rō-'mȯr-fik

homonym (*n.*)   word that sounds like another but differs in meaning and spelling
'häm-ə-ˌnim   Examples: *principal* and *principle*.

heteronym (*n.*)   word spelled like another, but differing in sound and meaning
'het-ə-rə-ˌnim   Examples: *bass* (the tone, pronounced "base") and *bass* (the fish, rhyming with "pass").

homocentric (*adj.*)   having the same center; concentric
hō-mō-'sen-trik

homophonic (*adj.*)   having the same sound
ˌhäm-ə-'fän-ik   (*ant.* **polyphonic,** ˌpäl-i-'fän-ik, having many sounds or voices)

heteroclite (*adj.*)   deviating from the common rule; abnormal; atypical
'het-ə-rə-ˌklīt

heteroclite (*n.*)   person or thing deviating from the common rule

heterodox (*adj.*)   opposed to accepted beliefs or established doctrines; unorthodox
'het-ə-rə-ˌdäks   (*ant.* **orthodox,** 'ȯr-thə-ˌdäks, conforming to accepted doctrines, especially in religion)

EXERCISE 4.13

In each blank, insert the most appropriate word from groups 15 and 16, *homo* and *hetero*.

1. The butterfly is _____; it goes through four stages in its life cycle, and in each of these it has a different form.

2. An archery target usually consists of several _____ circles.

3. People of many races and religions can be found in the _____ population of large American cities.

4. The words *write* and *right* are _____ .

5. The foreleg of a horse and the wing of a bird exhibit _____; they have a fundamental similarity of structure.

6. To escape persecution for his _____ views, Roger Williams fled from Massachusetts Bay Colony and founded the colony of Rhode Island.

7. *Lead*, as in "lead the way," and *lead*, as in "lead pipe," are a pair of _____s.

8. Stained-glass windows are _____; they are composed of glass sections of many colors.

9. The newly admitted students, though fairly _____ in age, were quite heterogeneous in ability.

10. One would not expect heteroclite opinions from a(n) _____ person.

---

17. HYPER: "over," "above," "beyond the ordinary"
18. HYPO: "under," "beneath," "less than the ordinary"

---

hyperacidity (*n.*) ˌhī-pər-ə-ˈsid-ət-ē	excessive acidity
hypoacidity (*n.*) ˌhī-pō-ə-ˈsid-ət-ē	weak acidity
hyperglycemia (*n.*) ˌhī-pər-glī-ˈsēm-ē-ə	excess of sugar in the blood
hypoglycemia (*n.*) ˌhī-pə-glī-ˈsēm-ē-ə	abnormally low level of sugar in the blood
hypertension (*n.*) ˌhī-pər-ˈten-shən	abnormally high blood pressure
hypotension (*n.*) ˌhī-pō-ˈten-shən	low blood pressure

hyperthermia (*n.*)　　　especially high fever; hyperpyrexia
ˌhī-pər-'thər-mē-ə

hypothermia (*n.*)　　　subnormal body temperature
ˌhī-pō-'thər-mē-ə

hyperthyroid (*adj.*)　　marked by excessive activity of the thyroid gland
ˌhī-pər-'thī-ˌroid

hypothyroid (*adj.*)　　marked by deficient activity of the thyroid gland
ˌhī-pō-'thī-ˌroid

hyperactive (*adj.*)　　overactive
ˌhī-pə-'rak-tiv

hyperbole (*n.*)　　　　extravagant exaggeration of statement
hī-'pər-bə-lē

hypercritical (*adj.*)　　overcritical
ˌhī-pər-'krit-i-kəl

hyperemia (*n.*)　　　　superabundance of blood
ˌhī-pə-'rē-mē-ə

hyperopia (*n.*)　　　　farsightedness
ˌhī-pə-'rō-pē-ə　　　　　(*ant.* **myopia,** mī-'ō-pē-ə, nearsightedness)

hypersensitive (*adj.*)　excessively sensitive; supersensitive
ˌhī-pər-'sen-sət-iv

hypertrophy (*n.*)　　　enlargement of a body part or organ, as from excessive use
ˌhī-'pər-trə-fē　　　　　(*ant.* **atrophy,** 'a-trə-fē, lack of growth from want of nourishment or from disease)

hypodermic (*adj.*)　　injected under the skin
ˌhī-pə-'dər-mik

hypothesis (*n.*)　　　　theory or supposition assumed as a basis for reasoning (something "placed
ˌhī-'päth-ə-səs　　　　　under")

hypothetical (*adj.*)　　assumed without proof for the purpose of reasoning; conjectural
ˌhī-pə-'thet-i-kəl

EXERCISE 4.14

In each blank, insert the most appropriate word from groups 17 and 18, *hyper* and *hypo.*

1. Try not to hurt Ann's feelings when you criticize her work, as she is _____.

2. In _____, the blood pressure is lower than normal.

3. The critic who judged the story was _____;
he exaggerated minor faults and gave no credit at all for the author's style and humor.

4. Nobody finished the lemonade because of its _____. Evidently, too much lemon juice had been used.

5. The following statement is an example of _____: "I've told you a *million* times to wear your boots when it rains."

6. A _____ syringe and needle are used to administer injections under the skin.

7. Billy is a _____ youngster; he won't sit still for a minute.

8. If your _____ is disproved by facts, you should abandon it.

9. In _____, the blood pressure is abnormally high.

10. Excessive activity of the thyroid gland is described as a _____ condition.

---

19. ENDO: "within"
20. EXO: "out of," "outside"

---

endocrine (*adj.*) 'en-də-krən	secreting internally
exocrine (*adj.*) 'ek-sə-krən	secreting externally
endogamy (*n.*) en-'däg-ə-mē	marriage within the tribe, caste, or social group
exogamy (*n.*) ek-'säg-ə-mē	marriage outside the tribe, caste, or social group
endogenous (*adj.*) en-'däj-ə-nəs	produced from within; due to internal causes
exogenous (*adj.*) ek-'säj-ə-nəs	produced from without; due to external causes
endoskeleton (*n.*) ˌen-dō-'skel-ət-ᵊn	internal skeleton or supporting framework in an animal
exoskeleton (*n.*) ˌek-sō-'skel-ət-ᵊn	hard protective structure developed outside the body, as the shell of a lobster
endosmosis (*n.*) ˌen-ˌdäs-'mō-səs	osmosis inward
exosmosis (*n.*) ˌek-ˌsäs-'mō-səs	osmosis outward

endocarditis (*n.*)　　inflammation of the lining of the heart
ˌen-dō-kär-'dīt-əs

endoderm (*n.*)　　membranelike tissue lining the digestive tract
'en-də-ˌdərm

endoparasite (*n.*)　　parasite living in the internal organs of an animal (*ant.* **ectoparasite,**
ˌen-dō-'par-ə-ˌsīt　　ˌek-tō-'par-ə-ˌsīt, parasite living on the exterior of an animal)

endophyte (*n.*)　　plant growing within another plant
'en-də-ˌfīt

exoteric (*adj.*)　　external; exterior; readily understandable
ˌek-sə-'ter-ik　　(*ant.* **esoteric,** ˌes-ə-'ter-ik, inner; private; difficult to understand)

exotic (*adj.*)　　1. introduced from a foreign country; not native
eg-'zät-ik　　2. excitingly strange

EXERCISE 4.15

In each blank, insert the most appropriate word from groups 19 and 20, *endo* and *exo*.

1. Algae that live within other plants are known as _____s.

2. Foreign visitors can often be identified by their _____ dress.

3. _____ glands discharge their secretions externally through ducts or tubes.

4. _____ glands, having no ducts or tubes, secrete internally.

5. Some primitive tribes observe _____, forbidding marriage outside the tribe.

6. The body louse is a most annoying _____, as it moves freely over the body of its host.

7. The lobster has a thick protective shell known as an _____.

8. Unlike lobsters, humans have an inside skeleton called an _____.

9. Refusing to admit that the rebellion was _____, the dictator blamed "foreign agitators."

10. Once established in the intestines of its host, an _____ leads a life of ease.

---

21. ARCHY: ''rule''

---

anarchy (*n.*)　　total absence of rule or government; confusion; disorder
'an-ər-kē

autarchy (*n.*)　　rule by an absolute sovereign
'ȯ-ˌtär-kē

hierarchy (*n.*)
'hī-ə-ˌrär-kē

body of rulers or officials grouped in ranks, each being subordinate to the rank above it

matriarchy (*n.*)
'mā-trē-ˌär-kē

form of social organization in which the mother rules the family or tribe, descent being traced through the mother

monarchy (*n.*)
'män-ər-kē

state ruled over by a single person, as a king or queen

oligarchy (*n.*)
'äl-ə-ˌgär-kē

form of government in which a few people have the power

patriarchy (*n.*)
'pā-trē-ˌär-kē

form of social organization in which the father rules the family or tribe, descent being traced through the father

EXERCISE 4.16

In each blank, insert the most appropriate word from group 21, *archy.*

1. In the naval _____, a rear admiral ranks below a vice admiral.

2. Many a supposedly "democratic" organization is controlled by a(n) _____ of three or four influential members.

3. In a constitutional _____, the power of the king or queen is usually limited by a constitution and a legislature.

4. A family in which the mother alone makes all the final decisions could be called a(n)

_____ .

5. Those who declare that the best form of government is no government at all are advocating

_____ .

---

22. GEO: "earth," "ground"

---

geocentric (*adj.*)
ˌjē-ō-'sen-trik

measured from the earth's center; having the earth as a center

geodetic (*adj.*)
ˌjē-ə-'det-ik

pertaining to *geodesy* (mathematics dealing with the earth's shape and dimensions)

geography (*n.*)
jē-'äg-rə-fē

study of the earth's surface, climate, continents, people, products, etc.

geology (*n.*)
jē-'äl-ə-jē

science dealing with the earth's history as recorded in rocks

geometry (*n.*) jē-'äm-ə-trē	mathematics dealing with lines, angles, surfaces, and solids (literally, ''measurement of land'')
geomorphic (*adj.*) ˌjē-ə-'mȯr-fik	pertaining to the shape of the earth or the form of its surface
geophysics (*n.*) ˌjē-ə-'fiz-iks	science treating of the forces that modify the earth
geopolitics (*n.*) ˌjē-ō-'päl-ə-ˌtiks	study of government and its policies as affected by physical geography
geoponics (*n.*) ˌjē-ə-'pän-iks	art or science of agriculture (literally, ''working of the earth'')
georgic (*adj.*) 'jȯr-jik	agricultural
georgic (*n.*)	poem on husbandry (farming)
geotropism (*n.*) jē-'ä-trə-ˌpiz-əm	response to earth's gravity, as the growing of roots downward in the ground

The form *gee* is used at the end of a word. For example:

apogee (*n.*) 'ap-ə-jē	farthest point from the earth in the orbit of a satellite
perigee (*n.*) 'per-ə-jē	nearest point to the earth in the orbit of a satellite

EXERCISE 4.17

In each blank, insert the most appropriate word from group 22, *geo.*

1. At its apogee the moon is nearly 252,000 miles from the earth; at its _____ it is less than 226,000 miles away.

2. Heliotropism attracts leaves to sunlight; _____ draws roots downward in the earth.

3. To make precise earth measurements, _____ engineers use sensitive instruments.

4. Some earthquakes have little effect on the form of the earth's surface, but others result in noticeable _____ changes.

5. The atmosphere, the sun, and other forces that modify the earth are dealt with in the science of _____ .

23. PATH (PATHO, PATHY): (1) "feeling," "suffering,"; (2) "disease"

FEELING, SUFFERING

antipathy (*n.*)
an-'tip-ə-thē

aversion ("feeling against"); dislike
(*ant.* **sympathy**)

apathy (*n.*)
'ap-ə-thē

lack of feeling, emotion, interest, or excitement; indifference

empathy (*n.*)
'em-pə-thē

the complete understanding of another's feelings, motives, etc.

pathetic (*adj.*)
pə-'thet-ik

arousing pity

pathos (*n.*)
'pā-thäs

quality in drama, speech, literature, music, or events that arouses a feeling of pity or sadness

sympathy (*n.*)
'sim-pə-thē

a sharing of ("feeling with") another's trouble; compassion
(*ant.* **antipathy**)

telepathy (*n.*)
tə-'lep-ə-thē

transference of the thoughts and feelings of one person to another by no apparent means of communication

DISEASE

homeopathy (*n.*)
ˌhō-mē-'äp-ə-thē

system of medical practice that treats disease by administering minute doses of a remedy which, if given to healthy persons, would produce symptoms of the disease treated

osteopath (*n.*)
'äs-tē-ə-ˌpath

practitioner of *osteopathy* (treatment of diseases by manipulation of bones, muscles, nerves, etc.)

pathogenic (*adj.*)
ˌpath-ə-'jen-ik

causing disease

pathological (*adj.*)
ˌpath-ə-'läj-i-kəl

due to disease

psychopathic (*adj.*)
ˌsī-kə-'path-ik

1. pertaining to mental disease
2. insane

EXERCISE 4.18

In each blank, insert the most appropriate word from group 23, *path* (*patho, pathy*).

1. Among the diseases caused by _____ bacteria are pneumonia and scarlet fever.

2. Sometimes, as if by _____, one may know the thoughts of an absent friend or relative.

3. The _____ expression on the youngster's face made everyone feel sorry for him.

4. Such intense _____ resulted from their quarrel that the sisters haven't spoken to each other for years.

5. The reunion of the rescued miners with their families was full of _____ .

---

24. MORPH: "form"

---

amorphous (*adj.*)
ə-'mȯr-fəs

without definite form; shapeless

anthropomorphic (*adj.*)
ˌan-thrə-pə-'mȯr-fik

attributing human form or characteristics to beings not human, especially gods

dimorphous (*adj.*)
dī-'mȯr-fəs

occurring under two distinct forms

endomorphic (*adj.*)
ˌen-də-'mȯr-fik

occurring within; internal

heteromorphic (*adj.*)
'het-ə-rō-'mȯr-fik

exhibiting diversity of form

metamorphosis (*n.*)
ˌmet-ə-'mȯr-fə-səs

change of form

monomorphic (*adj.*)
ˌmän-ō-'mȯr-fik

having a single form

morphology (*n.*)
mȯr-'fäl-ə-jē

1. branch of biology dealing with the form and structure of animals and plants
2. form and structure of an organism or any of its parts

EXERCISE 4.19

In each blank, insert the most appropriate word from group 24, *morph*.

1. As the fog slowly lifted, _____ objects began to assume definite shapes.

2. When you study cell _____ , you will learn about the nucleus, the cell membrane, and other features of cell structure.

3. The drastic _____ from forested area to attractive residential neighborhood was accomplished in less than three years.

4. Individual members of a(n) _____ species are identical or similar in form.

5. The ancient Greeks had a(n) _____ conception of deity; they gave their gods and goddesses the characteristics of men and women.

25. PERI: "around," "about," "near," "enclosing"

pericardium (*n.*) ˌper-ə-ˈkärd-ē-əm	membranous sac enclosing the heart
perigee (*n.*) ˈper-ə-jē	nearest point to the earth in the orbit of a satellite (*ant.* **apogee**, ˈap-ə-jē, farthest point from the earth in the orbit of a satellite)
perihelion (*n.*) ˌper-ə-ˈhēl-yən	nearest point to the sun in the orbit of a planet or comet (*ant.* **aphelion**, a-ˈfēl-yən, farthest point from the sun in the orbit of a planet or comet)
perimeter (*n.*) pə-ˈrim-ət-ə(r)	the whole outer boundary or measurement of a surface or figure
periodontics (*n.*) ˌper-ē-ō-ˈdänt-iks	branch of dentistry dealing with diseases of the bone and gum tissues supporting the teeth
peripheral (*adj.*) pə-ˈrif-ə-rəl	1. on the *periphery* (outside boundary); outside or away from the central part, as in *peripheral* vision 2. only slightly connected with what is essential; merely incidental
periphrastic (*adj.*) ˌper-ə-ˈfras-tik	expressed in a roundabout way
periscope (*n.*) ˈper-ə-ˌskōp	instrument permitting those in a submarine a view ("look around") of the surface
peristalsis (*n.*) ˌper-ə-ˈstȯl-səs	wavelike contraction of the walls of the intestines which propels contents onward
peristyle (*n.*) ˈper-ə-ˌstīl	1. row of columns around a building or court 2. the space so enclosed
peritonitis (*n.*) ˌper-ət-ᵊn-ˈīt-əs	inflammation of the *peritoneum* (membrane lining the abdominal cavity and covering the organs)

EXERCISE 4.20

In each blank, insert the most appropriate word from group 25, *peri*.

1. The _____ of a rectangle is twice its width plus twice its length.

2. At its aphelion, the earth is 152,516,120 kilometers (94,560,000 miles) from the sun; at its _____, it is only 147,496,770 kilometers (91,448,000 miles) away.

3. We will not be able to reach a decision on the main issue if we waste too much time on _____ matters.

4. By a series of wavelike contractions, known as _____, food is moved through the intestines.

5. Before changing its position, the cautious turtle raised its head like a _____ to survey surrounding conditions.

Review Exercises

REVIEW 8: GREEK PREFIXES AND ROOTS

In the space before each Greek prefix or root in column I, write the *letter* of its correct meaning from column II.

COLUMN I	COLUMN II
_____ 1. POD	*a.* different
_____ 2. EXO	*b.* life
_____ 3. HETERO	*c.* under; beneath; less than ordinary
_____ 4. GEO	*d.* one and the same; like
_____ 5. LOGY	*e.* rule
_____ 6. HYPO	*f.* around; about; near; enclosing
_____ 7. BIO	*g.* cutting; operation of incision
_____ 8. MORPH	*h.* feeling; suffering; disease
_____ 9. PATH (PATHO, PATHY)	*i.* earth; ground
_____ 10. ARCHY	*j.* within
_____ 11. PERI	*k.* foot
_____ 12. TOMY (TOM)	*l.* form
_____ 13. HYPER	*m.* out of; outside
_____ 14. ENDO	*n.* over; above; beyond the ordinary
_____ 15. HOMO	*o.* science; study; account

REVIEW 9: SYNONYMS

In the space provided, write the *letter* of the word that most nearly has the SAME MEANING as the italicized word or expression.

_____ 1. *hypercritical* reviewer: *a.* uncritical *b.* hypersensitive *c.* esoteric *d.* overcritical

_____ 2. complete *metamorphosis*: *a.* change *b.* course *c.* process *d.* misunderstanding

_____ 3. eminent *foot specialist*: *a.* criminologist *b.* world traveler *c.* podiatrist *d.* osteopath

_____ 4. trace one's *genealogy*: *a.* career *b.* descent *c.* downfall *d.* personality

_____ 5. *hypothetical* statement: *a.* conjectural *b.* introductory *c.* unbiased *d.* incontrovertible

_____ 6. *anatomical* defect: *a.* minor *b.* irremediable *c.* structural *d.* inherited

_____ 7. *homogeneous* in size: *a.* different *b.* perfect *c.* heteromorphic *d.* similar

_____ 8. seems *psychopathic*: *a.* pathetic *b.* indifferent *c.* insane *d.* unsympathetic

_____ 9. *exotic* customs: *a.* native *b.* foreign *c.* familiar *d.* cultured

_____ 10. *amorphous* ideas: *a.* organized *b.* original *c.* exaggerated *d.* shapeless

REVIEW 10: OPPOSITES

In the blank space, write the word that means the OPPOSITE of the word defined.

DEFINITION	WORD	OPPOSITE
1. differing in kind	heterogeneous	_____
2. conforming to an acknowledged standard	orthodox	_____
3. lack of growth from want of nourishment	atrophy	_____
4. a feeling of accord	sympathy	_____
5. having many sounds	polyphonic	_____
6. difficult to understand	esoteric	_____
7. fundamental similarity in structure	homology	_____
8. parasite living on the exterior of an animal	ectoparasite	_____
9. low blood pressure	hypotension	_____
10. nearsightedness	myopia	_____
11. excessive acidity	hyperacidity	_____
12. osmosis outward	exosmosis	_____
13. secreting internally	endocrine	_____
14. excess of sugar in the blood	hyperglycemia	_____
15. nearest point to the earth in the orbit of a satellite	perigee	_____
16. development of life from preexisting life	biogenesis	_____
17. due to external causes	exogenous	_____
18. nearest point to the sun in the orbit of a planet	perihelion	_____
19. exhibiting diversity of form	heteromorphic	_____
20. marriage outside the tribe, caste, or social group	exogamy	_____

REVIEW 11: BRAINTEASERS

Fill in the missing letters.

1. Many citizens do not bother to vote on Election Day. What is the reason for their

   __ **p a t h** __?

2. The __ __ **r i m** __ __ __ __ of a 7-inch square is 28 inches.

3. TV weather programs teach us a great deal about __ __ __ __ __ __ __ **l o g** __.

4. A country ruled by a(n) __ __ __ __ **a r c h** __ of three powerful officials is not a true democracy.

5. Continued progress in __ __ __ __ **n o** __ __ __ __ is enabling factories to turn out more and more products with fewer and fewer employees.

6. The feelings of a(n) __ __ __ __ __ __ __ __ **s i t** __ __ __ person are easily hurt.

7. If there were no laws, and we all could do as we pleased, our nation would be in a state of

   a n __ __ __ __ __.

8. Some of the lecturer's remarks were so __ **s o t** __ __ __ __ that nobody but advanced scholars could understand them.

9. When it is noon here, it is midnight in the __ __ **t i p** __ __ __ __.

10. Seals are **a m** __ __ __ __ __ __ __ __; they spend a part of the year on land.

REVIEW 12: CONCISE WRITING

Express the thought of each sentence below in no more than four words.

1. Shock may cause a person's body temperature to drop to a subnormal level.

   _____

2. Some wastes cannot readily be decomposed into harmless substances by living microorganisms.

   _____

3. Galileo had ideas that were contrary to the accepted beliefs of his time.

   _____

4. The science that deals with the study of living things is fascinating.

   _____

5. Some chiefs forbid the marriage of any member of their tribe to an outsider.

   _____

6. Is the supposition that you are making as a basis for your reasoning logical?

   _____

7. The operation for the surgical removal of her appendix was a success.

_____

8. These very minute living organisms are invisible to the naked eye.

_____

9. We are studying the science that deals with the earth's history as told in rocks.

_____

10. He goes to a physician who specializes in the treatment of foot problems.

_____

REVIEW 13: COMPOSITION

Answer in two or three sentences.

1. Is our nation's population more homogeneous or more heterogeneous than it was a hundred years ago? Explain.

_____

_____

_____

2. Why would most Americans have an antipathy to the establishment of a monarchy in their country?

_____

_____

_____

3. Would it encourage or discourage apathy in a lesson on amphibious animals if a living frog were brought into the classroom? Why?

_____

_____

_____

4. How would a hypersensitive individual react to criticism by a hypercritical person?

_____

_____

_____

5. Describe one metamorphosis in the way we live that was brought on by a technological discovery.

_____

_____

_____

REVIEW 14: ANALOGIES

Write the *letter* of the word that best completes the analogy.

1. *Environment* is to *ecology* as *skin* is to _____.
   a. osteopathy *b.* dermatology *c.* peritonitis *d.* neurology *e.* endoderm

2. *Lobotomy* is to *brain* as *phlebotomy* is to _____.
   a. throat *b.* nerve *c.* foot *d.* vein *e.* muscle

3. *Government* is to *anarchy* as *sympathy* is to _____.
   a. pathos *b.* compassion *c.* apathy *d.* empathy *e.* telepathy

4. *Pathology* is to *disease* as *morphology* is to _____.
   a. structure *b.* function *c.* descent *d.* health *e.* race

5. *Animal* is to *tapeworm* as *plant* is to _____.
   a. earthworm *b.* biota *c.* microbe *d.* ectoparasite *e.* endophyte

CHAPTER 5

Words Derived From Latin

When the Latin-speaking Romans ruled Britain, approximately 75–410 A.D., there was no English language. The native Britons spoke Celtic, a language akin to Irish and Welsh. After the Romans withdrew, the Britons were overwhelmed by Germanic invaders, the Angles and Saxons. The English we speak today is a continuation of the language of the Angles and Saxons.

Before invading Britain, the Angles and Saxons had adopted some Latin words from contacts with the vast neighboring Roman Empire. In Britain, they undoubtedly acquired a few more Latin words from the Britons, who had lived so long under Roman domination. And after 597, when the Roman monk St. Augustine introduced Christianity and the Holy Scripture—in Latin—to Britain, the Anglo-Saxons absorbed more words from Latin. But Latin had no major impact on English until 1066, when the Normans conquered England.

The Normans spoke French, a *Romance* language, i.e., a language developed from the language of the *Romans*. French, which is 85 per-cent descended from Latin, was England's official language for two hundred years after the Norman Conquest. The language of the Normans gradually blended with the Anglo-Saxon spoken by the common people. In the process, a considerable number of Latin words were incorporated into English indirectly, by way of French.

Later, a substantial number of other words came into English directly from Latin itself. From the Renaissance, in the sixteenth century, to the present day, as English-speaking authors and scientists have needed new words to express new ideas, they have been able to form them from Latin—or Greek.

It is no wonder, then, that more than 50 percent of the vocabulary of English derives directly or indirectly from Latin.

To boost your word power, study the common Latin prefixes and roots presented in this chapter. Each of them, as the following pages will show, can help you learn a cluster of useful English words.

Latin Prefixes 1–15

PREFIX	MEANING	SAMPLE WORDS
1. **a, ab**	away, from	*a*vert (turn *away*), *ab*duct (lead *from*)
2. **ad**	to	*ad*mit (grant entrance *to*)
3. **ante**	before	*ante*room (a room *before* another)
4. **bi**	two	*bi*cycle (a vehicle having *two* wheels)

PREFIX	MEANING	SAMPLE WORDS
5. **circum**	around	*circum*navigate (sail *around*)
6. **con (col, com, cor)**	together, with	*con*spire (plot *together* or *with*), *col*loquy (a talking *together*; conference), *com*pose (put *together*), *cor*respond (agree *with*; communicate *with* by exchange of letters)
7. **contra**	against	*contra*dict (speak *against*; deny)
8. **de**	from, down	*de*duction (a conclusion drawn *from* reasoning), *de*mote (move *down* in rank)
9. **dis**	apart, away	*dis*rupt (break *apart*), *dis*miss (send *away*)
10. **e, ex**	out	*e*mit (send *out*; utter), *ex*pel (drive *out*)
11. **extra**	beyond	*extra*ordinary (*beyond* the ordinary)
12. **in (il, im, ir)**	not	*in*significant (*not* significant), *il*legal (*not* legal), *im*moral (*not* moral), *ir*regular (*not* regular)
13. **in (il, im, ir)**	in, into, on	*in*ject (throw or force *in*), *il*luminate (direct light *on*; light up), *im*port (bring *into* one country from another), *ir*rigate (pour water *on*)
14. **inter**	between	*inter*rupt (break *between*; stop)
15. **intra**	within	*intra*mural (*within* the walls; inside)

EXERCISE 5.1

Fill in the prefix in column I and the new word in column III. (The answer to question 1 has been inserted as an example.)

COLUMN I	COLUMN II	COLUMN III
1. <u>in</u> *not*	+ tangible *able to be touched*	= <u>intangible</u> *not able to be touched*
2. _____ *against*	+ vene *come; go*	= _____ *go against or contrary to*
3. _____ *out*	+ hale *breathe*	= _____ *breathe out*
4. _____ *down*	+ mote *move*	= _____ *reduce to lower rank*
5. _____ *to*	+ here *stick*	= _____ *stick to*

6. _____   + gregate   = _____
   together   *gather*   *gather together; assemble*

7. _____   + normal   = _____
   from   *deviating from the normal*

8. _____   + scribe   = _____
   around   *write; draw*   *write or draw a line around;*
                                      encircle; limit

9. _____   + cede   = _____
   between   *go*   *go between arguing parties;*
                                      mediate

10. _____   + sect   = _____
   two   *cut*   *cut into two parts*

11. _____   + mural   = _____
   beyond   *pertaining to a wall*   *occurring beyond the walls*

12. _____   + diluvian   = _____
   before   *pertaining to a flood* *belonging to the period be-*
                                          fore the Biblical Flood;
                                          therefore, very old

13. _____   + venous   = _____
   within   *pertaining to a vein*   *within a vein*

14. _____   + pel   = _____
   apart   *drive*   *drive apart; scatter*

15. _____   + fuse   = _____
   in   *pour*   *pour in; fill; instill*

16. _____   + scend   = _____
   down   *climb*   *climb down*

17. _____   + sensory   = _____
   beyond   *pertaining to the senses*   *beyond the scope of the*
                                              senses

18. _____   + sect   = _____
   apart   *cut*   *cut apart*

19. _____   + solve   = _____
   from   *loose*   *loose from; release from*

20. _____   + pute   = _____
   apart   *think*   *think apart (differently from*
                                      others); argue

EXERCISE 5.2

In the space before each Latin prefix in column I, write the *letter* of its correct meaning from column II.

COLUMN I	COLUMN II
_____ **1.** contra	*a.* within
_____ **2.** ante	*b.* between
_____ **3.** de	*c.* in; into; on
_____ **4.** extra	*d.* from; down
_____ **5.** a, ab	*e.* out
_____ **6.** in (il, im, ir)	*f.* against
_____ **7.** bi	*g.* around
_____ **8.** intra	*h.* beyond
_____ **9.** dis	*i.* apart; away
_____ **10.** e, ex	*j.* to
_____ **11.** ad	*k.* together; with
_____ **12.** inter	*l.* before
_____ **13.** circum	*m.* two
_____ **14.** con (col, com, cor)	*n.* away; from

Latin Prefixes 16–30

PREFIX	MEANING	SAMPLE WORDS
16. **ob, op**	against	*obloquy* (a talking *against*; censure; *op*pose (set oneself *against*)
17. **per**	through, thoroughly	*per*ennial (lasting *through* the years; enduring), *per*vert (*thoroughly* turn from the right way; corrupt)
18. **post**	after	*post* war (*after* the war)
19. **pre**	before	*pre*monition (a warning *before*; forewarning)
20. **preter**	beyond	*preter*human (*beyond* what is human)
21. **pro**	forward	*pro*gressive (moving *forward*)
22. **re**	again, back	*re*vive (make alive *again*), *re*tort (hurl *back*; reply sharply)
23. **retro**	backward	*retro*gression (act of moving *backward*)
24. **se**	apart	*se*cede (move *apart*; withdraw)
25. **semi**	half	*semi*circle (*half* of a circle)

26.	**sub, sup**	under	*sub*merge (put *under* or plunge into water); *sup*port (uphold)
27.	**super**	above	*super*natural (*above* what is natural; miraculous)
28.	**trans**	across, through	*trans*continental (extending *across* a continent), *trans*mit (send *through*)
29.	**ultra**	beyond, exceedingly	*ultra*conservative (*exceedingly* conservative)
30.	**vice**	in place of	*vice* president (officer acting *in place of* the president)

EXERCISE 5.3

In the space before each Latin prefix in column I, write the *letter* of its correct meaning from column II.

	COLUMN I		COLUMN II
_____	**1.** semi	*a.*	against
_____	**2.** ob	*b.*	beyond; exceedingly
_____	**3.** sub	*c.*	again; back
_____	**4.** trans	*d.*	before
_____	**5.** vice	*e.*	after
_____	**6.** ultra	*f.*	half
_____	**7.** super	*g.*	apart
_____	**8.** re	*h.*	under
_____	**9.** pro	*i.*	in place of
_____	**10.** post	*j.*	above
_____	**11.** se	*k.*	forward
_____	**12.** pre	*l.*	across; through

EXERCISE 5.4

Fill in the prefix in column I and the new word in column III.

COLUMN I	COLUMN II	COLUMN III
1. _____ *in place of*	+ chancellor	= _____ *person acting in place of a chancellor*
2. _____ *half*	+ annual	= _____ *occurring every half year*
3. _____ *under*	+ vert *turn*	= _____ *turn under; undermine*

4. _____ + clude = _____
  apart   *shut*   shut or keep apart; isolate

5. _____ + sede = _____
  above   *sit*   sit above; take the place of; replace

6. _____ + mote = _____
  forward   *move*   move forward; raise in rank

7. _____ + durate = _____
  against   *hardened*   hardened against; unyielding;
                           stubborn

8. _____ + ient = _____
  through   *going*   going through (not staying);
                           short-lived

9. _____ + struct = _____
  against   *pile up*   pile up (an obstacle) against;
                           hinder

10. _____ + calcitrant = _____
  back   *kicking*   kicking back; rebellious

11. _____ + pone = _____
  after   *put*   put after; defer; delay

12. _____ + nationalistic = _____
  exceedingly   exceedingly nationalistic

13. _____ + requisite = _____
  before   *required*   required before; necessary as a
                           preliminary

14. _____ + active = _____
  backward   acting backward; effective in a
                           prior time

15. _____ + meate = _____
  through   *pass*   pass through

16. _____ + sume = _____
  again   *take*   take up or begin again

17. _____ + turb = _____
  thoroughly *disturb*   disturb thoroughly; agitate

18. _____ + natural = _____
  beyond   beyond what is natural

19. _____ + gregate = _____
  apart   *gather*   set apart; gather into separate
                           groups

20. _____ + marine = _____
  under   *pertaining to the sea*   used or existing under the sea's
                           surface

EXERCISE 5.5

Using your knowledge of the Latin prefixes and the hints given below, insert the basic meaning of these sixty English words. (The answer to question 1 has been inserted as an example.)

Hint: **-port** means "carry"

1. report ___carry back___

2. import _____

3. transport _____

4. deport _____

5. export _____

Hint: **-ject** means "throw"

6. interject _____

7. eject _____

8. object _____

9. project _____

10. inject _____

Hint: **-scribe** means "write"

11. superscribe _____

12. transcribe _____

13. prescribe _____

14. inscribe _____

15. subscribe _____

Hint: **-pel** means "drive"

16. dispel _____

17. propel _____

18. expel _____

19. impel _____

20. repel _____

Hint: **-voke** means "call"

21. evoke _____

22. convoke _____

23. provoke _____

24. revoke _____

25. invoke _____

Hint: **-mit** means "send"

26. permit _____

27. admit _____

28. transmit _____

29. emit _____

30. remit _____

Hint: **-tract** means "drag," "draw"

31. protract _____

32. subtract _____

33. distract _____

34. retract _____

35. detract _____

Hint: **-duce** means "lead," "draw"

36. seduce _____

39. deduce _____

37. induce _____

40. reduce _____

38. produce _____

Hint: **-cede** or **-ceed** means "go"

41. intercede _____

44. exceed _____

42. proceed _____

45. recede _____

43. secede _____

Hint: **-fer** means "carry," "bring," "bear"

46. transfer _____

49. infer _____

47. prefer _____

50. defer _____

48. refer _____

Hint: **-vert** means "turn"

51. avert _____

54. revert _____

52. advert _____

55. subvert _____

53. pervert _____

Hint: **-pose** means "put"

56. compose _____

59. propose _____

57. depose _____

60. transpose _____

58. interpose _____

Latin Roots

1. RUPT: "break," "burst"

WORD	MEANING
abrupt (*adj.*) ə-'brəpt	1. broken off; lacking in continuity; steep (*ant.* **sloping**) 2. sudden; quick and unexpected (*ant.* **leisurely; deliberate**)
corrupt (*adj.*) kə-'rəpt	changed ("broken to pieces") from good to bad; vicious

corrupt (*v.*)	change ("break to pieces") from good to bad; debase; pervert; falsify
disrupt (*v.*) dis-'rəpt	break apart; cause disorder
erupt (*v.*) i-'rəpt	burst or break out
incorruptible (*adj.*) ‚in-kə-'rəp-tə-bəl	inflexibly honest; incapable of being corrupted or bribed
interrupt (*v.*) ‚int-ə-'rəpt	break into or between; hinder; stop
rupture (*n.*) 'rəp-chə(r)	1. break; breaking 2. hostility

EXERCISE 5.6

In each blank, insert the most appropriate word from group 1, *rupt*.

1. The simmering antipathy between the rival groups may _____ into open combat.

2. The star's _____ withdrawal from the cast took the producer by surprise.

3. Both sides had faith in the judge's honesty, for he was known to be _____ .

4. Many homes were flooded as a result of a(n) _____ in a water main.

5. Please don't _____ me when I am speaking on the telephone.

2. CIDE: "killing," "killer"

bactericide (*n.*) bak-'tir-ə-‚sīd	substance that kills bacteria
biocide (*n.*) 'bī-ə-‚sīd	substance that destroys living microorganisms
fratricide (*n.*) 'fra-trə-‚sīd	act of killing (or killer of) one's brother
fungicide (*n.*) 'fən-jə-‚sīd	substance that kills fungi or inhibits their growth
genocide (*n.*) 'jen-ə-‚sīd	deliberate extermination of a racial or cultural group
germicide (*n.*) 'jər-mə-‚sīd	substance that kills germs

herbicide (*n.*) ˌ(h)ər-bə-ˌsīd	substance that kills plants
homicide (*n.*) ˈhäm-ə-ˌsīd	killing of one human by another
infanticide (*n.*) in-ˈfant-ə-ˌsīd	act of killing (or killer of) an infant
insecticide (*n.*) in-ˈsek-tə-ˌsīd	substance that kills insects
matricide (*n.*) ˈma-trə-ˌsīd	act of killing (or killer of) one's mother
patricide (*n.*) ˈpa-trə-ˌsīd	act of killing (or killer of) one's father
pesticide (*n.*) ˈpes-tə-ˌsīd	substance that kills rats, insects, bacteria, etc.
regicide (*n.*) ˈrej-ə-ˌsīd	act of killing (or killer of) a king
sororicide (*n.*) sə-ˈrȯr-ə-ˌsīd	act of killing (or killer of) one's sister
suicide (*n.*) ˈsü-ə-ˌsīd	act of killing (or killer of) one's self
tyrannicide (*n.*) tə-ˈran-ə-ˌsīd	act of killing (or killer of) a tyrant

EXERCISE 5.7

In each blank, insert the most appropriate word from group 2, *cide*.

1. The murderers planned to escape prosecution by making their deed appear like a(n)

_____ .

2. The assailant was told that he would be charged with _____ if his victim were to die.

3. To prevent the extermination of minorities, the United Nations voted in 1948 to outlaw

_____ .

4. Claudius, in Shakespeare's HAMLET, is guilty of _____, for he has slain his brother.

5. The attempt at _____ failed when the king's would-be assassins were arrested outside the palace.

6. One way to get rid of weeds is to spray them with a(n) _____ .

3. STRING (STRICT): "bind," "draw tight"

astringent (*adj.*) ə-'strin-jənt	1. drawing (the tissues) tightly together 2. stern; austere
astringent (*n.*)	substance that shrinks tissues and checks flow of blood by drawing together blood vessels
boa constrictor (*n.*) 'bō-ə-kən-'strik-tə(r)	snake that "constricts" or crushes its prey in its coils
constrict (*v.*) kən-'strikt	draw together; render narrower; shrink (*ant.* **expand**)
restrict (*v.*) ri-'strikt	keep within limits (literally, "keep back"); confine
stricture (*n.*) 'strik-chə(r)	adverse criticism (literally, "tightening"); censure
stringent (*adj.*) 'strin-jənt	strict (literally, "binding tight"); rigid; severe
unrestricted (*adj.*) ˌən-ri-'strikt-əd	1. not confined within bounds; free 2. open to all

EXERCISE 5.8

In each blank, insert the most appropriate word from group 3, *string* (*strict*).

1. All residents enjoy _____ use of the pool, except children under 16, who must leave at 5 P.M.

2. Unless you _____ your remarks to the topic on the floor, the chair will rule you "out of order."

3. Shavers use a styptic pencil or some other _____ to check the bleeding from minor cuts.

4. Jean Valjean's sentence of five years at hard labor for stealing a loaf of bread seems an unusually

   _____ punishment.

5. If you interpret a minor suggestion for improvement as a major _____,
   you are being hypersensitive.

4. VOR: "eat greedily"

carnivore (*n.*) 'kär-nə-ˌvȯ(ə)r	flesh-eating animal

carnivorous (*adj.*)   flesh-eating
kär-'niv-ə-rəs

devour (*v.*)   1. eat greedily or ravenously
di-'vaù-ə(r)   2. seize upon and destroy

frugivorous (*adj.*)   feeding on fruit
frü-'jiv-ə-rəs

herbivore (*n.*)   plant-eating animal
'(h)ər-bə-ˌvò(ə)r

herbivorous (*adj.*)   dependent on (literally, ''eating'') plants as food
ˌ(h)ər-'biv-ə-rəs

insectivorous (*adj.*)   dependent on (literally, ''eating'') insects as food
ˌin-ˌsek-'tiv-ə-rəs

omnivore (*n.*)   person or animal that eats everything (both flesh and plants)
'äm-ni-ˌvò(ə)r

omnivorous (*adj.*)   1. eating everything, both plant and animal substances
äm-'niv-ə-rəs   2. avidly taking in everything, as an *omnivorous* reader

voracious (*adj.*)   1. greedy in eating
vò-'rā-shəs   2. insatiable, as a *voracious* appetite

EXERCISE 5.9

In each blank, insert the most appropriate word from group 4, *vor*.

1. Spiders are _____; their principal food is insects.

2. Have you ever watched a ravenous eater _____ a sandwich in two or three gulps?

3. The diet of the _____ lion includes the zebra, antelope, buffalo, and ostrich.

4. Since human beings generally obtain food from both plants and animals, they may be described

   as _____ organisms.

5. The rabbit is _____; it eats grass, vegetables, and even the bark of trees.

6. _____ insects damage fruit crops.

5. VIV: ''live,'' ''alive''

convivial (*adj.*) kən-'viv-ē-əl	fond of eating and drinking with friends; jovial; hospitable (*ant.* **taciturn,** inclined to silence; **stolid,** unemotional)
revive (*v.*) ri-'vīv	bring back to life; restore
survive (*v.*) sər-'vīv	outlive; remain alive after (*ant.* **perish**)
vivacious (*adj.*) və-'vā-shəs	lively in temper or conduct (*ant.* **languid,** lacking in vigor)
vivacity (*n.*) və-'vas-ə-tē	liveliness of spirit
vivid (*adj.*) 'viv-əd	1. (used with things) having the vigor and spirit of life 2. sharp and clear; graphic
vivify (*v.*) 'viv-ə-ˌfī	enliven; make vivid
vivisection (*n.*) ˌviv-ə-'sek-shən	operation on a living animal for scientific investigation

EXERCISE 5.10

In each blank, insert the most appropriate word from group 5, *viv*.

1. A business must eliminate waste if it is to _____ in a competitive market.

2. When fashion designers can offer no new styles, they usually _____ old ones.

3. By using carefully chosen verbs and adjectives, you can turn a dull description into a _____ one.

4. David Copperfield found a warm welcome in the _____ Peggotty family.

5. A few inexpensive art reproductions, cleverly arranged, can _____ an otherwise drab wall.

6. I admire her _____ and zest for life.

6. TORT (TORS): "twist"

contortionist (*n.*) kən-'tòr-shə-nəst	person who can twist his or her body into odd postures
distort (*v.*) dis-'tòrt	1. twist out of shape; contort 2. twist out of the true meaning; misrepresent; pervert; falsify
extort (*v.*) ek-'stòrt	wrest (money, promises, etc.) from a person by force (literally, "twist out")
retort (*v.*) ri-'tòrt	reply quickly or sharply ("twist back")
retort (*n.*)	quick, witty, or cutting reply
torsion (*n.*) 'tòr-shən	act of twisting; twisting of a body by two opposing forces
tortuous (*adj.*) 'tòrch-ə-wəs	1. full of twists or curves; winding, as a *tortuous* road 2. tricky; crooked
torture (*v.*) 'tòr-chə(r)	1. wrench; twist 2. inflict severe pain upon
torture (*n.*)	anguish of body or mind; agony

EXERCISE 5.11

In each blank, insert the most appropriate word from group 6, *tort* (*tors*).

1. Soldiers know that if they are captured, the enemy will do its utmost to _____ military secrets from them.

2. It is very easy to _____ another person's ideas if you quote them out of context.

3. When teenagers are asked to help with the chores, they often _____ that they have no time.

4. _____ amaze us by their remarkable ability to throw their bodies into extraordinary postures.

5. Near its mouth, the Mississippi winds among numerous swamps in a(n) _____ course to the Gulf of Mexico.

7. VICT (VINC): "conquer," "show conclusively"

convict (*v.*) kən-'vikt	prove guilty; show conclusively to be guilty
convict (*n.*) 'kän-,vikt	person serving a prison sentence
conviction (*n.*) kən-'vik-shən	1. state of having been judged guilty of an offense 2. strong belief
convince (*v.*) kən-'vins	persuade or show conclusively by argument or proof
evict (*v.*) ē-'vikt	1. expel by legal process, as to *evict* a tenant 2. oust
evince (*v.*) ē-'vins	show clearly; disclose
invincible (*adj.*) in-'vin-sə-bəl	incapable of being conquered
vanquish (*v.*) 'vaŋ-kwish	overcome in battle; conquer
victor (*n.*) 'vik-tə(r)	winner; conqueror

EXERCISE 5.12

In each blank, insert the most appropriate word from group 7, *vict* (*vinc*).

1. Stadium police are empowered to _____ any spectator who creates a disturbance.

2. After the match, the _____ shook hands with the loser.

3. Students who _____ a talent for writing should be encouraged to contribute to the school newspaper and literary magazine.

4. Facts alone will usually not _____ a biased person that he or she is wrong.

5. Our apparently _____ swimming team has been neither beaten nor tied in the past two seasons.

8. FRACT (FRAG): "break"

fraction (*n.*) 'frak-shən	one or more of the equal parts of a whole; fragment
fractious (*adj.*) 'frak-shəs	apt to break out into a passion; cross; irritable (*ant.* **peaceable**)
fracture (*n.*) 'frak-chə(r)	1. break or crack 2. breaking of a bone
fragile (*adj.*) 'fraj-əl	easily broken; frail; delicate (*ant.* **tough; durable**)
fragment (*n.*) 'frag-mənt	part broken off
infraction (*n.*) in-'frak-shən	act of breaking; breach; violation, as an *infraction* of a law
refract (*v.*) ri-'frakt	bend (literally, "break back") a ray of light, a heat or sound wave, etc., from a straight course
refractory (*adj.*) ri-'frak-tə-rē	resisting; intractable; hard to manage, as a *refractory* mule (*ant.* **malleable, tractable, adaptable**)

EXERCISE 5.13

In each blank, insert the most appropriate word from group 8, *fract* (*frag*).

1. Glassware and other _____ materials require special packaging to prevent breakage.

2. Failure to stop at a full-stop sign is a(n) _____ of the traffic laws.

3. X-ray diagnosis disclosed that the child had sustained no _____.

4. If I could find the one missing _____, I would be able to restore the broken vase.

5. I was criticized for not reducing the _____ 3/12 to 1/4.

9. OMNI: "all," "every," "everywhere"

omnibus (*adj.*) 'äm-ni-bəs	covering many things at once, as an *omnibus* bill
omnibus (*n.*)	1. bus 2. book containing a variety of works by one author, as a Hemingway *omnibus*

omnifarious (*adj.*) ˌäm-nə-ˈfar-ē-əs	of all varieties, forms, or kinds
omnific (*adj.*) äm-ˈnif-ik	all-creating
omnipotent (*adj.*) äm-ˈnip-ət-ənt	unlimited in power; almighty
omnipresent (*adj.*) ˌäm-ni-ˈprez-ᵊnt	present everywhere at the same time; ubiquitous
omniscient (*adj.*) äm-ˈnish-ənt	knowing everything
omnivorous (*adj.*) äm-ˈniv-ə-rəs	1. eating everything, both plant and animal substances 2. avidly taking in everything, as an *omnivorous* reader

EXERCISE 5.14

In each blank, insert the most appropriate word from group 9, *omni*.

1. I cannot answer all questions, since I am not _____ .

2. With his magic lamp, Aladdin was _____ ; no feat was beyond his power.

3. Because of its _____ uses, a scout knife is indispensable equipment for a camping trip.

4. With several desirable invitations for the same evening, I regretted that I could not be

_____ .

5. It was a conviction of the ancient Egyptians that their sun god was _____ . They believed that he had created everything.

10. FLECT (FLEX): ''bend''

deflect (*v.*) di-ˈflekt	turn (''bend'') aside
flex (*v.*) ˈfleks	bend, as to *flex* a limb
flexible (*adj.*) ˈflek-sə-bəl	pliable (''capable of being bent''); not rigid; tractable (*ant.* **inflexible**)
flexor (*n.*) ˈflek-sə(r)	muscle that serves to bend a limb
genuflect (*v.*) ˈjen-yə-ˌflekt	bend the knee; touch the right knee to the ground, as in worship

inflection (*n.*) in-'flek-shən	change ("bend") in the pitch or tone of a person's voice
inflexibility (*n.*) in-ˌflek-sə-'bil-ət-ē	rigidity; firmness
reflect (*v.*) ri-'flekt	1. throw ("bend") back light, as from a prism 2. think
reflex (*n.*) 'rē-ˌfleks	involuntary response ("bending back") to a stimulus; for example, sneezing is a *reflex*

EXERCISE 5.15

In each blank, insert the most appropriate word from group 10, *flect* (*flex*).

1. The secretion of tears, as when a cinder enters the eye, is a(n) _____, since it is beyond our control.

2. Copper tubing is easy to shape but it is much less _____ than rubber hose.

3. Unable to catch the line drive, I managed to _____ the ball toward the infield, holding the batter to a single.

4. Obedient subjects were expected to _____ when admitted to the presence of an absolute monarch.

5. The _____ of both sides makes an early settlement unlikely.

11. TEN (TIN, TENT): "hold," "keep"

detention (*n.*) di-'ten-shən	act of keeping back or detaining
impertinent (*adj.*) im-'pərt-ᵊn-ənt	1. not pertinent; inappropriate (*ant.* **pertinent**) 2. rude
pertinacious (*adj.*) ˌpert-ᵊn-'ā-shəs	adhering ("holding") firmly to a purpose or opinion; very persistent
pertinent (*adj.*) ˌpərt-ᵊn-ənt	having to do with ("holding to") the matter at hand; relevant (*ant.* **impertinent**)
retentive (*adj.*) ri-'tent-iv	tenacious; able to retain or remember
retinue (*n.*) 'ret-ᵊn-ˌyü	group of followers or assistants attending a distinguished person
tenacity (*n.*) tə-'nas-ət-ē	firmness in holding fast; persistence

tenancy (*n.*) 'ten-ən-sē	period of a tenant's temporary holding of real estate
tenet (*n.*) 'ten-ət	principle, belief, or doctrine generally held to be true
tenure (*n.*) 'ten-yə(r)	1. period for which an office or position is held, as: "U.S. Supreme Court Justices enjoy life *tenure*." 2. status assuring an employee a permanent position
untenable (*adj.*) ˌən-'ten-ə-bəl	incapable of being held or defended (*ant.* **tenable**)

EXERCISE 5.16

In each blank, insert the most appropriate word from group 11, *ten* (*tin, tent*).

1. The _____ of a member of the House of Representatives is only two years.

2. Retreating from their _____ coastal positions, the rebels sought a more defensible foothold in the hills.

3. Your remark is not _____; it has nothing to do with the matter we are discussing.

4. Though she can't recall names, Sylvia has a(n) _____ memory for faces.

5. The basketball star was accompanied by a(n) _____ of admirers.

6. Freedom of speech is one of the _____s of democracy.

---

12. MON (MONIT): "warn"

---

admonish (*v.*) ad-'män-ish	warn of a fault; reprove; rebuke (*ant.* **commend**)
admonition (*n.*) ˌad-mə-'nish-ən	gentle reproof ("warning"); counseling against a fault or error
admonitory (*adj.*) ad-'män-ə-ˌtȯr-ē	conveying a gentle reproof
monitor (*n.*) 'män-ət-ə(r)	person or mechanical device that keeps track of, checks, or warns
monitor (*v.*) 'män-ət-ə(r)	keep track of, regulate, or control the operation of a machine or process
monument (*n.*) 'män-yə-mənt	a means of reminding us of a person or event; for example, a statue or a tomb
premonition (*n.*) ˌprē-mə-'nish-ən	forewarning; intuitive anticipation of a coming event

premonitory (*adj.*)   conveying a forewarning
prē-'män-ə-ˌtȯr-ē

EXERCISE 5.17

In each blank, insert the most appropriate word from group 12, *mon* (*monit*).

1. Had they heeded your _____ to fill the gas tank, they would not have been stranded on the road.

2. I must _____ you that you will be unable to vote if you do not register.

3. Some think that an early autumn snowstorm is a(n) _____ of a severe winter, but you really can't tell in advance.

4. A(n) _____ stands in the village square in memory of local veterans of foreign wars.

5. The approach of the storm was signaled by a low, _____ rumbling from the distant hills.

6. Intensive care patients are wired to devices that _____ their blood pressure, heart rate, and other vital body functions.

13. MAND (MANDAT): "order," "command," "commit"

countermand (*v.*)   issue a contrary order
'kau̇nt-ər-ˌmand

mandate (*n.*)   1. authoritative command
'man-ˌdāt   2. territory administered by a trustee (supervisory nation)

mandatory (*adj.*)   obligatory; required by command
'man-də-ˌtȯr-ē   (*ant.* **optional**)

remand (*v.*)   send ("order") back; recommit, as to a prison
ri-'mand

writ of mandamus (*n.*)   written order from a court to enforce the performance of some public
'ritəvman-'dā-məs   duty

EXERCISE 5.18

In each blank, insert the most appropriate word from group 13, *mand* (*mandat*).

1. The reelected candidate regarded her huge popular vote as a _____ from the people to continue the policies of her first term in office.

2. On learning of the colonel's ill-advised order to retreat, the general hastened to _____ it.

3. Several prominent citizens have applied for a _____
to compel the Mayor to publish the budget, as required by law.

4. The coach regards attendance at today's practice session as _____ ;
no one is excused.

5. Since the retrial resulted in a verdict of ''guilty,'' the judge was obliged to _____
the defendant to the state penitentiary.

---

14. CRED (CREDIT): ''believe''

---

accredited (*adj.*) ə-'kred-ət-id	officially authorized or recognized; provided with credentials
credence (*n.*) 'krēd-³ns	belief as to the truth of something
credentials (*n. pl.*) kri-'den-shəlz	documents, letters, references, etc., that inspire belief or trust
credible (*adj.*) 'kred-ə-bəl	believable (*ant.* **incredible**)
credit (*n.*) 'kred-ət	belief; faith; trust
credulous (*adj.*) 'krej-ə-ləs	too ready to believe; easily deceived (*ant.* **incredulous; skeptical**)
creed (*n.*) 'krēd or **credo** 'krēd-ō	summary of principles believed in or adhered to
discredit (*v.*) dis-'kred-ət	1. cast doubt on; refuse to believe 2. take trust or credit away from; disgrace
discredit (*n.*) dis-'kred-ət	loss of belief or trust; damage to one's reputation; disgrace
incredible (*adj.*) in-'kred-ə-bəl	not believable
incredulity (*n.*) ‚in-kri-'d(y)ü-lət-ē	disbelief

EXERCISE 5.19

In each blank, insert the most appropriate word from group 14, *cred(credit)*.

1. His rude behavior brought _____ not only upon himself, but also upon
his team.

2. I showed _____ negligence in not removing the pot fr*
   when the timer rang.

3. When applying for admission to college, you are likely to be asked for such _____
   as your high school transcript, standardized test scores, and letters of recommendation.

4. Gerald is too _____; he will believe anything a salesperson may tell
   him.

5. Olga greeted the announcement that she had won the door prize with a look of baffled

   _____ .

6. The diplomas and professional licenses in Dr. Green's office show that she is a(n) _____
   physician.

15. FID: "faith," "trust"

affidavit (*n.*)
ˌaf-ə-ˈdā-vət

sworn written statement made before an authorized official

bona fide (*adj.*)
ˈbō-nə-ˌfīd

made or carried out in good faith; genuine

confidant (*n.*)
ˈkän-fə-ˌdant

(*confidante*, if a woman) one to whom secrets are entrusted

confident (*adj.*)
ˈkän-fəd-ənt

having faith in oneself; self-reliant; sure
(*ant.* **apprehensive; diffident**)

confidential (*adj.*)
ˌkän-fə-ˈden-shəl

communicated in trust; secret; private

diffident (*adj.*)
ˈdif-əd-ənt

lacking faith in oneself; timid; shy
(*ant.* **confident**)

fidelity (*n.*)
fə-ˈdel-ət-ē

1. faithfulness to a trust or vow
(*ant.* **perfidy; infidelity**)
2. accuracy; faithfulness of sound reproduction

fiduciary (*adj.*)
fə-ˈd(y)ü-shē-ˌer-ē

1. held in trust (*fiduciary* property)
2. confidential (*fiduciary* duties of a trustee)

infidel (*n.*)
ˈin-fəd-ᵊl

one who does not accept a particular faith; unbeliever

perfidious (*adj.*)
pər-ˈfid-ē-əs

false to a trust; faithless

perfidy (*n.*)
ˈpər-fəd-ē

violation of a trust; treachery; faithlessness; disloyalty
(*ant.* **fidelity; fealty**)

EXERCISE 5.20

In each blank, insert the most appropriate word from group 15, *fid*.

1. Your disclosure of secrets you were sworn to keep is unforgivable _____.

2. Marie looks upon her cousin Nancy as a(n) _____ with whom she can freely discuss her personal problems.

3. At first, new motorists are usually nervous, but with experience they become more _____.

4. Our teacher recommends a particular translation of the ODYSSEY because of its _____ to the original.

5. Steve was very _____ as he mounted the platform, even though he knew his speech by heart.

6. The witness agreed to sign a(n) _____ and, if necessary, to testify in person.

7. The trustees were sued for having used _____ property for their own benefit.

Review Exercises

REVIEW 1: DEFINING LATIN ROOTS

In the space before each Latin root in column I, write the *letter* of its correct meaning from column II.

	COLUMN I		COLUMN II
_____	1. CIDE	*a.*	live; alive
_____	2. VOR	*b.*	break; burst
_____	3. FLECT (FLEX)	*c.*	order; command; commit
_____	4. TORT (TORS)	*d.*	bind; draw tight
_____	5. OMNI	*e.*	faith; trust
_____	6. VICT (VINC)	*f.*	warn
_____	7. TEN (TIN, TENT)	*g.*	killing; killer
_____	8. MAND (MANDAT)	*h.*	believe
_____	9. FID	*i.*	conquer; show conclusively
_____	10. FRACT (FRAG)	*j.*	bend
_____	11. VIV	*k.*	eat greedily
_____	12. MON (MONIT)	*l.*	twist
_____	13. CRED (CREDIT)	*m.*	hold; keep
_____	14. STRING (STRICT)	*n.*	all; every; everywhere

REVIEW 2: USING LATIN ROOTS

Enter the Latin roots needed to complete the partially spelled words below.

DEFINITION	WORD
1. break asunder	D I S _ _ _ _
2. germ-killing substance	G E R M I _ _ _ _
3. part broken off	_ _ _ _ M E N T
4. faithfulness to a trust	_ _ _ E L I T Y
5. one who conquers	_ _ _ _ O R
6. flesh-eating	C A R N I _ _ _ O U S
7. issue a contrary order	C O U N T E R _ _ _ _

8. forewarning   P R E _ _ _ _ _ I O N

9. muscle that serves to bend a limb   _ _ _ _ O R

10. readiness to believe on slight evidence   _ _ _ _ U L I T Y

11. snake that crushes (constricts) its prey   B O A C O N _ _ _ _ _ _ O R

12. bring back to life   R E _ _ _ E

13. adhering firmly to a purpose or opinion   P E R _ _ _ A C I O U S

14. present everywhere at the same time   _ _ _ _ P R E S E N T

15. throw (bend) back heat, light, sound, etc.   R E _ _ _ _ _

16. greedy in eating   _ _ _ A C I O U S

17. breaking of a bone   _ _ _ _ _ U R E

18. show conclusively by proof   C O N _ _ _ _ E

19. killing of a human by another   H O M I _ _ _ _

20. documents inspiring trust   _ _ _ _ E N T I A L S

REVIEW 3: SENTENCE COMPLETION

In the blank space, write the *letter* of the word (or set of words) that best completes the sentence.

1. Circus elephants are usually _____, but occasionally they are refractory.
   a. unmanageable *b.* stubborn *c.* tractable *d.* uncooperative *e.* resisting

2. Harvey believes he is omniscient, but we are not particularly impressed by his _____.
   a. power *b.* knowledge *c.* manners *d.* personality *e.* appearance

3. The promise had been extorted and, like all promises growing out of _____, it was _____.
   a. ignorance . . . perfidious *b.* haste . . . untenable *c.* rumor . . . false
   d. compulsion . . . unreliable *e.* friendship . . . dependable

4. An act of regicide always has a _____ as its victim.
   a. rebel *b.* general *c.* president *d.* prime minister *e.* monarch

5. I usually admonished my brother for distorting facts, but Mother seldom _____ him.
   a. reproved *b.* encouraged *c.* remanded *d.* praised *e.* supported

6. An omnibus bill deals with proposed legislation on _____ problems.
   a. economic *b.* many *c.* minor *d.* transportation *e.* few

7. The rapid withdrawal of your hand from the flame was a reflex, not a(n) _____ ,reaction.
   a. protective *b.* dangerous *c.* involuntary *d.* natural *e.* voluntary

8. The author read the critics' _____ with incredulity; they were too laudatory to be _____.
   a. censures . . . heeded *b.* strictures . . . ignored *c.* admonitions . . . challenged
   d. encomiums . . . believed *e.* rebukes . . . answered

9. It is advisable to take along plenty of sandwiches because hungry picnickers are _____ eaters.

    a. admonitory *b.* abstemious *c.* omnifarious *d.* heterogeneous *e.* voracious

10. No one would dare to offer a bribe to an official who is known to be thoroughly _____ .

    a. incorruptible *b.* invincible *c.* credulous *d.* retentive *e.* convivial

REVIEW 4: ANTONYMS

Each italicized word in column I has an ANTONYM in column II. Enter the *letter* of that ANTONYM in the space provided.

	COLUMN I		COLUMN II
_____	1. *perfidious* adviser	*a.*	languid
_____	2. *fragile* structure	*b.*	optional
_____	3. probably *survived*	*c.*	expanded
_____	4. *credulous* audience	*d.*	peaceable
_____	5. *confident* of the outcome	*e.*	durable
_____	6. *constricted* passageways	*f.*	commended
_____	7. *fractious* neighbors	*g.*	faithful
_____	8. *admonished* for their deed	*h.*	perished
_____	9. *vivacious* appearance	*i.*	apprehensive
_____	10. *mandatory* attendance	*j.*	skeptical

REVIEW 5: SYNONYMS

In the space provided, write the *letter* of the word that has most nearly the SAME MEANING as the italicized word.

_____ 1. *fragile* flower: *a.* fragrant *b.* broken *c.* colorful *d.* frail

_____ 2. cling *tenaciously*: *a.* stubbornly *b.* dangerously *c.* hopefully *d.* timidly

_____ 3. beyond *credence*: *a.* detention *b.* doubt *c.* belief *d.* recall

_____ 4. *omnipotent* ruler: *a.* almighty *b.* wise *c.* cruel *d.* greedy

_____ 5. *mandatory* increase: *a.* deserved *b.* required *c.* temporary *d.* substantial

_____ 6. surprising *impertinence*: *a.* firmness *b.* unreliability *c.* impatience *d.* rudeness

_____ 7. *breach* of trust: *a.* atmosphere *b.* testing *c.* breaking *d.* abundance

_____ 8. *unvanquished* foe: *a.* defeated *b.* exhausted *c.* treacherous *d.* unbeaten

_____ 9. in a *fiduciary* capacity: *a.* confidential *b.* special *c.* professional *d.* important

_____ 10. refused to *genuflect*: *a.* admit *b.* kneel *c.* cooperate *d.* disclose

REVIEW 6: CONCISE WRITING

Express the thought of each sentence below in no more than four words.

1. Jim twisted the plan that we had presented out of its true meaning.

   _____

2. Laura submitted a sworn statement made before an authorized official.

   _____

3. Coughing is an act that is not subject to the control of the will.

   _____

4. Do not take roads that are full of twists and turns.

   _____

5. What is the reason that you have no faith in yourself?

   _____

6. The remark that Pat made has nothing to do with the matter at hand.

   _____

7. Sally had words of praise for our firmness in holding fast.

   _____

8. The position that we found ourselves in could not be defended.

   _____

9. George did not have anyone to whom he could entrust secrets.

   _____

10. The aim of logic is to show conclusively by means of argument or proof.

   _____

REVIEW 7: BRAINTEASERS

Fill in the missing letters.

1. We usually listen to rumors with __ __ __ **r e d** __ __ __ __ __.

2. To everyone's surprise, the __ __ __ **t o r t** __ __ __ __ __ __ squeezed himself into a small metal box.

3. My brother uses a(n) __ __ __ **r i n g** __ __ __ after shaving.

4. The __ __ __ **d e n t** __ __ __ __ of nominees to fill important vacancies are sometimes checked not too carefully.

5. The dictator is suspected of __ **r a t** __ __ __ __ __ __, though some say that he could not have murdered his own brother.

6. Elephants never hunt; they are not **c a r** __ __ __ __ __ __ __ __.

7. Many oppose __ __ __ __ **s e c t** __ __ __ because they feel animals have the same right to live as humans have.

8. Some who claim to be honest turn out to be __ __ __ __ **u p** __.

9. The Pilgrims had to leave their native land because they refused to surrender their __ __ **n e t s**.

10. Foolish humans who may consider themselves __ __ __ __ __ __ **t e n t** will soon learn that they are not gods.

REVIEW 8: COMPOSITION

Answer in two or three sentences.

1. Should the death penalty be mandatory for all persons convicted of homicide? Explain.

_____

_____

2. Why should we not put too much credence in the opinions of those who claim to be omniscient?

_____

_____

3. Discuss two precautions that might help a driver survive a collision with another vehicle.

_____

_____

4. Should an ordinary citizen take it upon himself or herself to admonish someone about to commit an infraction? Explain.

_____

_____

5. Discuss a possible result of the unrestricted use of pesticides.

_____

_____

REVIEW 9: ANALOGIES

Write the *letter* of the word that best completes the analogy.

1. *Matricide* is to *mother* as *genocide* is to _____.
   a. uncle *b.* country *c.* race *d.* tyrant *e.* general

2. *Flesh* is to *carnivorous* as *fruit* is to _____.

   a. omnivorous *b.* insectivorous *c.* vegetarian *d.* frugivorous *e.* agricultural

3. *Fraction* is to *whole* as *follower* is to _____.

   a. creed *b.* retinue *c.* tenure *d.* fragment *e.* torsion

4. *Reservation* is to *cancel* as *directive* is to _____.

   a. command *b.* proclaim *c.* flex *d.* demand *e.* countermand

5. *Orphan* is to *guardian* as *mandate* is to _____.

   a. victor *b.* monitor *c.* trustee *d.* confidant *e.* commission

---

16. GRAT: "pleasant," "thank," "favor"

---

congratulate (*v.*) kən-'grach-ə-ˌlāt	express one's pleasure to another person at that person's success
gracious (*adj.*) 'grā-shəs	pleasant; courteous; kindly (*ant.* **ungracious**)
grateful (*adj.*) 'grāt-fəl	feeling or expressing gratitude; thankful; obliged (*ant.* **ungrateful**)
gratify (*v.*) 'grat-ə-ˌfī	give or be a source of pleasure or satisfaction
gratis (*adv.*) 'grāt-əs	without charge or payment; free
gratitude (*n.*) 'grat-ə-ˌt(y)üd	thankfulness (*ant.* **ingratitude**)
gratuitous (*adj.*) grə-'t(y)ü-ət-əs	1. given freely; gratis 2. unwarranted, as a *gratuitous* remark
gratuity (*n.*) grə-'t(y)ü-ət-ē	present of money in return for a favor or service; tip
ingrate (*n.*) 'in-ˌgrāt	ungrateful ("not thankful") person
ingratiate (*v.*) in-'grā-shē-ˌāt	establish (oneself) in the favor or good graces of another

EXERCISE 5.21

In each blank, insert the most appropriate word from group 16, *grat.*

1. I would consider myself a(n) _____ if I did not express my gratitude to those who have helped me.

2. Some restaurants charge for a second cup of coffee, but others provide it _____ .

3. We were so pleased with the service that we left a generous _____ .

4. Keeping your TV on extremely loud until three in the morning is no way to _____ yourself with the neighbors.

5. I am sorry I was so discourteous. I shall try to be more _____ .

6. Compliments are meant to _____ .

---

17. MOR (MORT): "death"

---

immortal (*adj.*) im-'ort-ᵊl	1. not subject to death (*ant.* **mortal**) 2. not subject to oblivion (being forgotten); imperishable (*ant.* **mortality**)
immortality (*n.*) ͺim-or-'tal-ət-ē	1. eternal life 2. lasting fame
moribund (*adj.*) 'mor-ə-bənd	dying; near death
mortal (*adj.*) 'mort-ᵊl	1. destined to die (*ant.* **mortal**) 2. human 3. causing death; fatal, as a *mortal* blow
mortal (*n.*) 'mort-ᵊl	human being; person; individual
mortality (*n.*) mor-'tal-ət-ē	1. death rate 2. mortal nature (*ant.* **immortality**)
mortician (*n.*) mor-'tish-ən	undertaker
mortification (*n.*) ͺmort-ə-fə-'kā-shən	shame; humiliation; embarrassment
mortify (*v.*) 'mort-ə-ͺfī	embarrass; shame; humiliate (literally, "make dead," "kill")
mortuary (*n.*) 'mor-chə-ͺwer-ē	funeral home
rigor mortis (*n.*) ͺrig-ər-'mort-əs	stiffness of the body that sets in several hours after death (literally, "stiffness of death")

EXERCISE 5.22

In each blank, insert the most appropriate word from group 17, *mor (mort)*.

1. Patrick Henry's _____ rests on a speech ending "Give me liberty, or give me death!"

2. Infant _____ is relatively high in nations that have few physicians and hospitals.

3. The proprietor did not realize what _____ she caused her assistant when she scolded him in the presence of the entire staff.

4. Though the mountain climber's injury is critical, it may not be _____; he has a chance of recovery.

5. The _____ community has been given a new lease on life since the re-opening of two large factories that were shut down three years ago.

---

18. CORP: "body"

---

corporal (*adj.*) 'kȯr-p(ə-)rəl	bodily, as *corporal* punishment
corporation (*n.*) ˌkȯr-pə-'rā-shən	body authorized by law to carry on an activity with the rights and duties of a single person
corps (*n.*) 'kȯ(ə)r	1. organized body of persons 2. branch of the military, as the Marine *Corps*
corpse (*n.*) 'kȯrps	dead body
corpulent (*adj.*) 'kȯr-pyə-lənt	bulky; obese; very fat
corpus (*n.*) 'kȯr-pəs	general collection or body of writings, laws, etc.
corpuscle (*n.*) 'kȯr-pəs-əl	1. blood cell (literally, a "little body") 2. minute particle
corpus delicti (*n.*) ˌkȯr-pəs-di-'lik-ˌtī	1. facts proving that a crime has been committed 2. body of the victim in a murder case
esprit de corps (*n.*) es-ˌprēd-ə-'kȯ(ə)r	spirit of a body of persons; group spirit
habeas corpus (*n.*) ˌhā-bē-ə-'skȯr-pəs	1. writ (order) requiring a detained person to be brought before a court to investigate the legality of that person's detention (the writ begins with the words **habeas corpus,** meaning "you should have the body") 2. right of a citizen to secure court protection against illegal imprisonment
incorporate (*v.*) in-'kȯr-pə-ˌrāt	combine so as to form one body

EXERCISE 5.23

In each blank, insert the most appropriate word from group 18, *corp.*

1. The executive in charge of administration has a(n) _____ of able assistants.

2. Criminals were flogged or put in the stocks in olden times, but such _____ punishment is rare today.

3. The _____ patient was advised by a physician to try to lose weight.

4. Publishers often _____ two or more works of an author into one volume.

5. Until the _____ is produced, it cannot be established that a crime has been committed.

6. The residents proudly support their block association; they have a fine _____ .

7. In countries where there is no _____ , a suspect can be kept in prison without ever being brought to trial.

---

19. DUC (DUCT): "lead," "conduct," "draw"

---

aqueduct (*n.*) 'ak-wə-ˌdəkt	artificial channel for conducting water over a distance
conducive (*adj.*) kən-'d(y)ü-siv	tending to lead to; contributive; helpful
conduct (*v.*) kən-'dəkt	lead; guide; escort
deduction (*n.*) di-'dək-shən	1. taking away; subtraction (*ant.* **addition**) 2. reasoning from the general to the particular
duct (*n.*) 'dəkt	tube or channel for conducting a liquid, air, etc.
ductile (*adj.*) 'dək-tᵊl	1. able to be drawn out or hammered thin (said of metal) 2. easily led; docile
induce (*v.*) in-'d(y)üs	lead on; move by persuasion
induct (*v.*) in-'dəkt	admit ("lead in") as a member; initiate
induction (*n.*) in-'dək-shən	1. ceremony by which one is made a member; initiation 2. reasoning from the particular to the general
seduction (*n.*) si-'dək-shən	enticement; leading astray into wrongdoing

traduce (*v.*) tra-'d(y)üs	(literally, "lead along" as a spectacle to bring into disgrace); malign; slander; vilify; calumniate
viaduct (*n.*) 'vī-ə-ˌdəkt	bridge for conducting a road or railroad over a valley, river, etc.

EXERCISE 5.24

In each blank, insert the most appropriate word from group 19, *duc* (*duct*).

1. A(n) _____ conducts water from a source of supply to a point of distribution.

2. How much of a(n) _____ is made from your weekly salary for taxes?

3. Though John had said that he wouldn't join, I was able to _____ him to become a member.

4. As the train passed over the _____, we had an excellent view of the valley below.

5. When films that exaggerate the luxury and idleness of American life are shown abroad, they _____ our good name.

20. SECUT (SEQU): "follow"

consecutive (*adj.*) kən-'sek-yət-iv	following in regular order; successive
consequence (*n.*) 'kän-sə-ˌkwens	1. that which follows logically; result 2. importance, as a person of *consequence*
execute (*v.*) 'ek-sə-ˌkyüt	1. follow through to completion; carry out 2. put to death
inconsequential (*adj.*) in-ˌkän-sə-'kwen-shəl	of no consequence; trivial; unimportant
prosecute (*v.*) 'präs-i-ˌkyüt	1. follow to the end or until finished 2. conduct legal proceedings against; sue
sequel (*n.*) 'sē-kwəl	something that follows; continuation; consequence; outcome
sequence (*n.*) 'sē-kwəns	the following of one thing after another; succession; orderly series
sequential (*adj.*) si-'kwen-chəl	arranged in a sequence; serial

EXERCISE 5.25

In each blank, insert the most appropriate word from group 20, *secut* (*sequ*).

1. If the vandals refuse to pay for the damage they caused, the town will _____ them.

2. After a string of seven _____ victories, we suffered our first loss.

3. The book about the clever detective proved so popular that the author was induced to write a(n)

_____ .

4. The cards in the card catalog are arranged in strict alphabetical _____ .

5. The shortage of water during dry spells is a matter of serious _____ in affected communities.

21. CUR (CURR, CURS): ''run''

concur (*v.*) kən-'kə(r)	1. agree; be of the same opinion (literally, ''run together'') (*ant.* **contend**) 2. happen together; coincide
concurrent (*adj.*) kən-'kər-ənt	running together; occurring at the same time
current (*adj.*) 'kər-ənt	1. running or flowing (said of water or electricity) 2. now in progress, prevailing
curriculum (*n.*) kə-'rik-yə-ləm	course of study in a school or college
cursive (*adj.*) 'kər-siv	running or flowing (said of handwriting in which the letters are joined)
cursory (*adj.*) 'kərs-ə-rē	running over hastily; superficially done, as a *cursory* glance
discursive (*adj.*) dis-'kər-siv	wandering (''running'') from one topic to another; rambling; digressive
excursion (*n.*) ik-'skər-zhən	going (''running'') out or forth; expedition
incur (*v.*) in-'kə(r)	1. meet with (''run into'') something undesirable 2. bring upon oneself
incursion (*n.*) in-'kər-zhən	1. a rushing into 2. hostile invasion; raid
precursor (*n.*) pri-'kər-sə(r)	forerunner; predecessor
recur (*v.*) ri-'kə(r)	happen again (literally, ''run again'')

EXERCISE 5.26

In each blank, insert the most appropriate word from group 21, *cur* (*curr, curs*).

1. If you are habitually late, you will _____ the displeasure of your employer.

2. Does your school _____ include a course in driver training?

3. The _____ film at the Bijou is a western; the war drama is no longer playing there.

4. A difficult passage requires much more than a(n) _____ reading if it is to be fully understood.

5. Our conversation, as usual, was _____, ranging from the latest popular tunes to the prospects of our favorite teams.

---

22. GRESS (GRAD): "step," "walk," "go"

aggressive (*adj.*) ə-'gres-iv	disposed to attack (literally "step toward"); militant; assertive; pushing
egress (*n.*) 'ē-,gres	means of going out; exit (*ant.* **access**)
gradation (*n.*) grā-'dā-shən	1. a change by steps or stages 2. act of grading
grade (*n.*) 'grād	step; stage; degree; rating
gradient (*n.*) 'grād-ē-ənt	1. rate at which a road, railroad track, temperature, voltage, etc., rises ("steps" up) 2. slope
gradual (*adj.*) 'graj-ə-wəl	step-by-step; bit by bit (*ant.* **abrupt**)
graduate (*v.*) 'graj-ə-,wāt	complete all the steps of a course and receive a diploma or degree
graduated (*adj.*) 'graj-ə-,wāt-əd	arranged in regular steps, stages, or degrees
progressive (*adj.*) prə-'gres-iv	going forward to something considered better (*ant.* **reactionary; retrogressive**)
regressive (*adj.*) ri-'gres-iv	disposed to move ("step") backward; retrogressive
retrograde (*adj.*) 're-trə-,grād	1. going backward 2. becoming worse

retrogression (*n.*)   act of going from a better to a worse state
ˌre-trə-ˈgresh-ən   (*ant.* **progress**)

transgress (*v.*)   step beyond the limits or barriers; go beyond; break a law
trans-ˈgres

EXERCISE 5.27

In each blank, insert the most appropriate word from group 22, *gress* (*grad*).

1. Learning to play an instrument is a(n) _____ process; it cannot be achieved overnight.

2. The offenders know that they will be dealt with severely if they should _____ again.

3. When the game ended, hordes of spectators jammed the stadium exits, making _____ painfully slow.

4. The medical report showed _____ rather than progress, for the patient's blood pressure had gone up.

5. In a string of _____ pearls, the individual pearls are arranged in the order of increasing size on both halves of the string.

23. PED: "foot"

biped (*n.*)   two-footed animal
ˈbī-ˌped

centipede (*n.*)   (literally, "hundred-legged" creature); wormlike animal with one pair of
ˈsent-ə-ˌpēd   legs on most of its segments

expedite (*v.*)   1. facilitate (literally, "extricate someone caught by the foot")
ˈek-spə-ˌdīt   2. accelerate or speed up (*ant.* **delay**)

impede (*v.*)   hinder (literally, "entangle the feet"); obstruct; block
im-ˈpēd   (*ant.* **assist; aid**)

impediment (*n.*)   1. hindrance; obstacle (literally, "something entangling the feet")
im-ˈped-ə-mənt   2. defect

millipede (*n.*)   (literally, "thousand-legged" creature); wormlike animal with two pairs
ˈmil-ə-ˌpēd   of legs on most of its segments

pedal (*n.*)   lever acted on by the foot
ˈped-ᵊl

pedestal (*n.*)   1. support or foot of a column or statue
ˈped-əst-ᵊl   2. foundation

pedestrian (*n.*) pə-'des-tre-ən	person traveling on foot
pedestrian (*adj.*)	commonplace or dull, as a *pedestrian* performance
velocipede (*n.*) və-'läs-ə-ˌpēd	1. child's tricycle (literally, "swift foot") 2. early form of bicycle

EXERCISE 5.28

In each blank, insert the most appropriate word from group 23, *ped*.

1. A supervisor is expected to _____, not impede, production.

2. It is foolhardy for a(n) _____ to cross a busy thoroughfare against the light.

3. For a smooth stop, apply foot pressure to the brake _____ gradually, not abruptly.

4. As a youth, Demosthenes, the famous orator, is said to have suffered from a speech
_____.

5. At the age of six, Judy abandoned her _____ and learned to ride a bicycle.

24. TACT (TANG): "touch"

contact (*n.*) 'kän-ˌtakt	touching or meeting; association; connection
contiguous (*adj.*) kən-'tig-yə-wəs	touching; in physical contact; adjoining
contingent (*adj.*) kən-'tin-jənt	1. dependent on something else (literally, "touching together") 2. accidental
intact (*adj.*) in-'takt	untouched or uninjured; kept or left whole (*ant.* **defective**)
intangible (*adj.*) in-'tan-jə-bəl	1. not capable of being perceived by the sense of touch 2. hard to grasp or define exactly (*ant.* **tangible**)
tact (*n.*) 'takt	sensitive mental perception of what is appropriate on a given occasion (literally, "sense of touch")
tactful (*adj.*) 'takt-fəl	having or showing tact (*ant.* **tactless**)
tactile (*adj.*) 'tak-t°l	1. pertaining to the sense of touch 2. tangible

tangent (*adj.*) 'tan-jənt	touching
tangent (*n.*)	line or surface meeting a curved line or surface at one point, but not intersecting it
tangential (*adj.*) tan-'jen-chəl	merely touching; slightly connected; digressive

EXERCISE 5.29

In each blank, insert the most appropriate word from group 24, *tact* (*tang*).

1. To discuss your admission to college in the presence of someone who has just received a rejection notice is _____ .

2. The missing sum was found _____ ; not a penny had been spent.

3. The Federal grant is _____ on our raising a matching sum; if we fail to raise that sum, we will not qualify.

4. A firm's goodwill with its clients is a most valuable, though _____ , asset.

5. If you wish to maintain _____ with your classmates after graduation, join the Alumni Association.

25. PREHEND (PREHENS): "seize," "grasp"

apprehend (*v.*) ,ap-ri-'hend	1. seize or take into custody 2. understand
apprehensive (*adj.*) ,ap-ri-'hen-siv	1. quick to understand or grasp 2. fearful of what may come; anxious (*ant.* **confident**)
comprehensible (*adj.*) ,käm-pri-'hen-sə-bəl	able to be grasped mentally; understandable (*ant.* **incomprehensible**)
comprehensive (*adj.*) ,käm-pri-'hen-siv	including ("seizing") very much; extensive
prehensile (*adj.*) prē-'hen-səl	adapted for seizing, as a *prehensile* claw
reprehend (*v.*) ,rep-ri-'hend	(literally, "hold back"); find fault with; rebuke; reprimand; censure
reprehensible (*adj.*) ,rep-ri-'hen-sə-bəl	deserving of censure; culpable

EXERCISE 5.30

In each blank, insert the most appropriate word from group 25, *prehend* (*prehens*).

1. Aggression is utterly _____ .

2. From the observation deck at the top of the south tower of the World Trade Center, you can get

a(n) _____ view of New York City and its environs.

3. A coded message is _____ only to those who know the code.

4. Before the curtain rose, I was _____ about my performance, even though
I had rehearsed my part many times.

5. Law enforcement officials are doing their best to _____ the escaped convict.

6. The instructor is quick to _____ us when we violate safety regulations.

---

26. JECT: "throw," "cast"

---

abject (*adj.*)
'ab-ˌjekt

sunk or cast down to a low condition; downtrodden; deserving contempt

conjecture (*n.*)
kən-'jek-chə(r)

a guess; supposition; inference

dejected (*adj.*)
di-'jek-təd

downcast ("thrown down"); discouraged; depressed

eject (*v.*)
ē-'jekt

throw out or expel; evict

inject (*v.*)
in-'jekt

force or introduce ("throw in") a liquid, a remark, etc.

interject (*v.*)
ˌint-ər-'jekt

throw in between; insert; interpose

projectile (*n.*)
prə-'jek-tᵊl

1. object (bullet, shell, etc.) designed to be shot forward
2. anything thrown forward

reject (*v.*)
ri-'jekt

refuse to take; discard ("throw back")
(*ant.* **accept**)

subject (*v.*)
səb-'jekt

force (someone) to undergo something unpleasant or inconvenient; expose; make liable to

EXERCISE 5.31

In each blank, insert the most appropriate word from group 26, *ject*.

1. My friend is _____ over the damage to her new car.

2. A wise policy in buying shares of stock is to be guided by fact rather than _____ .

3. The umpire was obliged to _____ a player who refused to accept his decision.

4. A hypodermic syringe is used to _____ a dose of medicine beneath the skin.

5. The mob hurled stones, bricks, bottles, eggs, and anything else that could serve as a(n) _____ .

6. We tend to avoid rude people because we do not wish to _____ ourselves to their insults.

---

27. VERT (VERS): ''turn''

---

aversion (*n.*) ə-'vər-zhən	feeling of repugnance toward something with a desire to turn away from it; strong dislike; antipathy
avert (*v.*) ə-'vərt	1. turn away 2. prevent; avoid
controversy (*n.*) 'kän-trə-ˌvər-sē	dispute (literally, a ''turning against''); debate; quarrel
diversion (*n.*) di-'vər-zhən	entertainment; amusement
divert (*v.*) də-'vərt	1. turn aside 2. amuse; entertain
extrovert (*n.*) 'ek-strə-ˌvərt	one more interested in matters outside the self than in one's own thoughts and feelings
inadvertently (*adv.*) ˌin-əd-'vərt-ᵊnt-lē	without turning one's mind to the matter at hand; carelessly; unintentionally
incontrovertible (*adj.*) in-ˌkän-trə-'vərt-ə-bəl	not able to be ''turned opposite'' or disputed; not open to question (*ant.* **controvertible; disputable**)
introvert (*n.*) 'in-trə-ˌvərt	one more interested in one's own thoughts and feelings than in matters outside oneself
introvert (*v.*)	turn inward
invert (*v.*) in-'vərt	turn upside down
obverse (*n.*) 'äb-ˌvərs	side turned toward the observer; therefore, the front of a coin, medal, etc. (*ant.* **reverse**)

perverse (*adj.*) pər-'vərs	turned away from what is right or good; corrupt; wrongheaded
pervert (*v.*) pər-'vərt	turn away from right or truth; give a wrong meaning to
revert (*v.*) ri-'vərt	return; go back, as: ''The property will *revert* to the owner when the lease is up.''
versatile (*adj.*) 'vər-sət-ᵊl	able to turn with ease from one thing to another
verse (*n.*) 'vərs	line of poetry (literally, ''a turning around.'' After a fixed number of syllables, the poet has to ''turn around'' to begin a new line.)
vertigo (*n.*) 'vərt-i-ˌgō	condition in which one feels that one's surroundings are turning about; dizziness

EXERCISE 5.32

In each blank, insert the most appropriate word from group 27, *vert* (*vers*).

1. Between Thanksgiving and Christmas most department-store employees work overtime; then

    they _____ to their normal working hours.

2. The words ''In God We Trust'' appear above Lincoln's image on the _____
    of a cent.

3. No sooner did we settle one quarrel than we became involved in another _____.

4. The first _____ of Katherine Lee Bates' ''America, the Beautiful'' begins ''O
    beautiful for spacious skies.''

5. A(n) _____ musician can play several instruments.

6. The proof of his guilt was so _____ that the defendant confessed
    to the crime.

---

28. MIS (MISS, MIT, MITT): ''send''

---

commitment (*n.*) kə-'mit-mənt	1. consignment (''sending'') to prison or a mental institution 2. pledge
demise (*n.*) di-'mīz	death (literally, ''sending or putting down'')
emissary (*n.*) 'em-ə-ˌser-ē	person sent out on a mission
emit (*v.*) ē-'mit	send out; give off

intermittent (*adj.*) ˌint-ər-'mit-ᵊnt	coming and going at intervals, as an *intermittent* fever (literally, ''sending between'')
missile (*n.*) 'mis-əl	weapon (spear, bullet, rocket, etc.) capable of being propelled (''sent'') to hit a distant object
missive (*n.*) 'mis-iv	written message sent; a letter
remiss (*adj.*) ri-'mis	negligent (literally, ''sent back''); careless; lax (*ant.* **scrupulous**)
remission (*n.*) ri-'mish-ən	period of lessening or disappearance of the symptoms of a disease
remit (*v.*) ri-'mit	1. send money due 2. forgive, as to have one's sins *remitted*

EXERCISE 5.33

In each blank, insert the most appropriate word from group 28, *mis* (*miss, mit, mitt*).

1. This morning's rain was _____, starting and stopping several times.

2. It was my fault. I was _____ in not writing sooner.

3. A distinguished veteran diplomat has been chosen as the President's _____ to the international conference.

4. Unless you _____ the mortgage payment by the tenth of the month, you must pay a late fee.

5. My large searchlight can _____ a powerful beam.

6. We gave you our word; we will not go back on our _____.

7. Three months ago, the patient's recovery seemed unlikely, but then, miraculously, there was a(n) _____.

29. LOCUT (LOQU): ''speak,'' ''talk''

circumlocution (*n.*) ˌsər-kəm-lō-'kyü-shən	roundabout way of speaking
colloquy (*n.*) 'käl-ə-kwē	a talking together; conference; conversation
elocution (*n.*) 'el-ə-'kyü-shən	art of speaking out or reading effectively in public

eloquent (*adj.*) 'el-ə-kwənt	speaking with force and fluency; movingly expressive
grandiloquent (*adj.*) gran-'dil-ə-kwənt	using lofty or pompous words; bombastic
interlocutor (*n.*) ˌint-ə(r)-'läk-yət-ə(r)	1. questioner 2. one who participates in a conversation
loquacious (*adj.*) lō-'kwā-shəs	talkative; garrulous
obloquy (*n.*) 'äb-lə-kwē	1. a speaking against; censure 2. public reproach (*ant.* **praise**)

EXERCISE 5.34

In each blank, insert the most appropriate word from group 29, *locut* (*loqu*).

1. "Your services will be terminated if you persist in disregarding our requirement of punctuality"

   is a(n) _____ . It would be more direct to say, "You will be dismissed if you come late again."

2. _____ students who carry on noisy conversations in the library prevent others from concentrating.

3. A course in _____ can help one to become an effective public speaker.

4. The referee held a short _____ with the judges before announcing the winner.

5. Witnesses appearing before the investigating committee found that its chief counsel was the principal

   _____ ; the committee members asked very few questions.

---

30. FER(ous): "bearing," "producing," "yielding"

---

auriferous (*adj.*) ȯ-'rif-ə-rəs	bearing or yielding gold
coniferous (*adj.*) kō-'nif-ə-rəs	bearing cones, as the pine tree
odoriferous (*adj.*) ˌōd-ə-'rif-ə-rəs	yielding an odor, usually fragrant
pestiferous (*adj.*) pe-'stif-ə-rəs	1. infected with or bearing disease; pestilential 2. evil
proliferous (*adj.*) prə-'lif-ə-rəs	producing new growth rapidly and extensively

somniferous (*adj.*)   bearing or inducing sleep
säm-'nif-ə-rəs

vociferous (*adj.*)   producing a loud outcry; clamorous; noisy
vō-'sif-ə-rəs

EXERCISE 5.35

In each blank, insert the most appropriate word from group 30, *fer(ous)*.

1. The infant emitted so _____ a protest when placed in the crib that his mother took him up at once.

2. A bunch of _____ lilacs in a vase on the table gave the room an inviting fragrance.

3. Some people who have difficulty falling asleep have found that a glass of warm milk taken before retiring has a(n) _____ effect.

4. The settlers were heartbroken to see their fields of corn and wheat devastated by swarms of _____ locusts.

5. The seed-bearing part of pines, cedars, firs, and other _____ trees is known as a cone.

6. _____ weeds are a serious problem for gardeners.

7. The lucky miner struck a(n) _____ vein.

Review Exercises

REVIEW 10: DEFINING LATIN ROOTS

In the space before each Latin root in column I, write the *letter* of its correct meaning from column II.

COLUMN I   COLUMN II

_____ **1.** MOR (MORT)   *a.* body

_____ **2.** TACT (TANG)   *b.* step; walk; go

_____ **3.** LOCUT (LOQU)   *c.* run

_____ **4.** GRAT   *d.* bearing; producing; yielding

_____ **5.** SECUT (SEQU)   *e.* speak; talk

_____ **6.** CORP   *f.* throw

_____ **7.** CUR (CURR, CURS)   *g.* touch

_____ **8.** PED   *h.* pleasant; thank; favor

_____ **9.** PREHEND (PREHENS)   *i.* lead; conduct; draw

_____ **10.** JECT   *j.* death

_____ **11.** VERT (VERS)   *k.* send

_____ **12.** FER(ous)   *l.* turn

_____ **13.** GRESS (GRAD)   *m.* seize; grasp

_____ **14.** MIS (MISS, MIT, MITT) *n.* foot

_____ **15.** DUC (DUCT)   *o.* follow

REVIEW 11: USING LATIN ROOTS

Enter the Latin roots needed to complete the partially spelled words below.

DEFINITION	WORD
1. moved forward to something better	P R O __ __ __ __ E D
2. person traveling on foot	__ __ __ E S T R I A N
3. combine so as to form one body	I N __ __ __ __ __ A T E
4. something that follows; continuation	__ __ __ __ E L
5. artificial channel for conducting water	A Q U E __ __ __ __
6. undertaker	__ __ __ __ I C I A N

7. gift of money in return for a favor   _ _ _ _ _ U I T Y

8. producing a loud outcry   V O C I _ _ _ _ _ _

9. turning away; repugnance   A _ _ _ _ _ I O N

10. pertaining to the sense of touch   _ _ _ _ _ I L E

11. a speaking against; censure   O B _ _ _ _ Y

12. running or flowing (handwriting)   _ _ _ _ I V E

13. by steps or degrees   _ _ _ _ U A L

14. a written message   _ _ _ _ I V E

15. talkative   _ _ _ _ A C I O U S

16. throw in between; interpose   I N T E R _ _ _ _

17. tending to lead to; contributive   C O N _ _ _ I V E

18. person sent on a mission   E _ _ _ _ A R Y

19. running together; occurring simultaneously   C O N _ _ _ _ E N T

20. turning easily from one thing to another   _ _ _ _ A T I L E

REVIEW 12: SENTENCE COMPLETION

Which of the two terms makes the sentence correct? Write the *letter* of your answer in the space provided.

1. The _____ speaker moved the audience deeply in her brief address.

   a. loquacious *b.* eloquent

2. Andrew is too much of an _____; he doesn't show enough interest in what is going on around him.

   a. extrovert *b.* introvert

3. The authorities know the identity of the _____ and expect to apprehend him soon.

   a. transgressor *b.* precursor

4. Larry's diverting account of his experiment _____ the class.

   a. confused *b.* amused

5. The entire foreign diplomatic _____ was present at the funeral rites for the distinguished leader.

   a. corpse *b.* corps

6. For all the kindness you have shown us, we are extremely _____.

   a. grateful *b.* gratuitous

7. Since Emily's motion was adopted by a 12-to-2 vote, it was clear that most of the members

   _____ .

   a. incurred   *b.* concurred

8. If you had used fewer technical terms, your explanation would have been more _____ .

   a. comprehensible   *b.* comprehensive

9. The employer explained that salary increases are not automatic but _____ on satisfactory service.

   a. contiguous   *b.* contingent

10. The following is an example of _____: "Swimmers come to the surface within seconds after a dive; when Dee didn't come up immediately, we knew she was in trouble."

    a. induction   *b.* deduction

REVIEW 13: OPPOSITES

Write the word that means the OPPOSITE of the defined word by adding, dropping, or changing a prefix or a suffix. (The first answer has been filled in as an example.)

	DEFINITION	WORD	OPPOSITE
1.	important	consequential	inconsequential
2.	unbelievable	incredible	
3.	having no tact	tactless	
4.	discourteous, rude	ungracious	
5.	disposed to move backward	regressive	
6.	thrown in	injected	
7.	yielding no odor	odorless	
8.	indefensible	untenable	
9.	having faith in oneself	confident	
10.	unrelated to the matter in hand	impertinent	
11.	front of a coin	obverse	
12.	capable of being corrupted	corruptible	
13.	a going ("running") out	excursion	
14.	touchable	tangible	
15.	reasoning from particular to general	induction	
16.	understandable	comprehensible	
17.	trust in the truth of	credit	
18.	faithfulness to a trust	fidelity	

19. unconquered   unvanquished   _____

20. person more interested in own thoughts

than in outside matters   introvert   _____

REVIEW 14: MEANINGS

In the space before each word or expression in column I, write the *letter* of its correct meaning from column II.

	COLUMN I		COLUMN II
_____	1. death rate	*a.*	invert
_____	2. turn upside down	*b.*	grandiloquent
_____	3. felicitate	*c.*	retrograde
_____	4. adapted for seizing	*d.*	congratulate
_____	5. give a wrong meaning to	*e.*	mortality
_____	6. bombastic	*f.*	pervert
_____	7. interpose	*g.*	ductile
_____	8. going backward	*h.*	corpuscle
_____	9. minute particle	*i.*	interject
_____	10. able to be hammered thin	*j.*	prehensile

REVIEW 15: CONCISE WRITING

Express the thought of each sentence below in no more than four words.

1. He never appreciates a favor and he never says "thank you."

_____

2. Is it possible for the process of growth to be speeded up?

_____

3. The talk that you gave kept wandering from one topic to another.

_____

4. It is important for us to have a sensitive mental perception of what is appropriate on a given occasion.

_____

5. There are few individuals who can speak with force and fluency.

_____

6. We drove by several people who were traveling on foot.

_____

7. No evidence exists to prove that a crime has been committed.

_____

8. The opinion that she has expressed is open to question.

_____

9. You are so absorbed with your own thoughts and feelings that you pay little attention to what is going on in the world around you.

_____

10. Some of the artificial channels that the Romans built for conducting water over a distance survive to this day.

_____

REVIEW 16: BRAINTEASERS

Fill in the missing letters.

1. The proprietor's purchase of a computer is __ __ __ **t i n g e** __ __ on her being able to get a loan from a bank.

2. The horse-drawn carriage was a(n) __ __ __ **c u r** __ __ __ of the automobile.

3. After his defeat by an unknown young newcomer, the ex-champion could not conceal his

__ __ __ __ __ __ __ **c a t** __ __ __ .

4. A United Nations __ **m i s s** __ __ __ is being sent to help mediate the dispute between the two nations.

5. As a result of the six __ __ __ __ __ __ **c u t** __ __ __ days of rain, we have had severe flooding.

6. My neighbor is a(n) __ __ __ **r a t e**. I washed his car and he didn't even thank me.

7. Because of the legislator's __ __ __ __ __ **h e n s** __ __ __ __ conduct, the voters overwhelmingly rejected his bid for a second term.

8. Benjamin Franklin—printer, author, scientist, inventor, philosopher, and diplomat—was one of

the most __ __ __ **s a t** __ __ __ people of his time.

9. Charges against the defendant were dropped when her defense attorney presented

__ __ __ __ __ __ **r o v e r** __ __ __ __ __ evidence of her innocence.

10. Some department stores have posted signs stating that all shoplifters who are apprehended will

be __ __ __ __ __ **c u t e** __ .

REVIEW 17: COMPOSITION

Answer in two or three sentences.

1. If you were Mayor, how might you expedite the settlement of a labor-management controversy in your town?

_____

_____

2. Would you be remiss if you made an important decision on the basis of conjecture? Explain.

_____

_____

3. Must the gradual loss of population to the suburbs be a mortal blow to a city? Why, or why not?

_____

_____

4. Explain how a gratuitous remark incurred someone's displeasure.

_____

_____

5. Would it be a sign of retrogression or of progress for a nation to abolish the death penalty? Explain.

_____

_____

REVIEW 18: ANALOGIES

Write the *letter* of the word that best completes the analogy.

1. *River* is to *bridge* as *valley* is to _____ .
   a. viaduct *b.* mountain *c.* pontoon *d.* projectile *e.* road

2. *Olfactory* is to *smell* as *tactile* is to _____ .
   a. see *b.* grasp *c.* touch *d.* hear *e.* taste

3. *Birth* is to *demise* as *preface* is to _____ .
   a. foreword *b.* conclusion *c.* footnote *d.* introduction *e.* outline

4. *Corpse* is to *life* as *ingrate* is to _____ .
   a. fear *b.* ingratitude *c.* unkindness *d.* dejection *e.* gratitude

5. *Plan* is to *execution* as *outline* is to _____ .
   a. summary *b.* organization *c.* killing *d.* composition *e.* topic

CHAPTER 6

Words From Classical Mythology and History

This chapter will teach you to use important words taken from classical (ancient Greek and Roman) mythology. The beautiful and profoundly significant myths created by the Greeks and adopted by the Romans have contributed words that an educated person is expected to know. All the words discussed below originate from myths, except the following which are based on historical fact: *Draconian, forum, laconic, Lucullan, Marathon, philippic, Pyrrhic, solon, Spartan,* and *thespian.*

Study Your New Words

WORD	MEANING	TYPICAL USE
Adonis (*n.*) ə-'dän-əs	very handsome young man (from *Adonis*, a handsome youth loved by Aphrodite, goddess of love)	Joanna's former boyfriend was not exactly handsome, but her new one is quite an *Adonis*.
aegis (*n.*) 'ē-jəs	shield or protection; auspices; sponsorship (from *aegis*, the protective shield of Zeus, king of the Greek gods)	An international force under the *aegis* of the United Nations has been dispatched to the troubled area.
amazon (*n.*) 'am-ə-ˌzän	tall, strong, masculine woman (from the *Amazons*, a mythological race of women warriors)	The laborious work that pioneer women had to do would have challenged an *amazon*.
ambrosial (*adj.*) am-'brō-zhəl	exceptionally pleasing to taste or smell; extremely delicious; excellent (from *ambrosia*, the literally ''not mortal'' food of the gods)	The *ambrosial* aroma of the roast whetted our appetites.

atlas (*n.*)
'at-ləs

book of maps (from *Atlas*, a giant who supported the heavens on his shoulders. The figure of Atlas supporting the world was prefaced to early map collections; hence the name *atlas*.)

For reliable information about present national boundaries, consult an up-to-date *atlas*.

auroral (*adj.*)
ə-'ror-əl

pertaining to or resembling the dawn; rosy (from *Aurora*, goddess of the dawn)

The darkness waned, and a faint *auroral* glow began to appear in the east.

bacchanalian (*adj.*)
ˌbak-ə-'nāl-yən
(or **bacchic**)

jovial or wild with drunkenness (from *Bacchus*, the god of wine)

At 2 A.M. the neighbors called the police to quell the *bacchanalian* revelry in the upstairs apartment.

Cassandra (*n.*)
kə-'san-drə

one who prophesies doom or disaster; pessimist (from *Cassandra*, who was given the power of prophecy by Apollo. When she spurned his love, he could not take back his gift, but he added the stipulation that no one would ever believe her.)
(*ant.* **Pollyanna**)

Many say we will lose, but the coach is urging us to pay no attention to those *Cassandras*.

chimerical (*adj.*)
kī-'mer-i-kəl
(or **chimeric**)

fantastic; unreal; impossible; absurd (from the *Chimera*, a fire-breathing monster with a lion's head, goat's body, and serpent's tail)

At first, Robert Fulton's plans for his steamboat were derided as *chimerical* nonsense.

Draconian (*adj.*)
drə-'kō-nē-ən
(or **draconian**)

cruel; harsh; severe; ironhanded (from *Draco*, an Athenian lawmaker who drew up a harsh code of laws)

The dictator took *Draconian* measures against those he suspected of plotting a rebellion.

echolalia (*n.*)
ˌek-ō-'lā-lē-ə

automatic and immediate repetition (echoing) of what others say (from *Echo*, a maiden who loved Narcissus. When he rejected her, she pined away until nothing was left of her but her voice.)

The *echolalia* of infants is part of the process by which they learn to speak.

Elysian (*adj.*)
i-'lizh-ən

delightful; blissful; heavenly (from *Elysium*, the mythological paradise where the brave and good dwell after death)

Students yearn for the *Elysian* leisure of the summer vacation.

eristic (*adj.*)
i-'ris-tik

prone to controversy; disputatious; argumentative (from *Eris*, the goddess of discord)

It is extremely difficult to reach an agreement with anyone who has an *eristic* temperament.

fauna (*n.*)
'fȯn-ə

animal life; animals of a particular region or period (from *Faunus*, Roman god of animals)

Our careless use of pesticides threatens to remove the bald eagle from our nation's *fauna*.

flora (*n.*)
'flȯr-ə

plant life; plants of a particular region or period (from *Flora*, Roman goddess of flowers)

Pollution is harming not only the residents of the area, but also its *fauna* and *flora*.

forum (*n.*)
'fôr-əm

any medium or place for open discussion and expression of ideas—a public meeting, a radio or TV discussion, editorial page, etc. (from *Forum*, the marketplace and place of assembly for the people in Ancient Rome)

A dictatorship permits no *forum* where ideas can be freely and openly discussed.

hector (*v.*)
'hek-tər

bully; intimidate with threats; bluster (from *Hector*, bravest of the Trojans)

The pickets did not allow themselves to be provoked, despite the unruly crowds that gathered to *hector* them.

herculean (*adj.*)
,hər-kyə-'lē-ən
(or **Herculean**)

very difficult; requiring the strength of *Hercules* (a hero of superhuman strength)

Among the *herculean* tasks confronting our nation is the rebuilding of roads, bridges, and tunnels.

hermetic (*adj.*)
hər-'met-ik

airtight (from *Hermes*, messenger of the gods and reputed inventor of a magic seal to keep a vessel airtight)

To get a vitamin pill from a new bottle, you must unscrew the cap and break the *hermetic* seal.

iridescent (*adj.*)
,ir-ə-'des-ᵊnt

having colors like the rainbow (from *Iris*, goddess of the rainbow)

Children enjoy blowing *iridescent* soap bubbles.

jovial (*adj.*)
'jo-vē-əl

jolly; merry; good-humored (from *Jove*, or Jupiter, king of the Roman gods. The planet Jupiter was believed to make persons born under its influence cheerful or *jovial*.)

Our *jovial* hostess entertained us with some amusing anecdotes about her family.

labyrinthine (*adj.*)
lab-ə-'rin-thən

full of confusing passageways; intricate; complicated, like the *Labyrinth* (a fabled maze in Crete)

Out-of-towners may easily lose their way in New York City's *labyrinthine* subway passages.

laconic (*adj.*)
lə-'kän-ik

using words sparingly; terse; concise (from *Lakonikos*, meaning "Spartan." The Spartans were known for their terseness.)

All I received in response to my request was the *laconic* reply "Wait."

lethargic (*adj.*)
li-'thär-jik

unnaturally drowsy; sluggish; dull (from *Lethe*, river in Hades whose water, when drunk, caused forgetfulness of the past)

For several hours after the operation, the patient was *lethargic* because of the anesthetic.

Lucullan (*adj.*)
lü-'kəl-ən

sumptuous; luxurious (from *Lucullus*, a Roman who gave lavish banquets)

Thanksgiving dinner is almost a *Lucullan* feast.

marathon (*n.*)
'mar-ə-,thän

1. long-distance footrace of 26 miles 385 yards (from *Marathon*, where the Greeks defeated the Persian invaders in 490 B.C. The fleet-footed Pheidippides raced to Athens with the joyous news, but fell dead after announcing the victory.)

Roadrunners from all over the world compete in the annual Boston and New York City *marathons*.

2. endurance contest, as a dance *marathon*

martial (*adj.*) 'mär-shəl	pertaining to war; warlike (from *Mars*, god of war)	The Helvetians were a *martial* people who tried to conquer southern Gaul.
mentor (*n.*) 'men-ˌtȯ(r)	1. wise and trusted adviser (from *Mentor*, to whom Odysseus entrusted the education of his son) 2. tutor; coach	The retiring supervisor was persuaded to stay on for a month as *mentor* to her successor. The basketball *mentor* says that our team is the best he has ever coached.
mercurial (*adj.*) mər-'kyu̇r-ē-əl	1. quick; vivacious; active; lively (*ant.* **saturnine**) (from *Mercury*, the Roman counterpart of *Hermes*. *Mercury* was the messenger of the gods, the god of commerce, eloquence, and magic, and also the patron of travelers, rogues, and thieves. His name designates a planet as well as a metal.) 2. inconstant; unstable; capricious; subject to rapid and unpredictable mood changes	The older partner is rather dull and morose, but the younger has a *mercurial* temperament that appeals to customers. Someone with a *mercurial* disposition may at any moment turn from contentment to dissatisfaction, or from friendliness to hostility.
myrmidon (*n.*) 'mər-mə-ˌdän	obedient and unquestioning follower (from the *Myrmidons*, a martial tribe who accompanied Achilles to the Trojan War)	The dictator was surrounded by *myrmidons* who could be trusted to execute all orders loyally and pitilessly.
narcissistic (*adj.*) ˌnär-sə-'sis-tik	in love with oneself; excessively fascinated and gratified by one's own physical and mental qualities; egocentric (from *Narcissus*, a handsome youth who didn't even look at any of the many maidens who loved him. However, when he saw his own image in a pool, he fell madly in love with it. His futile longing for himself caused him such suffering that he died soon thereafter.)	*Narcissistic* individuals tend to overevaluate their own merits and to see no desirable qualities in others.
nectar (*n.*) 'nek-tər	something exceptionally delicious to drink (from *nectar*, the literally "death-overcoming" drink that made the gods immortal)	The juice of that freshly squeezed grapefruit is like *nectar*.
nemesis (*n.*) 'nem-ə-səs	1. due punishment for evil deeds (from *Nemesis*, goddess of vengeance) 2. one who inflicts such punishment	A conviction for tax evasion has been the *nemesis* of many a criminal who had previously escaped justice. Napoleon crushed many opponents, but Wellington was his *nemesis*.

odyssey (*n.*)
'äd-ə-sē

any long series of wanderings or travels (from the *Odyssey*, the poem dealing with Odysseus' ten years of wandering on his way home from the Trojan War)

A travel agent will gladly plan a year's *odyssey* to places of interest around the world.

Olympian (*adj.*)
ə-'lim-pē-ən
(or **Olympic**)
ə-'lim-pik

1. Majestic; godlike; lofty (from *Mt. Olympus*, highest mountain in Greece. Its summit, obscured by clouds from human view, was the home of the gods.)
2. having to do with the *Olympic Games*, an international athletic competition held every four years

Chief executive officers are usually given offices and staffs that are commensurate with their *Olympian* responsibilities.

paean (*n.*)
'pē-ən

song or hymn of praise, joy, or triumph (A *paean* was a hymn in praise of Apollo, the god of deliverance.)

When the crisis was resolved, people danced in the streets and sang *paeans* of joy.

palladium (*n.*)
pə-'lād-ē-əm

safeguard or protection (from *Palladium*, the statue of Pallas Athena, which was thought to protect the city of Troy)

The little girl habitually fell asleep clutching a battered doll, her *palladium*.

panic (*n.*)
'pan-ik

unreasoning, sudden fright that grips a multitude (from *Pan*, a god believed to cause fear)

A *panic* ensued when someone in the crowded auditorium yelled "Fire!"

philippic (*n.*)
fə-'lip-ik

bitter denunciation; tirade (from the *Philippics*, orations by Demosthenes denouncing King Philip of Macedon)

In an hour-long *philippic*, the legislator denounced the lobbyists opposing her bill.

plutocratic (*adj.*)
ˌplüt-ə-'krat-ik

having great influence because of one's wealth (from *Plutus*, god of wealth)

A handful of *plutocratic* investors, each owning several million shares, determined the policies of the corporation.

procrustean (*adj.*)
prə-'krəs-tē-ən
(or **Procrustean**)

cruel or inflexible in enforcing conformity (from *Procrustes*, a robber who made his victims fit the length of his bed, either stretching them if they were too short, or cutting off their legs if they were too tall)

The magistrate dispensed a *procrustean* kind of justice, imposing a fine of $200 on everyone who had received a summons, regardless of the circumstances.

protean (*adj.*)
'prōt-ē-ən

exceedingly variable; readily assuming different forms or shapes (from *Proteus*, a sea god who could readily change his shape to elude capture)

The microscopic ameba, a *protean* organism, is continually changing its shape.

Pyrrhic (*adj.*)
'pir-ik

ruinous; gained at too great a cost (from *Pyrrhus*, who suffered enormous losses in a "victory" over the Romans)

We won, but it was a *Pyrrhic* victory, as our leading scorer was injured and put out of action for the balance of the season.

saturnine (*adj.*)
'sat-ər-ˌnīn

heavy; dull; gloomy; morose (*ant.* **mercurial**) (from *Saturn,* father of Jupiter. Though Saturn's reign was supposedly a golden age, he has become a symbol of heaviness and dullness because the alchemists and astrologers associated his name with the metal lead.)

The research assistant was a *saturnine* scholar who said very little and smiled rarely.

siren (*n.*)
'sī-rən

1. dangerous, attractive woman (from the *Sirens,* creatures half woman and half bird, whose sweet singing lured sailors to destruction on the rocks)
2. a woman who sings sweetly

3. apparatus for sounding loud warnings

The enemy employed a redhaired *siren* as a spy.

One of the entertainers was a nightclub *siren* with a melodious voice.
Emergency vehicles raced to the scene with *sirens* screaming.

solon (*n.*)
'sō-lən

legislator; wise lawgiver (from *Solon,* noted Athenian lawgiver)

Next week the *solons* will return to the capital for the opening of the legislative session.

Spartan (*adj.*)
'spärt-ᵊn

marked by self-discipline, bravery, ability to endure pain, and avoidance of comfort (from *Sparta,* a city-state in ancient Greece, whose people had the above characteristics)

The rooms had neither rugs nor sofas nor easy chairs; they were furnished with *Spartan* simplicity.

stentorian (*adj.*)
sten-'tȯr-ē-ən

very loud (from *Stentor,* a legendary herald whose voice was as loud as fifty voices)

Speak softly; you don't need a *stentorian* voice to be heard in this small room.

Stygian (*adj.*)
'stij-ē-ən

infernal; especially dark; gloomy (from *Styx,* a river of the lower world leading into Hades, or Hell)

A power failure at 11:30 P.M. plunged the city into *Stygian* blackness.

tantalize (*v.*)
'tant-ᵊl-ˌīz

excite a hope but prevent its fulfillment; tease (from *Tantalus,* who was kept hungry and thirsty in the lower world with food and water very near but just beyond his reach)

We removed the strawberry shortcake from the table so as not to *tantalize* our weight-conscious guest.

terpsichorean (*adj.*)
ˌtərp-sik-ə-'rē-ən

pertaining to dancing (from *Terpsichore,* the muse of dancing)

The reviewers lauded the ballet troupe for its *terpsichorean* artistry.

thespian (*adj.*)
'thes-pē-ən
(or **Thespian**)

pertaining to the drama or acting (from *Thespis,* reputed father of Greek drama)

If you enjoy acting in plays, join a *thespian* club.

titanic (*adj.*)
tī-'tan-ik

of enormous strength, size, or power (from the *Titans,* lawless, powerful giants defeated by Zeus)

By a *titanic* effort, our football team halted an onrush at our one-yard line.

Apply What You Have Learned

EXERCISE 6.1: MEANINGS

In the blank space, enter the *letter* of the best definition of the italicized word.

_____ 1. *ambrosial* fare: *a.* expensive *b.* cut-rate *c.* railroad *d.* delicious

_____ 2. unemployed *thespians*: *a.* musicians *b.* actors *c.* dancers *d.* loafers

_____ 3. *martial* airs: *a.* matrimonial *b.* tuneful *c.* military *d.* soothing

_____ 4. impassioned *philippic*: *a.* plea *b.* message *c.* praise *d.* tirade

_____ 5. *plutocratic* associates: *a.* loyal and wealthy *b.* jovial *c.* carefree *d.* rich and influential

_____ 6. *Draconian* laws: *a.* democratic *b.* ironhanded *c.* unpopular *d.* unenforced

_____ 7. *hermetic* compartments: *a.* rigid *b.* tiny *c.* airtight *d.* labyrinthine

_____ 8. road *atlas*: *a.* traveler *b.* map collection *c.* network *d.* surface

_____ 9. endless *odyssey*: *a.* story *b.* wanderings *c.* sufferings *d.* errands

_____ 10. new *Adonis*: *a.* lover *b.* movie actor *c.* myrmidon *d.* handsome youth

EXERCISE 6.2: SENTENCE COMPLETION

In the blank space, enter the *letter* of the choice that best completes the sentence.

1. Photographs of _____ celebrities decorated the walls of the dance studio.
   a. operatic *b.* Olympic *c.* thespian *d.* eristic *e.* terpsichorean

2. The wrestler's _____ maneuvers made it difficult for an opponent to obtain a hold.
   a. hermetic *b.* protean *c.* titanic *d.* procrustean *e.* philippic

3. In a locker-room speech between halves, the _____ reaffirmed his confidence in his _____.
   a. conductor . . . myrmidons *b.* amazon . . . team *c.* myrmidon . . . adherents *d.* mentor . . . squad *e.* conductor . . . mentors

4. Many literatures describe a paradise where the _____ dwell in _____ repose.
   a. heroic . . . Stygian *b.* unvanquished . . . bacchanalian *c.* sirens . . . abject *d.* perfidious . . . ambrosial *e.* brave . . . Elysian

5. When people become _____, their ability to reason gives way to fear.
   a. lethargic *b.* saturnine *c.* panicky *d.* Draconian *e.* plutocratic

6. The audience laughed to see the burly actor _____ by his puny companion's hectoring.
   a. convinced *b.* betrayed *c.* tripped *d.* intimidated *e.* encouraged

7. The Pyrrhic victory was cause for widespread _____.
   a. dejection *b.* optimism *c.* paeans *d.* satisfaction *e.* promotions

8. Only a person with a _____ voice could have been heard above the din of the angry crowd.

   a. herculean *b.* stentorian *c.* jovial *d.* laconic *e.* titanic

9. Our _____ host always enjoys having friends to share his Lucullan suppers.

   a. cursive *b.* martial *c.* fractious *d.* convivial *e.* sanguine

10. Psychoanalysis can help patients recall long-forgotten experiences from the _____ recesses of their minds.

    a. labyrinthine *b.* chimerical *c.* iridescent *d.* auroral *e.* mercurial

EXERCISE 6.3: CONCISE WRITING

Express the thought of each sentence below in no more than four words.

1. Those who make predictions of doom and disaster are not popular.

   _____

2. Some people are inclined to be too much in love with themselves.

   _____

3. You aroused their hopes, and at the same time you made it impossible for them to realize those hopes.

   _____

4. This is not an ordinary beverage; it is exceptionally delicious.

   _____

5. Grownups should avoid the practice of automatically and instantly repeating what others say.

   _____

6. We attended a meeting at which there was open discussion and audience participation.

   _____

7. Make an effort to be sparing in your use of words.

   _____

8. Her cousin is the sort of person who likes to engage in disputes.

   _____

9. Tell us about the long series of wanderings that you were involved in.

   _____

10. Rumors can be the cause of sudden and unreasoning fright.

    _____

EXERCISE 6.4: BRAINTEASERS

Fill in the missing letters.

1. Feeling **l e t** __ __ __ __ __ __, the driver stopped for a short nap.

2. To lift the heavy weight that was pressing down upon the victim would have required __ __ __ __ __ **l e a n** strength.

3. Sometimes, after a summer shower, a(n) __ **r i d** __ __ __ __ __ __ arc appears in the sky.

4. __ __ __ **m e t** __ __ seals help to make some products tamper-proof.

5. Larry Smith's home run in the bottom of the nineteenth inning won the game for the home team and ended the six-hour __ __ **r a t** __ __ __.

6. Our __ **t e n t** __ __ __ __ __ instructor needs no microphone to be heard in our gym.

7. No one expects a(n) __ __ **c u l l** __ __ dinner to be served in a fast food restaurant.

8. Long before the first __ __ __ **o r a l** light, the farmer is up and ready for the day's chores.

9. Law-abiding people breathe a sigh of relief when notorious evildoers who have never been convicted finally meet their __ __ **m e** __ __ __.

10. As we kept going through the __ __ __ __ __ __ __ **t h i n e** corridors, we thought we would never be able to find our way back.

EXERCISE 6.5: COMPOSITION

Answer in two or three sentences.

1. Would you be in a jovial mood after achieving a victory? Why, or why not?

_____

_____

_____

2. Why is it normal for someone exploring a labyrinthine cave to be gripped with panic?

_____

_____

_____

3. Of all the foods you have tasted, name one that was ambrosial, and another that was like nectar. Give reasons for your choices.

_____

_____

_____

4. Are Draconian penalties an effective palladium against crime? Why, or why not?

_____

_____

_____

5. Would you withdraw from an election campaign if your rival's myrmidons hectored you at every place you tried to speak? Explain.

_____

_____

_____

EXERCISE 6.6: ANALOGIES

Write the _letter_ of the word-pair that best expresses a relationship similar to that existing between the capitalized word-pair.

_____ **1.** SOLON : LAWS

    _a._ atlas : maps   _d._ artisan : trade
    _b._ ruler : subjects   _e._ composer : operas
    _c._ philosopher : credentials

_____ **2.** SIREN : BEAUTY

    _a._ victim : trap   _d._ alarm : confidence
    _b._ temptress : prey   _e._ worm : fish
    _c._ hunter : bait

_____ **3.** CASSANDRA : POLLYANNA

    _a._ amazon : myrmidon   _d._ pessimist : optimist
    _b._ Spartan : laconic   _e._ titanic : herculean
    _c._ Olympian : majestic

_____ **4.** NEMESIS : EVILDOER

    _a._ avenger : victim   _d._ justice : misdeed
    _b._ retribution : culprit   _e._ penalty : evil
    _c._ punishment : benefactor

_____ **5.** AMAZON : STRENGTH

    _a._ comedienne : humor   _d._ warrior : civilian
    _b._ river : jungle   _e._ servant : indifference
    _c._ nurse : invalid

_____ **6.** PALLADIUM : DANGER

    _a._ rumor : panic   _d._ experience : skill
    _b._ arena : excitement   _e._ vaccination : smallpox
    _c._ investigation : truth

_____ 7. MERCURIAL : CAPRICIOUS

    a. procrustean : rigid   *d.* saturnine : hilarious
    b. protean : uniform   *e.* narcissistic : unselfish
    c. ethereal : earthly

_____ 8. PAEAN : ECSTASY

    a. anthem : nation   *d.* sadness : joy
    b. suffering : rejoicing   *e.* hymn : congregation
    c. lament : sorrow

_____ 9. THESPIAN : TERPSICHOREAN

    a. painter : dancer   *d.* actress : ballerina
    b. orator : musician   *e.* composer : singer
    c. comedian : sculptor

_____ 10. AURORAL : DAWN

    a. fragile : care   *d.* annual : season
    b. autumnal : fall   *e.* juvenile : delinquency
    c. visual : ear

CHAPTER 7

Anglo-Saxon Vocabulary

About 25 percent of our modern English vocabulary comes from the language of the Angles and Saxons, Germanic tribes who invaded Britain beginning about the year 450. The Anglo-Saxons ruled until 1066, when Harold, their last king, was defeated at the Battle of Hastings by an army from France led by William, Duke of Normandy. For the next two centuries, French was England's official language, but the common people continued to use Anglo-Saxon. The basic words of English today are of Anglo-Saxon origin. They include the articles (*a, an, the*), the words for numbers, the verb *to be*, prepositions (*at, by, from, in, out, with,* etc.), conjunctions (*and, but, as, when,* etc.), many commonly used verbs (*to go, to fight, to sleep, to eat,* etc.), many commonly used nouns (*father, mother, land, house, water,* etc.), and most pronouns.

After 1066, a wealth of Latin-derived parallels for Anglo-Saxon words came into our language through French. These borrowings, and others directly from Latin, endowed English with a rich supply of synonyms and near-synonyms. For example, for the Anglo-Saxon verb *lighten*, we have (1) the synonym *relieve*, borrowed from the language of the French-speaking invaders who had earlier gotten it from Latin, and (2) the synonym *alleviate*, borrowed directly from Latin.

This brief chapter deals with (1) Anglo-Saxon elements selected to help you increase your store of words, and (2) Latin-derived synonyms and near-synonyms for Anglo-Saxon words.

Anglo-Saxon Prefixes

1. A-: "on," "in," "in a state of"

WORD	MEANING
aboard (*adv.*) ə-'bòrd	on a ship, train, bus, etc. (Come *aboard*!)
aboard (*prep.*) ə-'bòrd	on (A stowaway was *aboard* the freighter.)
Also: **ashore, afoot**	

afoul (*adj.*) ə-ʼfaůl	in a state of entanglement (fishermen with their lines *afoul*)
afoul of (*prep.*) ə-ʼfaů-ləv	in or into collision or entanglement with (They ran *afoul* of the law.)
aloof (*adv.*) ə-ʼlüf	in the state of being at a distance (I stood *aloof*.)
aloof (*adj.*) ə-ʼlüf	withdrawn (Join us. Don't be *aloof*.)
amiss (*adv.*) ə-ʼmis	in a missing-the-mark manner; wrong (Something went *amiss*.)
amiss (*adj.*) ə-ʼmis	wrong; imperfect; faulty (Is anything *amiss*?)
asunder (*adv.*) ə-ʼsən-dər	in an apart position; apart (Friends were torn *asunder*.)

Also: **abed, adrift, afield, afire, afloat, aloft,** etc.

---

2. WITH-: ''against,'' ''back''

---

withdraw (*v.*) with-ʼdrȯ	draw back; take back
withhold (*v.*) with-ʼhōld	hold back
withstand (*v.*) with-ʼstand	stand up against; resist
notwithstanding (*prep.*) ˌnät-with-ʼstan-diŋ	despite (*Notwithstanding* her inexperience, she was hired.)

---

3. BE- has these meanings:

---

a. ''all around,'' ''on all sides,'' ''thoroughly''

beset (*v.*) bi-ʼset	attack on all sides; surround

Also: **begrudge, belabor, bemuddle, besiege, besmirch,** etc.

b."affect with," "cover with"

begrime (*v.*) bi-'grīm	cover with grime; make dirty
benighted (*adj.*) bi-'nīt-ˌəd	overtaken by darkness of night; unenlightened; intellectually or morally ignorant

    Also: **becloud, bedevil, befog, belie, bewitch,** etc.

c. "cause to be"

belittle (*v.*) bi-'lit-ᵊl	cause to be or seem little or unimportant; disparage

    Also: **becalm, bedim, bewilder,** etc.

Anglo-Saxon Suffixes and Combining Forms

---

1. -WISE: "way," "manner"

---

contrariwise (*adv.*) 'kän-ˌtrer-ē-ˌwīz	on the contrary (*ant.* **likewise**)
nowise (*adv.*) 'nō-ˌwīz	in no way; not at all

    Also: **breadthwise, lengthwise, otherwise,** etc.

---

2. -DOM: "dignity," "office," "realm," "state of being," "those having the character of"

---

earldom (*n.*) 'ərl-dəm	realm or dignity of an earl
martyrdom (*n.*) 'märt-ərd-əm	state of being a martyr
officialdom (*n.*) ə-'fish-əl-dəm	those having the authority of officials; officials collectively

    Also: **dukedom, fiefdom, kingdom, serfdom, sheikdom, stardom,** etc.

3. -SOME has these meanings:

a. **"full of the thing or quality denoted in the first part of the -SOME word"**

cumbersome (*adj.*)
'kəm-bər-səm

full of encumbrances; burdensome

fulsome (*adj.*)
'fúl-səm

offensive because of excessive display or obvious insincerity (literally, "full of fullness")

lissom(e) (*adj.*)
'lis-əm

lithesome (literally, "full of a lithe or supple quality"); nimble

mettlesome (*adj.*)
'met-ᵊl-səm

full of mettle (courage); spirited

noisome (*adj.*)
'nȯi-səm

offensive to the sense of smell (literally, "full of an annoying quality"); unwholesome

winsome (*adj.*)
'win-səm

full of a winning quality (literally, "full of *wynn*," the Anglo-Saxon word for *joy*); cheerful; merry

Also: **awesome, bothersome, fearsome, frolicsome, gruesome, irksome, lonesome, quarrelsome, toothsome, troublesome,** etc.

b. **"group of"**

twosome (*n.*)
tü-səm

group of two

Also: **threesome, foursome,** etc.

4. -LING has these meanings:

a. **"one pertaining to or concerned with whatever is denoted in the first part of the -LING word"**

hireling (*n.*)
'hī-ə(r)-liŋ

one whose only interest in his or her work is the *hire* (pay)

starveling (*n.*)
'stärv-liŋ

one who is thin from lack of food

suckling (*n.*)
'sək-liŋ

child or animal that is nursed (sucks)

yearling (*n.*)
'yi-ə(r)-liŋ

one who is a year old

b. **"little"**

changeling (*n.*)
'chānj-liŋ

child secretly exchanged for another in infancy (literally, "a little change")

duckling (*n.*)   little duck
'dək-liŋ

foundling (*n.*)   infant found after being deserted by its unknown parents
'faún-dliŋ

gosling (*n.*)   young goose
'gäz-liŋ

sibling (*n.*)   brother or sister (literally, "a little *sib*," a synonym for *blood relative*)
'sib-liŋ

stripling (*n.*)   lad (literally, "a little strip" from the main stem)
'strip-liŋ

    Also: **fledgling, princeling, sapling,** etc.

Miscellaneous Anglo-Saxon Words

anent (*prep.*)   about; concerning; in respect to
ə-'nent

anon (*adv.*)   soon; presently
ə-'nän

behest (*n.*)   command; order
bi-'hest

beholden (*adj.*)   bound in gratitude; indebted
bi-'hōl-dən

behoove (*v.*)   be necessary for; be proper for
bi-'hüv

betimes (*adv.*)   early
bi-'tīmz

heath (*n.*)   tract of wasteland
'hēth

wane (*v.*)   decrease gradually in size
'wān

warlock (*n.*)   sorcerer or wizard
'wòr-ˌläk

warp (*n.*)   the threads running lengthwise in the loom, crossed by the woof
'wòrp

wax (*v.*)   grow in size, as in "to wax and wane"
'waks

withal (*adv.*)   with it all; as well
wi<u>th</u>-'òl

woof (*n.*)   the threads running from side to side in a woven fabric
'wŭf

yclept (*adj.*)   named; called
or **ycleped**
i-'klept

EXERCISE 7.1: WORD COMPLETION

In each sentence, fill in the missing letters of the incomplete word. Each dash stands for one missing letter.

1. Do not **b** __ __ __ __ __ __ (*obscure, as with clouds*) the issue.

2. A **n** __ __ __ __ __ __ __ (*offensive to the sense of smell*) odor filled the chemistry laboratory.

3. Jim is friendly but his uncle holds himself **a** __ __ __ __ __ (*at a distance*).

4. Try as I might, I could not **b** __ __ __ __ __ (*cause to be quiet*) the anxious mother.

5. In the fog, we ran **a** __ __ __ __ of (*came in collision with*) a stalled car.

6. A public official should be cautious about accepting favors so as not to be

   b __ __ __ __ __ __ __ (*bound in gratitude*) to anybody.

7. Don't you agree they make an attractive **t** __ __ __ __ __ __ (*group of two*)?

8. Present your passbook to the teller whenever you deposit or **w** __ __ __ __ __ __ __ (*take back*) funds.

9. The monarch seemed not at all displeased by the obviously **f** __ __ __ __ __ __ (*offensively insincere*) compliments of his fawning subjects.

10. From her first performance, it was obvious she was destined for **s** __ __ __ __ __ __ (*the state of being a star*).

11. She is an only child; she has no **s** __ __ __ __ __ __ (*brother or sister*).

EXERCISE 7.2: ANGLO-SAXON SYNONYMS

In the space provided, write an Anglo-Saxon synonym for the word or expression in italics. The letters of each synonym appear in scrambled form in the parentheses. (The first answer has been filled in as an example.)

1. It *is necessary for* (VESHOOBE) students to be attentive.   behooves

2. She rose before dawn and retired *early* (MESBETI).   _____

3. Nothing was said *concerning* (TENNA) the proposal to grant a pardon.   _____

4. The witches in Shakespeare's play MACBETH usually met on the *wasteland* (TEHAH).   _____

5. We are *indebted* (HODNEBLE) to no one.   _____

6. The moon *grows* (XESWA) and wanes.   _____

7. With a small stone, the *lad* (GRINPLITS) David slew the giant Goliath.   _____

8. Richard I, *named* (PLETCY) the Lion-Hearted, was a twelfth-century king of England.   _____

9. I'll be there *soon* (NANO).   _____

10. The guard around the palace was doubled at the monarch's *command* (SETHEB).   _____

11. Let us help those who are *in a state of ignorance* (THINGBEED).   _____

EXERCISE 7.3: COMPOSITION

Answer in two or three sentences.

1. Why would it belittle someone to be called a hireling?

_____

_____

2. Is it likely that a person can achieve stardom without being beholden to anyone? Explain.

_____

_____

3. Suggest a possible solution for a particularly noisome problem that besets us today.

_____

_____

4. Would you be able to withstand the flatteries of fulsome admirers? Why, or why not?

_____

_____

5. Briefly describe a situation that resulted in tearing siblings asunder.

_____

_____

Latin-Derived Synonyms and Near-Synonyms for Anglo-Saxon Words

Because English has incorporated so many Latin words into its vocabulary, it often has two or more words for an idea: one from Anglo-Saxon (for example, *brotherly*) and another from Latin (for example, *fraternal*). The two words, however, are seldom exactly synonymous.

To illustrate, both *brotherly* and *fraternal* have the general meaning "pertaining to brothers." Yet, *brotherly* conveys a greater warmth of feeling than *fraternal*, which is less intimate and more formal. Thus, we speak of "brotherly love," but "fraternal organizations." This abundance of synonyms enables us to express varying shades of meaning.

In the pages that follow, Anglo-Saxon-derived adjectives, verbs, and nouns will be presented side by side with similar but not exactly synonymous Latin-derived adjectives, verbs, and nouns.

---

1. Adjectives

FROM ANGLO-SAXON

FROM LATIN

fatherly
pertaining to a father (warmer than *paternal*)

paternal pə-'tərn-ᵊl
1. fatherly
2. inherited from or related to the father's side

motherly
pertaining to a mother (warmer than *maternal*)

maternal mə-'tərn-ᵊl
1. motherly
2. inherited from or related to the mother's side

brotherly
pertaining to a brother (more affectionate than *fraternal*)

fraternal frə-'tərn-ᵊl
1. brotherly
2. having to do with a *fraternal* society (a group organized to pursue a common goal in brotherly union)

daughterly
pertaining to a daughter (less formal than *filial*)

filial 'fil-ē-əl
of or befitting a daughter or son, as *filial* respect

childlike
of or like a child in a good sense, as *childlike* innocence

infantile 'in-fən-ˌtīl
of or like a very young child; babyish

childish
of or like child in a bad sense, as *childish* mentality

puerile 'pyü(-ə)r-əl
foolish for a grown-up to say or do, as a *puerile* remark

manly
having the qualities usually considered
desirable in a man, as *manly* independence

womanly
having the qualities usually considered
desirable in an adult woman, as *womanly*
intuition

devilish
like a devil; mischievous

bearish
1. like a bear; rough
2. tending to depress stock prices
3. expecting a fall in stock prices

bullish
1. like a bull; obstinate
2. tending to cause rises in stock prices
3. expecting a rise in stock prices

catlike
like a cat; stealthy

cowlike
resembling a cow
oxlike
resembling an ox

doggish
doglike

donkeyish
like a donkey

fishy
like a fish in smell or taste

foxy
foxlike; wily; sly

goatish
goatlike; coarse; lustful

horsy
having to do with horses or horse racing as
horsy talk

masculine 'mas-kyə-lən
1. denoting the opposite gender of feminine
2. having qualities appropriate to a man

virile 'vir-əl
having the physical capabilities of a male
(stronger word than *masculine*)

feminine
1. denoting the opposite gender of masculine
2. having the features, qualities, and
characteristics belonging to women

diabolic(al) ˌdī-ə-'bäl-ik(-i-kəl)
very cruel; wicked; fiendish (stronger word
than *devilish*)

ursine 'ər-ˌsīn
of or like a bear

taurine 'tȯr-ˌin
1. of or like a bull
2. relating to Taurus (a sign of the zodiac)

feline 'fē-ˌlīn
of or pertaining to the cat family (cat, lion,
tiger, leopard, etc.); sly; stealthy

bovine 'bō-ˌvīn
1. of or like the cow or ox
2. sluggish and patient, as a *bovine* disposition

canine 'kā-ˌnīn
1. of or pertaining to the dog family (dog,
wolf, jackal, etc.)
2. designating one of the four pointed teeth
next to the incisors

asinine 'as-ᵊn-ˌin
like an ass or donkey (thought to be the most
stupid beast of burden); stupid; silly

piscine 'pi-ˌsēn
of or like a fish

vulpine 'vəl-ˌpīn
of or like a fox; crafty; cunning

hircine 'hər-ˌsīn
goatlike, especially in smell

equine 'ē-ˌkwīn
of or like a horse

piggish
hoggish, swinish

porcine 'pȯr-ˌsīn
of or like a pig

sheepish
1. like a sheep in timidity or stupidity
2. awkwardly bashful or embarrassed

ovine 'ō-ˌvīn
of or like a sheep

wolfish
characteristic of a wolf; ferocious

lupine 'lü-ˌpīn
of or like a wolf; ravenous

bloody
smeared with blood; involving bloodshed

sanguine 'saŋ-gwən
1. having a ruddy color, as a *sanguine* complexion
2. confident, as *sanguine* of success

sanguinary 'saŋ-gwə-ˌner-ē
bloody; as a *sanguinary* battle

EXERCISE 7.4: ANALOGIES

Write the *letter* of the word or words that best completes the analogy.

1. *Canine* is to *dog* as *feline* is to _____ .

   a. ox *b.* wolf *c.* bull *d.* tiger *e.* donkey

2. *Fraternal* is to *brother* as *filial* is to _____ .

   a. son *b.* son-in-law *c.* daughter *d.* son or daughter
   e. daughter-in-law

3. *Neigh* is to *equine* as *bleat* is to _____ .

   a. horsy *b.* bashful *c.* sanguinary *d.* zodiacal *e.* ovine

4. *Mature* is to *puerile* as *intelligent* is to _____ .

   a. paternal *b.* asinine *c.* cunning *d.* porcine *e.* infantile

5. *Courageous* is to *mettle* as *sanguine* is to _____ .

   a. success *b.* despair *c.* battle *d.* complexion *e.* hope

6. *Bullish* is to *bearish* as *up* is to _____ .

   a. above *b.* under *c.* down *d.* over *e.* beyond

7. *Devilish* is to *diabolical* as *interested* is to _____ .

   a. spoiled *b.* enthusiastic *c.* ruddy *d.* cherubic *e.* clever

8. *Cow* is to *bull* as *feminine* is to _____ .

   a. masculine *b.* ferocity *c.* bovine *d.* manly *e.* virile

9. *Bear* is to *ursine* as *fox* is to _____ .

   a. vulpine *b.* taurine *c.* lupine *d.* wily *e.* stealthy

10. *Hircine* is to *goat* as *piscine* is to _____ .

    a. leopard *b.* speed *c.* lion *d.* fish *e.* swine

EXERCISE 7.5: SENTENCE COMPLETION

Fill each blank with the most appropriate word from the vocabulary list at the end of the exercise.

1. Joe's only response when confronted with his blunder was a _____ (*awkwardly bashful*) grin.

2. The child followed her older sister with a kind of _____ (*pertaining to the dog family*) devotion.

3. My cousin is selling her shares; she is no longer _____ (*expecting a rise in stock prices*).

4. The blackmailer had devised a _____ (*fiendish*) scheme for extorting money from his victim.

5. Some parents do not know how to cope with _____ (*of a son or daughter*) disobedience.

6. Rarely have we witnessed such _____ (*foolish*) behavior from a mature person.

7. The _____ (*used to denote a female*) form of "confidant" is "confidante."

8. My _____ (*on my mother's side*) grandfather was a Senator.

9. At the close of THE CALL OF THE WILD, the dog Buck gradually lapses into _____ (*wolfish*) characteristics.

10. The fratricidal Battle of Gettysburg was one of the world's most _____ (*bloody*) conflicts.

VOCABULARY LIST

sanguinary	canine	puerile
diabolical	bearish	feminine
lupine	filial	bullish
fraternal	vulpine	feline
sheepish	masculine	maternal

2. Verbs

FROM ANGLO-SAXON	FROM LATIN		FROM LATIN	
beget	procreate	'prō-krē-ˌāt	generate	'jen-ə-ˌrāt
begin	originate	ə-'rij-ə-ˌnāt	initiate	in-'ish-ē-ˌāt
behead	decapitate	di-'kap-ə-ˌtāt		
bless	consecrate	'kän-sə-ˌkrāt		
bow, stoop	condescend	ˌkän-di-'send	prostrate	'präs-ˌtrāt
break	disintegrate	dis-'int-ə-ˌgrāt	invalidate	in-'val-ə-ˌdāt
chew	masticate	'mas-tə-ˌkāt		
curse	execrate	'ek-sə-ˌkrāt		

drink	imbibe	im-'bīb		
eat	devour	di-'vaù(ə)r	consume	kən-'süm
flay, fleece, skin	excoriate	ek-'skòr-e-,āt		
free	emancipate	i-'man-sə-,pāt	liberate	'lib-ə-,rāt
frighten	intimidate	in-'tim-ə-,dāt		
lie	prevaricate	pri-'var-ə-,kāt		
lighten	relieve	ri-'lēv	alleviate	ə-'lē-vē-,āt
sail	navigate	'nav-ə-,gāt		
shorten	abridge	ə-'brij	abbreviate	ə-'brē-vē-,āt
show	demonstrate	'dem-ən-,strāt		
soothe	assuage	ə-'swāj	pacify	'pas-ə-,fī
spit	expectorate	ek-'spek-tə-,rāt		
steal	peculate	'pek-yə-,lāt		
strengthen	corroborate	kə-'räb-ə-,rāt	invigorate	in-'vig-ə-,rāt
sweat	perspire	pər-'spī-ə(r)		
take (for oneself)	appropriate	ə-'prō-prē-,āt		
think	cogitate	'käj-ə-,tāt	ratiocinate	,rat-ē-'ōs-ᵊn-,āt
twinkle, sparkle	scintillate	'sint-ᵊl-,āt		
understand	comprehend	,käm-pri-'hend		
withstand	resist	ri-'zist	oppose	ə-'pōz
worship	venerate	'ven-ə-,rāt	revere	ri-'vi-ə(r)
yield	capitulate	kə-'pich-ə-,lāt	succumb	sə-'kəm

EXERCISE 7.6: LATIN-DERIVED SYNONYMS

Replace the italicized Anglo-Saxon word with a Latin-derived synonym from the verb list just presented.

1. Tell the truth. Don't *lie*. _____

2. The young acrobat gave a *sparkling* performance. _____

3. Your opponents will *flay* you if you accuse them without proof. _____

4. We cannot *understand* how you can be intimidated by such a small dog. _____

5. Don't gulp down your food; take the time to *chew* it. _____

6. At the end of the play, Macbeth is *beheaded* by Macduff. _____

7. *Spitting* in a public place is an offense punishable by a fine. _____

8. I am not afraid of you; you can't *frighten* me. _____

9. Sir Toby Belch's excessive *drinking* got him into trouble with his niece. _____

10. We shall evict those who have illegally *taken* our homes and our land. _____

3. Nouns

FROM ANGLO-SAXON	FROM LATIN		FROM LATIN	
blessing	benediction	ˌben-ə-'dik-shən		
breach	infraction	in-'frak-shən	rupture	'rəp-chə(r)
burden	obligation	ˌäb-lə-'gā-shən		
curse	execration	ˌek-sə-'krā-shən	malediction	ˌmal-ə-'dik-shən
fire	conflagration	ˌkän-flə-'grā-shən		
food	nutriment	'n(y)ü-trə-mənt		
greed	avarice	'av-(ə-)rəs		
heaven	firmament	'fər-mə-mənt		
home	domicile	'däm-ə-ˌsīl	residence	'rez-əd-əns
mirth	hilarity	hil-'ar-ət-ē		
name	appellation	ˌap-ə-'lā-shən		
oath	affirmation	ˌaf-ə(r)-'mā-shən		
shame	ignominy	'ig-nə-ˌmin-ē		
shard	fragment	'frag-mənt		
smear	vilification	ˌvil-ə-fə-'kā-shən		
snake	reptile	'rep-tᵊl		
sorrow	contrition	kən-'trish-ən	remorse	ri-'mȯrs
speed	velocity	və-'läs-ət-ē	celerity	sə-'ler-ət-ē
strength	impregnability	im-ˌpreg-nə-'bil-ət-ē		
theft	larceny	'lars-ə-nē	peculation	ˌpek-yə-'lā-shən
thread	filament	'fil-ə-mənt		
threat	menace	'men-əs		
truth	verity (of things)	'ver-ət-ē		
truthfulness	veracity (of persons)	və-'ras-ət-ē		
wedding	nuptials	'nəp-shəlz		

EXERCISE 7.7: SENTENCE COMPLETION

Which of the two terms makes the sentence correct? Write the *letter* of your answer in the space provided.

1. It is a well-known _____ that the early bird catches the worm.

　　a. verity *b.* veracity

2. The guillotine was an instrument of _____ .

　　a. capitulation *b.* decapitation

3. It was difficult to carry the _____ crowbar.

　　a. lissome *b.* cumbersome

4. Cats, leopards, and tigers belong to the _____ family.

 a. feline *b.* canine

5. Dan's brawl with the umpire was a serious _____ of the rules of the game.

 a. fragment *b.* breach

6. Shares of stock are relatively cheaper in a _____ market.

 a. bullish *b.* bearish

7. If you have attended regularly and done the assignments, you should feel _____ of passing.

 a. sanguinary *b.* sanguine

8. Do not interfere in matters that are not your concern, or you will be called _____ .

 a. meddlesome *b.* mettlesome

9. The hungry hiker _____ his sandwiches quickly.

 a. consumed *b.* imbibed

10. The drowning woman was saved by a _____ of 16.

 a. yearling *b.* stripling

EXERCISE 7.8: BRAINTEASERS

Fill in the missing letters.

1. The Rock of Gibraltar is a symbol of __ __ __ __ __ __ __ **n a b** __ __ __ __ __ .

2. How can we forgive those who feel no __ __ __ **o r** __ __ for their misdeeds?

3. The hunger striker drank some water but refused __ __ **t r i m** __ __ __ .

4. We have no faith in the __ **e r a** __ __ __ __ of a prevaricator.

5. There was not a cloud in the **f i r** __ __ __ __ __ __ .

6. The thief looked so innocent that one would not have thought him capable of

 __ **a r c** __ __ __ .

7. Light travels at a much higher __ __ __ __ __ **c i t y** than sound.

8. There is no __ __ **n o** __ __ __ __ in defeat if one has done one's best.

9. ''The Father of his Country'' is an __ __ __ **e l l** __ __ __ __ __ conferred on George Washington by his fellow Americans.

10. The vase fell and shattered into a hundred __ **h a r d** __ .

EXERCISE 7.9: CONCISE WRITING

Express the thought of each sentence below in no more than four words.

1. She paid no attention to her brothers and her sisters.

_____

2. Many of those who invest are expecting a fall in the price of stocks.

_____

3. Your friend had an awkwardly bashful grin on his face.

_____

4. Their praise was offensive because it obviously was not sincere.

_____

5. Don't do or say things that are foolish for a grown-up to do or say.

_____

6. The ones who had been digging were covered with grime.

_____

7. The plan that you are presenting is full of encumbrances.

_____

8. Who are the individuals who took our bicycles for their own personal use?

_____

9. The remarks that they made caused us to seem little and unimportant.

_____

10. Those who have the authority of officials often move at a slow pace.

_____

EXERCISE 7.10: COMPOSITION

Answer in two or three sentences.

1. How serious a menace are drivers who imbibe? Why?

_____

_____

_____

2. Under what circumstances, if any, might it be forgiveable for an individual to appropriate a vacant domicile? Explain.

_____

_____

_____

3. Why do some candidates stoop to vilification in the closing hours of a political campaign?

_____

_____

_____

4. Should the shortage of jail space influence judges in sentencing those who have committed larceny but no other infractions? Explain.

_____

_____

_____

5. Under what circumstances would it be ignominy to capitulate? Explain.

_____

_____

_____

CHAPTER 8

French Words in English

English has never hesitated to adopt useful French words. Any French expression that describes an idea better than the corresponding English expression may sooner or later be incorporated into English. The process has been going on for centuries.

This chapter will teach you how to use some of the more important French words and expressions that are today part of an educated person's English vocabulary.

1. Terms Describing Persons

WORD	MEANING	TYPICAL USE
au courant (*adj.*) ˌō-ˌku-'rä^n	well-informed; up-to-date	By reading reviews, you can keep *au courant* with the latest in literature, films, television, and the theater.
blasé (*adj.*) blä-'zā	tired of pleasures; bored	After a while, Edna had had her fill of mountain scenery, and when the guide pointed out some additional peaks, she reacted in a *blasé* manner.
bourgeois (*adj.*) 'burzh-ˌwä	1. having to do with the middle class 2. concerned with petty, materialistic interests; lacking in culture or refinement	At first, the aristocrat firmly opposed his daughter's prospective marriage into a *bourgeois* family.
chic (*adj.*) 'shēk	stylish	You looked very *chic* in your new outfit.
clairvoyant (*adj.*) kler-'voi-ənt	clear-sighted; unusually perceptive	If General Braddock had listened to George Washington, his *clairvoyant* young subordinate, he would not have been caught in an ambush.
complaisant (*adj.*) kəm-'plāz-ᵊnt	willing to please; obliging; amiable	We were sorry to hear that the Reeds were moving because they had been very *complaisant* neighbors.

debonair (*adj.*) ˌdeb-ə-'ne(ə)r	courteous, gracious, and charming	The headwaiter was *debonair* with the guests but firm with the waiters.
gauche (*adj.*) 'gōsh	lacking social grace; crude; tactless; awkward	It would be *gauche* for a host or hostess to begin eating before their guests have been served.
maladroit (*adj.*) ˌmal-ə-'drȯit	unskillful; clumsy (*ant.* **adroit**)	Our new supervisor is clever in many matters in which his predecessor was *maladroit*.
naive (*adj.*) nä-'ēv	simple in nature; artless; ingenuous	You are *naive* if you believe implacable foes can be reconciled easily.
nonchalant (*adj.*) ˌnän-shə-'länt	without concern or enthusiasm; indifferent	I am amazed that you can be so *nonchalant* about the coming test when everyone else is so worried.

EXERCISE 8.1

In each blank, insert the most appropriate word or expression from group 1.

1. Some advertising is so exaggerated that only a(n) _____ person would believe it.

2. If every meal were a banquet, we should soon greet even the most delicious food with a(n) _____ expression.

3. Read a good daily newspaper to keep _____ with what is going on in the world.

4. The cuts on Ralph's face show that he is _____ in the use of his razor.

5. Unlike her discourteous predecessor, the new office manager is quite _____.

2. Terms for Persons

attaché (*n.*) ˌat-ə-'shā	member of the diplomatic staff of an ambassador or minister	We were unable to see the ambassador, but we spoke to one of the *attachés*.
bourgeoisie (*n.*) ˌbùrzh-wä-'zē	the middle class	A strong *bourgeoisie* contributes to a nation's prosperity.
chargé d'affaires (*n.*) 'shär-ˌzhäd-ə-'fe(ə)r	temporary substitute for an ambassador	Whom did the President designate as *chargé d'affaires* when he recalled the ambassador?
concierge (*n.*) kōⁿ'syerzh	doorkeeper; custodian; janitor	We had notified the *concierge* that we were expecting visitors, and he admitted them as soon as they arrived.

confrere (*n.*) 'kōⁿ-ˌfre(ə)r	colleague; co-worker; comrade	The attorney introduced us to his *confrere*, Mr. Quinones; they share the same office.
connoisseur (*n.*) ˌkän-ə-'sər	expert; critical judge	To verify the gem's value, we consulted a *connoisseur* of rare diamonds.
coterie (*n.*) 'kōt-ə-rē	set or circle of acquaintances; clique	Helen won't bowl with us; she has her own *coterie* of bowling friends.
debutante (*n.*) 'deb-yu̇-ˌtänt	young woman who has just had her *debut* (first introduction into society)	The *debutante's* photograph was at the head of the society page.
devotee (*n.*) ˌdev-ə-'tē	zealous follower; ardent adherent of something or someone; fan	Eva is a *devotee* of the guitar.
elite (*n.*) ā-'lēt	group of individuals thought to be superior; aristocracy; choice part	Fred likes to consider himself a member of the intellectual *elite*.
émigré, *masc.* (*n.*) 'em-i-ˌgrā (**émigrée,** *fem.*)	refugee; person who has fled (*emigrated*) from his or her native land because of political conditions	A committee was formed to find housing and employment for the anxious *émigrés*.
entourage (*n.*) ˌän-tu̇-'räzh	group of attendants, assistants, or associates accompanying a person	Several dignitaries were at the airport to welcome the Prime Minister and his *entourage*.
entrepreneur (*n.*) än-trə-prə-'nər	one who assumes the risks and management of a business	What *entrepreneur* will invest capital unless there is some prospect of a profit?
envoy (*n.*) 'en-ˌvȯi	diplomatic agent or messenger	The President's *envoy* to the conference has not yet been chosen.
fiancé, *masc.* (*n.*) ˌfē-än-'sä (**fiancée,** *fem.*)	person engaged to be married	Madeline introduced Mr. Cole as her *fiancé*.
gendarme (*n.*) 'zhän-ˌdärm	armed police officer, especially in France and other European countries	The chargé d'affaires requested that extra *gendarmes* be posted outside the embassy.
gourmand (*n.*) 'gu̇(ə)r-ˌmänd	person excessively fond of eating and drinking; glutton	The food was so good that I ate more than I should have. I behaved like a *gourmand*.
gourmet (*n.*) 'gu̇(ə)r-ˌmā	connoisseur in eating and drinking	Valerie can recommend a good restaurant; she is a *gourmet*.
ingenue (*n.*) 'an-jə-ˌnü	actress playing the role of a naive young woman; naive young woman	She was as simple and pretty as a film *ingenue*.
maître d'hôtel (*n.*) ˌmā-trə-dō-'tel or **maître d'** mā-trə-'dē	headwaiter	The *maître d'hôtel* supervises the waiters.

martinet (*n.*) ˌmärt-ᵊn-ˈet	person who enforces very strict discipline	Our dean is an understanding counselor, not a *martinet*.
nonpareil (*n.*) nän-pə-ˈrel	person of unequalled excellence; paragon	Few can compare with Stella as a speller. Her classmates regard her as the *nonpareil*.
nouveaux riches (*n. pl.*) ˌnü-vō-ˈrēsh	persons newly rich	An unexpected inheritance lifted him into the ranks of the *nouveaux riches*.
parvenu, *masc.* (*n.*) ˈpär-və-ˌn(y)ü (**parvenue,** *fem.*)	person suddenly risen to wealth or power who lacks the proper social qualifications; upstart	When the entrepreneur first moved into the exclusive area, his aristocratic neighbors regarded him as a *parvenu*.
protégé, *masc.* (*n.*) ˈprōt-ə-ˌzhā (**protégée,** *fem.*)	person under the care and protection of another	The veteran infielder passed on numerous fielding hints to his young *protégé*.
raconteur (*n.*) ˌrak-än-ˈtər	person who excels in telling stories, anecdotes, etc.	Mark Twain was an excellent *raconteur*.
valet (*n.*) ˈval-ət	manservant who attends to the personal needs of his employer, as by taking care of his employer's clothes	That morning, the old gentleman got dressed without the help of his *valet*.

EXERCISE 8.2

In each blank, insert the most appropriate word or expression from group 2.

1. After a particularly unpleasant quarrel with her _____, Rita considered breaking their engagement.

2. Between the nobles on one extreme and the peasants on the other, a middle class known as the _____ emerged.

3. The _____ brushed his employer's clothes.

4. Sherlock Holmes collaborated on the case with his _____, Dr. Watson.

5. Louise can relate an anecdote better than I; she is a fine _____.

6. Though the food was delicious, Ed refused a second helping; he is no _____.

7. If I were a(n) _____, I would be able to tell whether the cheese in this salad is imported or domestic.

8. When the young attorney was elected to a seat on the board of directors, some of the veteran members considered her a(n) _____.

9. A man who flees his native land to escape political oppression is a(n) _____.

10. Though the Allens are friendly with everyone, they have rarely visited with anyone outside their tightly knit _____.

3. Terms for Traits or Feelings of Persons

aplomb (*n.*)
ə-'pläm

absolute confidence in oneself; poise; self-possession

At the public hearing, the mayor met all challenges with his customary *aplomb.*

éclat (*n.*)
ā-'klä

brilliancy of achievement

The violinist performed with rare *éclat.*

élan (*n.*)
ā-'läⁿ

enthusiasm; eagerness for action

Because the cast had rehearsed with such *élan*, the director had few apprehensions about the opening-night performance.

ennui (*n.*)
än-'wē

feeling of weariness and discontent; boredom; tedium

You too might suffer from *ennui* if you had to spend months in a hospital bed.

esprit de corps (*n.*)
es-ˌprēd-ə-'kȯ(ə)r

feeling of union and common interest pervading a group; devotion to a group or to its ideals

The employees showed extraordinary *esprit de corps* when they volunteered to work Saturdays for the duration of the crisis.

finesse (*n.*)
fə-'nes

skill and adroitness in handling a difficult situation

The adroit prosecutor conducted the cross-examination with admirable *finesse.*

legerdemain (*n.*)
ˌlej-ərd-ə-'mān

sleight of hand; artful trick

By a feat of *legerdemain*, the magician produced a rabbit from her hat.

malaise (*n.*)
ma-'lāz

vague feeling of bodily discomfort or illness

After the late, heavy supper, he experienced a feeling of *malaise.*

noblesse oblige (*n.*)
nō-ˌbles-ə-'blēzh

principle that persons of high rank or birth are obliged to act nobly

In the olden days, kings and other nobles, observing the principle of *noblesse oblige*, fought at the head of their troops.

rapport (*n.*)
ra-'pȯ(ə)r

relationship characterized by harmony, conformity, or affinity

A common interest in gardening brought Molly and Loretta into closer *rapport.*

sangfroid (*n.*)
'säⁿ-frwä

coolness of mind or composure in difficult circumstances; equanimity

The quarterback's *sangfroid* during the last tense moments of the game enabled him to call the winning play.

savoir faire (*n.*)
ˌsav-ˌwär-'fe(ə)r

knowledge of just what to do; tact

You need both capital and *savoir faire* to be a successful entrepreneur.

EXERCISE 8.3

In each blank, insert the most appropriate word or expression from group 3.

1. Joel is tactful; he has plenty of _____.

2. Your physician may help you obtain some relief from the _____ that accompanies a severe cold.

3. Instead of reducing their subordinates' salaries, the executives cut their own compensation substantially, in accordance with the principle of _____.

4. To do card tricks, you have to be good at _____.

5. If you are bored, try reading detective stories; they help to overcome _____.

---

4. Terms Dealing With Conversation and Writing

adieu (*n.*) ə-'d(y)ü	good-bye; farewell	On commencement day we shall bid *adieu* to our alma mater.
au revoir (*n.*) ˌȯr-əv-'wär	good-bye till we meet again	Since I hope to see you again, I'll say *au revoir* rather than adieu.
billet-doux (*n.*) ˌbil-ā-'dü	love letter	A timely *billet-doux* patched up the lovers' quarrel.
bon mot (*n.*) bōⁿ-'mō	clever saying; witty remark	The jester Yorick often set the table a-roaring with a well-placed *bon mot*.
brochure (*n.*) brō-'shü(ə)r	pamphlet; treatise	This helpful *brochure* explains the procedures for obtaining a driver's license.
canard (*n.*) kə-'närd	false rumor; absurd story; hoax	It took a public appearance by the monarch to silence the *canard* that he had been assassinated.
cliché (*n.*) klē-'shā	trite or worn-out expression	Two *clichés* that we can easily do without are "first and foremost" and "last but not least."
entre nous (*adv.*) ˌän-trə-'nü	between us; confidentially	The Wildcats expect to win, but *entre nous* their chances are not too good.
mot juste (*n.*) mō-zhūēst	the exactly right word	To improve your writing, try to find the *mot juste* for each idea. Also, avoid clichés.
nom de plume (*n.*) ˌnäm-di-'plüm	pen name; pseudonym	Benjamin Franklin used the *nom de plume* "Silence Dogood" when he submitted essays to his brother's newspaper.

précis (*n.*) 'prā-sē	brief summary	Include only the essential points when you write a *précis*.
repartee (*n.*) ˌrep-ər-'tē	skill of replying quickly, cleverly, and humorously; witty reply	Dorothy Parker was known for her *repartee*.
résumé (*n.*) 'rez-ə-ˌmā	1. brief account of personal, educational, and professional qualifications and experience submitted by an applicant for a position	Martha sent copies of her *résumé* to fourteen prospective employers.
	2. summary	The teacher asked us to write a *résumé* of the last act.
riposte (*n.*) ri-'pōst	1. quick retort or repartee	When Dan was criticized for his error, his *riposte* was ''All of us make mistakes.''
	2. in fencing, a quick return thrust after a parry	The fencing instructor showed us how to defend ourselves against *ripostes*.
tête-à-tête (*n.*) ˌtāt-ə-'tāt	private conversation between two persons	Before answering, the witness had a *tête-à-tête* with his attorney.

EXERCISE 8.4

In each blank, insert the most appropriate word or expression from group 4.

1. There are valuable hints on safe driving in this sixteen-page _____ .

2. Avoid the expression ''old as the hills''; it is a(n) _____ .

3. Investigation proved the story was unfounded; it was just a(n) _____ .

4. The manager went out to the mound for a brief _____ with his faltering pitcher.

5. Everyone supposes this diamond is genuine, but _____ it's only an imitation.

5. Terms Dealing With Situations

bête noire (*n.*) ˌbāt-nə-'wär	object or person dreaded; bugbear	He enjoyed all his subjects except mathematics, his *bête noire*.
carte blanche (*n.*) 'kärt-'bläⁿsh	full discretionary power; freedom to use one's own judgment	Ms. Mauro gave her assistant *carte blanche* in managing the office while she was away.
cause célèbre (*n.*) ˌkōz-sā-'lebrᵊ	famous case in law that arouses considerable interest; an incident or situation attracting much attention	The trial of John Peter Zenger, a *cause célèbre* in the eighteenth century, helped to establish freedom of the press in America.

contretemps (*n.*) inopportune occurrence; embarrass- The proctor arrived late but that wasn't
'kän-trə-ˌtäⁿ ing situation or mishap the only *contretemps*; the examination
  sent to our room was not the one we
  were supposed to take.

cul-de-sac (*n.*) blind alley Painting proved to be a *cul-de-sac* for
ˌkəl-di-'sak   Philip Carey, as he had no real talent.

debacle (*n.*) collapse, overthrow; rout The *debacle* at Waterloo signaled the
di-'bäk-əl   end of Napoleon's power.

fait accompli (*n.*) thing already done A reconciliation between the bitter
ˌfā-ta-kōⁿ-'plē   foes, once thought an impossibility,
  may soon become a *fait accompli*.

faux pas (*n.*) misstep or blunder in conduct, man- One of the guests got no dessert be-
(')fō-'pä ners, speech, etc. cause Dolores had committed the *faux
  pas* of serving herself too generous a
  helping.

impasse (*n.*) deadlock; predicament affording no The judge was informed that the jury
'im-ˌpas escape; impassable road had reached an *impasse* and could deliberate no further.

liaison (*n.*) bond; linking up; coordination of ac- By joining the alumni association,
'lē-ə-ˌzän tivities graduates can maintain their *liaison*
  with the school.

mélange (*n.*) mixture; medley; potpourri The last amateur show was a *mélange*
mā-'läⁿzh   of dramatic skits, acrobatics, ballet,
  popular tunes, and classical music.

mirage (*n.*) optical illusion The sheet of water we thought we saw
mə-'räzh   on the road ahead turned out to be
  only a *mirage*.

EXERCISE 8.5

In each blank, insert the most appropriate word or expression from group 5.

1. Your flippant remark to Mrs. Lee about her ailing son was a(n) _____.

2. The inhabitants of the remote Eskimo village had practically no _____
   with the outside world.

3. Mr. Briggs never concerned himself with hiring or dismissing employees, having given his plant

   manager _____ in these matters.

4. Despite seventeen hours of continuous deliberations, the weary negotiators still faced a(n)

   _____ over wages.

5. Alice's position turned out to be a(n) _____, since it offered no opportunity
   for advancement.

Review Exercises

REVIEW 1: MEANINGS

In the space before each word or expression in column I, write the *letter* of its correct meaning from column II.

	COLUMN I	COLUMN II
_____	**1.** refugee	*a.* devotee
_____	**2.** till we meet again	*b.* debacle
_____	**3.** well-informed	*c.* bête noire
_____	**4.** partisan	*d.* concierge
_____	**5.** brief summary	*e.* sangfroid
_____	**6.** hoax	*f.* nom de plume
_____	**7.** bugbear	*g.* émigré
_____	**8.** rout	*h.* précis
_____	**9.** love letter	*i.* au revoir
_____	**10.** equanimity	*j.* canard
_____	**11.** doorkeeper	*k.* au courant
_____	**12.** pen name	*l.* billet-doux

REVIEW 2: SENTENCE COMPLETION

In the space provided, enter the *letter* of the choice that best completes the sentence.

1. In serving the soup, the _____ waitress spilled some of it on the guest of honor.
   a. chic *b.* maladroit *c.* debonair

2. Monotonous repetition usually brings on _____.
   a. ennui *b.* éclat *c.* savoir faire

3. I'll be glad to give my opinion, but you must realize I am no _____.
   a. raconteur *b.* martinet *c.* connoisseur

4. A bibliophile is usually a _____ of good literature.
   a. protégée *b.* devotee *c.* repartee

5. We made a right turn into the next street, but it proved to be a _____.
   a. mélange *b.* cul-de-sac *c.* canard

6. The President was represented at the state funeral in Paris by a special _____ .

   a. ingenue b. bourgeoisie c. envoy

7. We had a _____ over a couple of ice-cream sodas.

   a. bête noire b. tête-à-tête c. mirage

8. Do not commit the _____ of seating Frank next to Rhoda because they are not on speaking terms.

   a. faux pas b. impasse c. riposte

9. Today, my biology teacher began with a _____ of yesterday's lesson.

   a. rapport b. résumé c. brochure

10. Because of her excellent training, she has developed remarkable _____ at the piano.

    a. sangfroid b. élan c. finesse

11. The launch of the space shuttle was delayed by one _____ after another.

    a. mirage b. contretemps c. brochure

12. It would be _____ to come to an employment interview in a jogging suit.

    a. chic b. complaisant c. gauche

REVIEW 3: BRAINTEASERS

Fill in the missing letters.

1. The celebrity was surrounded by a **c o t** __ __ __ __ of admirers.

2. She was as nervous as a(n) __ __ __ __ **t a n** __ __ at a coming-out party.

3. You don't have to be so strict. Don't be a(n) __ __ __ __ __ **n e t**.

4. No further progress is possible. We are at a(n) __ __ **p a s s** __ .

5. They get along poorly. There is little **r a p** __ __ __ __ between them.

6. A(n) __ **l a i r** __ __ __ __ __ person could have seen that trouble was coming.

7. A conceited person who has no talent often thinks that he or she is the

   __ __ __ **p a r** __ __ __.

8. To be a food columnist, you must be a writer and a(n) __ __ __ __ **m e t**.

9. Most of our school's intellectual __ **l i t** __ is in the Honor Society.

10. She enjoys opera, and she is also a(n) __ __ __ **v o t e** __ of the ballet.

REVIEW 4: COMPOSITION

Answer in two or three sentences.

1. Can a naive entrepreneur succeed in business? Why, or why not?

_____

_____

_____

2. Describe a situation in which it might not be a faux pas to give someone else carte blanche to make decisions for you.

_____

_____

_____

3. Is it normal for employees who consider themselves in a cul-de-sac to show ennui? Explain.

_____

_____

_____

4. How would a club's esprit de corps be affected if its president were a martinet?

_____

_____

_____

5. Why must you have rapport with your audience to succeed as a raconteur?

_____

_____

_____

6. Terms Dealing With History and Government

coup d'etat (*n.*) ˌküd-ö-'tä or **coup** 'kü	sudden violent, or illegal overthrow of a government	Napoleon seized power by a *coup d'etat*.
demarche (*n.*) dā-'märsh	course of action, especially one involving a change of policy	Hitler's attack on Russia, shortly after his pact with Stalin, was a stunning *demarche*.
détente (*n.*) dā-'tänt	a relaxing, as of strained relations between nations	An effective world disarmament treaty should bring a *détente* in international tensions.
entente (*n.*) än-'tänt	understanding or agreement between governments	Canada and the United States have a long-standing *entente* on border problems.
laissez-faire (*n.*) ˌles-ˌā-'fe(ə)r	absence of government interference or regulation	Adam Smith believed a policy of *laissez-faire* toward business would benefit a nation.
lettre de cachet (*n.*) ˌle-trə-də-ˌka-'shā	sealed letter obtainable from the King of France (before the Revolution) ordering the imprisonment without trial of the person named in the letter	Dr. Manette was imprisoned through a *lettre de cachet*.
premier (*n.*) ˌprē-mē-ər	prime minister	A *premier* can be forced out of office at any time by a vote of no confidence.
rapprochement (*n.*) ˌrap-ˌrōsh-'män	establishment or state of cordial relations; coming together	The gradual *rapprochement* between these two nations, long traditional enemies, cheered all Europeans.
regime (*n.*) rā-'zhēm	system of government or rule	The coup d'etat brought to power a *regime* that restored civil liberties to the oppressed people.

EXERCISE 8.6

In each blank, insert the most appropriate word or expression from group 6.

1. Do you favor strict regulation of business or a policy of _____?

2. The tyrannical ruler was eventually overthrown by a(n) _____.

3. The newly elected officials will face many problems left by the outgoing _____.

4. Before 1789, a French nobleman could have an enemy imprisoned without trial by obtaining a(n)

   _____.

5. Hopes for world peace rose sharply with reports of a(n) _____ in the strained relations between the two major powers.

7. Terms Dealing With the Arts

avant-garde (*n.*)
͵äv-͵än-'gärd

experimentalists or innovators in any art

Walt Whitman was no conservative; his daring innovations in poetry place him in the *avant-garde* of nineteenth-century writers.

bas-relief (*n.*)
͵bä-ri-'lēf
͵

carving or sculpture in which the figures project only slightly from the background

The ancient Greek Parthenon is famed for its beautiful sculpture in *bas-relief*.

baton (*n.*)
ba-'tän

stick with which a conductor beats time for an orchestra or band

A downbeat is the downward stroke of the conductor's *baton*, denoting the principally accented note of a measure.

chef d'oeuvre (*n.*)
shā-'dəvrᵊ

masterpiece in art, literature, etc.

Many connoisseurs regard HAMLET as Shakespeare's *chef d'oeuvre*.

denouement (*n.*)
͵dā-nü-'mäⁿ
͵

solution ("untying") of the plot in a play, story, or complex situation; outcome; end

In the *denouement* of GREAT EXPECTATIONS, Pip's benefactor is identified as the escaped convict whom Pip had once befriended.

encore (*n.*)
'än-͵kȯ(ə)r

repetition of a performance (or the rendition of an additional selection) in response to the demand from an audience

In appreciation of the enthusiastic applause, the vocalist sang an *encore*.

genre (*n.*)
'zhän-rə

1. kind; sort; category

2. style of painting depicting scenes from everyday life

The literary *genre* to which Virginia Woolf contributed most is the novel. Painters of *genre* choose scenes from everyday life as their subject matter.

musicale (*n.*)
͵myü-zi-'kal
͵

social gathering, with music as the featured entertainment

Last night's *musicale* at the White House featured entertainment by a popular folk singer.

palette (*n.*)
'pal-ət

thin board (with a thumb hole at one end) on which an artist lays and mixes colors

After a few strokes on the canvas, an artist reapplies the brush to the *palette* for more paint.

repertoire (*n.*)
'rep-ə(r)-͵twär

1. stock of plays, operas, roles, compositions, etc., that a company or performer is prepared to perform
2. collection

The guitarist apologized for not playing the requested number, explaining that it was not in his *repertoire*.
Whenever I hear a good joke, I add it to my *repertoire*.

vignette (*n.*)
vin-'yet

short verbal description; small, graceful literary sketch

James Joyce's DUBLINERS offers some unforgettable *vignettes* of life in Dublin at the turn of the century.

EXERCISE 8.7

In each blank, insert the most appropriate word or expression from group 7.

1. After studying poetry, we turned our attention to another _____, short stories.

2. A novel with a suspenseful plot makes the reader impatient to get to the _____.

3. If audience reaction is favorable, Selma is prepared to play a(n) _____.

4. Beethoven's NINTH SYMPHONY is regarded by many as his _____.

5. By diligent study, the young singer added several new numbers to his _____.

---

8. Terms Dealing With Food

---

a la carte (*adv.*) ‚al-ə-'kärt	according to the bill of fare; dish by dish; with a stated price for each dish	If you order *a la carte*, you select whatever you wish from the bill of fare, paying only for the dishes ordered.
a la mode (*adj.*) 'al-ə-'mōd	1. according to fashion; stylish 2. with ice cream	Most shoppers buy only the latest fashions because they want their clothes to be *a la mode*. We enjoy apple pie *a la mode*.
aperitif (*n.*) ‚ap-‚er-ə-'tēf	alcoholic drink taken before a meal as an appetizer	Select a nonalcoholic appetizer, such as tomato juice, if you do not care for an *aperitif*.
bonbon (*n.*) 'bän-‚bän	piece of candy	For St. Valentine's Day, we gave Mother a heart-shaped box of delicious *bonbons*.
consommé (*n.*) ‚kän-sə-'mā	clear soup; broth	Ask the waiter if we may order some *consommé* instead of the *soup du jour*.
croissant (*n.*) ‚kwä-'sä^n	rich, flaky crescent-shaped roll	*Croissants* are more tasty than ordinary rolls.
cuisine (*n.*) kwi-'zēn	style of cooking or preparing food	Around the corner is a restaurant specializing in French *cuisine*.
demitasse (*n.*) 'dem-ē-‚tas	small cup for, or of, black coffee	Aunt Dorothy always takes cream with her coffee; she is not fond of *demitasse*.
entrée (*n.*) 'än-trā	main dish at lunch or dinner	We had a choice of the following *entrées*: roast beef, fried chicken, or baked mackerel.
filet (*n.*) fi-'lā	slice of meat or fish without bones or fat	Because they contain no bones or excess fat, *filets* are more expensive than ordinary cuts of meat.

hors d'oeuvres (*n. pl.*) ȯr-'dərvz	light food served as an appetizer before the regular courses of a meal	Malcolm purchased olives, celery, and anchovies for the *hors d'oeuvres*.
pièce de résistance (*n.*) pē-ˌes-də-rə-ˌzē-'stäns	1. main dish	If you eat too much of the introductory dishes, you will have little appetite for the *pièce de résistance*.
	2. main item of any collection, series, program, etc.	The preliminaries were followed by the *pièce de résistance*, the title bout.
soup du jour (*n.*) ˌsüp-də-'zhu̇r	special soup served in a restaurant on a particular day	Often, the only soup a restaurant offers is the *soup du jour*.
table d'hôte (*n.*) ˌtäb-əl-'dōt	complete meal of several courses offered in a hotel or restaurant at a fixed price	If you order the *table d'hôte*, you pay the fixed price for the entire dinner, even if you do not have some of the dishes.

EXERCISE 8.8

In each blank, insert the most appropriate word or expression from group 8.

1. Before dinner, our hostess brought in a large tray of appetizing _____.

2. Though this chef's style of cooking is quite interesting, it cannot compare with my grandmother's _____.

3. When I do not care to have a complete dinner, I order a couple of dishes _____.

4. My little sister was so fond of candy that she had to be restricted to one _____ after each meal.

5. If you like flounder without fishbones, order _____ of flounder.

6. We would have had some split pea soup, but unfortunately it was not the _____.

---

9. Terms Dealing With Dress

---

bouffant (*adj.*) bü-'fänt	puffed out; full	Corridors and stairways would have to be widened considerably if all women were to wear *bouffant* skirts.
boutique (*n.*) bü-'tēk	small shop specializing in fashionable clothes	Rhoda found her outfit in a midtown *boutique*.
chemise (*n.*) shə-'mēz	loose-fitting, sacklike dress	Though more comfortable than most other dresses, the *chemise* has often been ridiculed for its shapelessness.
coiffure (*n.*) kwä-'fyu̇(ə)r	style of arranging the hair; headdress	Sally's *coiffure* was created for her by my sister's hair stylist.

corsage (*n.*) kor-'säzh	small bouquet worn by a woman	Holly *corsages* are often worn at Christmas.
cravat (*n.*) krə-'vat	necktie	He wore a light blue shirt and a navy blue *cravat*.
ensemble (*n.*) än-'säm-bəl	complete costume of harmonious clothing and accessories	Her red blouse, black skirt, and matching red slippers made an attractive *ensemble*.
flamboyant (*adj.*) flam-'boi-ənt	flamelike; very ornate; showy	To add a touch of bright color to his outfit, Jack wore a *flamboyant* scarf.
toupee (*n.*) tü-'pā	wig	The actor's blond hair was cleverly concealed by a grey *toupee*.
vogue (*n.*) 'vōg	fashion; accepted style	Fashions change rapidly; today's style may be out of *vogue* tomorrow.

EXERCISE 8.9

In each blank, insert the most appropriate word from group 9.

1. The excessive heat made George untie his _____ and unbutton his shirt collar.

2. After trying several elaborate hair styles, Marie has returned to a simple _____.

3. On your visit to Mount Vernon in Virginia, you will see furniture styles that were in _____ in George and Martha Washington's time.

4. It was easy to identify the guest of honor because of the beautiful _____ at her shoulder.

5. The gowns in the dress salon include sedate blacks, as well as _____ reds and golds.

---

10. Miscellaneous Terms

---

ambience (*n.*) än-'byäns	surrounding atmosphere; environment	We enjoyed the restaurant for its food, as well as its *ambience*; never had we dined in pleasanter surroundings.
apropos (*adv.*) ‚ap-rə-'pō	by the way; incidentally	We'll meet you at the station. *Apropos*, when does your train arrive?
apropos (*adj.*)	appropriate; relevant; pertinent	So far, none of your comments are *apropos*; everything you have said is off the topic.

avoirdupois (*n.*) ˌav-ərd-ə-'pȯiz	weight; heaviness	Dieters constantly check their *avoirdupois*.
bagatelle (*n.*) ˌbag-ə-'tel	trifle	Pay attention to important matters; don't waste time on *bagatelles*.
coup de grace (*n.*) ˌküd-ə-'gräs	decisive finishing blow	We won, 5-1, thanks to Pat. He administered the *coup de grace* by homering with the bases loaded.
en route (*adv.* or *adj.*) äⁿ-'rüt	1. on the way	My friends are *en route*; they will be here shortly.
	2. along the way	We left before breakfast but stopped for an early lunch *en route*.
etiquette (*n.*) 'et-i-kət	conduct and manners of polite society	According to the rules of *etiquette*, a person should not come to a party to which he or she has not been invited.
facade (*n.*) fə-'säd	face or front of a building, or of anything	The patient's cheerful smile was just a *facade*; actually, she was suffering from ennui.
fete (*n.*) 'fāt	festival; entertainment; party	Our block party last year was a memorable *fete*.
fete (*v.*)	honor with a fete	Retiring employees are often *feted* at a special dinner.
foyer (*n.*) 'fȯi(-ə)r	entrance hall; lobby	Let's meet in the *foyer* of the public library.
milieu (*n.*) mēl-'yə	environment; setting	David found it much easier to make friends in his new *milieu*.
parasol (*n.*) 'par-ə-ˌsȯl	umbrella for protection against the sun	In summer when you stroll on the boardwalk in the noonday sun, it is advisable to take along a *parasol*.
par excellence (*adj.*) ˌpär-ˌek-sə-'läⁿs	above all others of the same sort (follows the word it modifies)	Charles Dickens was a raconteur *par excellence*.
passé (*adj.*) pa-'sā	old-fashioned; behind the times; outmoded	Recently bought equipment may quickly become *passé*, thanks to the rapid pace of technological innovation.
pince-nez (*n.*) paⁿs-'nā	eyeglasses clipped to the nose by a spring	Since they are held in place by a spring that pinches the nose, *pince-nez* may not be as comfortable as ordinary eyeglasses.
premiere (*n.*) pri-'mye(ə)r	first performance	The second performance was even better than the *premiere*.
queue (*n.*) 'kyü	line of persons waiting their turn	The *queue* at the box office was so long that I decided to come back another time.

raison d'être (*n.*) ‚rā-‚zōⁿ-'detrᵊ	reason or justification for existing	Apparently, Alice lives just for dancing; it is her *raison d'être*.
rendezvous (*n.*) 'rän-di-‚vü	1. meeting place fixed by prior agreement	We agreed to meet after the test at the handball courts, our usual *rendezvous*.
	2. appointment to meet at a fixed time and place	Our *rendezvous* with the coach and captain of the visiting team was set for 2 P.M.
silhouette (*n.*) ‚sil-ə-'wet	shadow; outline	I knew Jonah was coming to let me in because I recognized his *silhouette* behind the curtained door.
sobriquet (*n.*) or **soubriquet** 'sō-bri-‚kā	nickname	Andrew Jackson was known by the *sobriquet* ''Old Hickory.''
souvenir (*n.*) 'sü-və-‚ni(ə)r	reminder; keepsake; memento	The Yearbook, in time to come, will be a treasured *souvenir* of high school days.
tour de force (*n.*) ‚tü(ə)rd-ə-'fȯrs	feat of strength, skill, or ingenuity	The sixty-yard run was the *tour de force* that won the game for us.
vis-à-vis (*prep.*) ‚vē-zə-'vē	face to face; opposite	At the banquet table, I had the good fortune to sit *vis-à-vis* an old friend.

EXERCISE 8.10

In each blank, insert the most appropriate word or expression from group 10.

1. Carmela brought me a print of the Lincoln Memorial as a(n) _____ of her visit to Washington.

2. Paul mounts the scale morning and night to check his _____.

3. After class, my friends gather at our _____ outside the pizza parlor.

4. Agnes is a mimic _____; no one else in our club can do impersonations as well as she.

5. Because of his flaming hair, Harvey is popularly known by the _____ ''Red.''

6. The small merchants in our area are fearful that the opening of another shopping mall will be the _____ for them.

7. Our club is planning a(n) _____ in honor of the outgoing president.

8. On the first day in a new school, arriving students find themselves in a bewildering _____.

9. I did not recognize the hotel because its _____ and foyer had been modernized since I was last there.

10. Winning the league pennant is an outstanding achievement, but going on to capture the World Series in four straight victories is an even greater _____.

11. When the film had its premiere at our local theater, the _____ stretched half way around the block.

12. Blanche, we're glad to see you. _____, how is your brother?

Review Exercises

REVIEW 5: MEANINGS

In the space before each word or expression in column I, write the *letter* of its correct meaning from column II.

COLUMN I	COLUMN II
_____ 1. piece of candy	*a.* silhouette
_____ 2. nickname	*b.* coup d'etat
_____ 3. relaxing of strained relations	*c.* consommé
_____ 4. full; puffed out	*d.* coup de grace
_____ 5. style of cooking	*e.* apropos
_____ 6. masterpiece	*f.* bonbon
_____ 7. shadow	*g.* chef d'oeuvre
_____ 8. weight	*h.* cuisine
_____ 9. decisive finishing stroke	*i.* avoirdupois
_____ 10. sudden overthrow of a regime	*j.* sobriquet
_____ 11. relevant	*k.* détente
_____ 12. broth	*l.* bouffant

REVIEW 6: MORE MEANINGS

In the space provided, write the *letter* of the choice that correctly defines the italicized word or expression.

_____ 1. prosperous *bourgeoisie* *a.* elite *b.* entrepreneur *c.* middle class *d.* citizenry *e.* officialdom

_____ 2. *flamboyant* jacket *a.* debonair *b.* warm *c.* sanguinary *d.* showy *e.* stylish

_____ 3. happy *denouement* *a.* ending *b.* vignette *c.* milieu *d.* event *e.* episode

_____ 4. sudden *demarche* *a.* détente *b.* reversal *c.* entrée *d.* discovery *e.* aggression

_____ 5. attitude of *laissez-faire* *a.* boredom *b.* equanimity *c.* eagerness *d.* cordiality *e.* noninterference

_____ 6. enduring *entente* a. influence b. understanding c. bitterness d. cause célèbre
e. entrance

_____ 7. serve *hors d'oeuvres* a. entrée b. appetizers c. desserts d. pièce de résistance
e. table d'hôte

_____ 8. join the *avant-garde* a. gendarmes b. protégés c. devotees d. underground
e. innovators

_____ 9. welcome *encore* a. cancellation b. delay c. repetition d. refund
e. improvement

_____ 10. flavor *par excellence* a. new b. unsurpassed c. spicy d. mild e. inferior

_____ 11. has become *passé* a. popular b. fashionable c. outmoded d. unnecessary
e. acceptable

_____ 12. delayed *en route* a. for a short time b. before departure c. somewhere
d. on arrival e. on the way

REVIEW 7: SENTENCE COMPLETION

Complete the sentence by inserting the correct word or expression from the vocabulary list below.

VOCABULARY LIST

coiffure	chargé d'affaires	regime
au courant	pièce de résistance	raison d'être
envoy	éclat	avant-garde
genre	bagatelle	nouveaux riches
laissez-faire	facade	souvenir

1. At one time or another, some hobby or interest becomes so important to us that it is practically

   our only _____ (*reason for existence*).

2. This piece of driftwood is a(n) _____ (*something that serves as a reminder*) of
   last summer's camping trip.

3. The reason you were not ready is that you spent too much time on a mere _____
   (*unimportant, trifling matter*).

4. What _____ (*style of arranging the hair*) is most in vogue today?

5. The _____ (*persons who had newly become rich*) felt ill at ease in
   their new social milieu.

6. In her letters Susan kept me _____ (*up to date*) about events in my old
   neighborhood.

7. The _____ (*main number on the program*) of the musicale was a
   medley of Gilbert and Sullivan airs.

8. It is an unwise parent who follows a policy of _____
   (*absence of interference*) in bringing up children.

9. The United States has encouraged nations everywhere to install a democratic _____
   (*system of government or rule*).

10. The _____ (*ambassador's substitute*) has had years of experience in the diplomatic service.

REVIEW 8: BRAINTEASERS

Fill in the missing letters.

1. Don't change your hair style. We like your present __ __ __ __ **f u r** __.

2. Is __ __ **l e t** of sole on today's menu?

3. The matter is of little importance. It is a mere **b a g** __ __ __ __ __ __.

4. They enjoy simple cooking; they don't care for fancy __ __ __ **s i n** __.

5. Only the __ __ **c a d** __ has been renovated. The interior is unchanged.

6. We didn't stick to the topic. Little that was said was __ **p r o p** __ __.

7. Residents complain that the park has become a **r e n d** __ __ __ __ __ __ for drug traffickers.

8. A(n) __ __ __ __ **b o y** __ __ __ ensemble is not for a conservative dresser.

9. The **r a p** __ __ __ __ __ __ __ __ __ __ between the rivals suggests that an era of harmony may be beginning.

10. We were told that the tune we had asked for was, regrettably, not in the band's __ __ **p e r t** __ __ __ __.

REVIEW 9: CONCISE WRITING

Express the thought of each sentence below in no more than four words.

1. We went into a small shop that specializes in fashionable clothes.

   _____

2. The line of persons waiting their turn kept getting longer and longer.

   _____

3. People who travel on foot sometimes carry umbrellas for protection against the sun.

   _____

4. We arranged an appointment to meet at a fixed time and place.

   _____

5. The loose-fitting sacklike dress that she wore is not expensive.

   _____

6. What is the time at which the first performance will be presented?

_____

7. Sometimes, people who assume the risks and management of a business go bankrupt.

_____

8. Give us full discretionary power to use our own judgment.

_____

9. The vague feeling of illness that I was having is gone.

_____

10. Do you know anyone who is fond of eating and drinking to excess?

_____

REVIEW 10: COMPOSITION

Answer in two or three sentences.

1. Who are more likely to have trouble with their avoirdupois, gourmands or gourmets? Explain.

_____

_____

_____

2. Though the hazards of overexposure to the sun have been widely publicized, parasols do not seem to be in vogue. Why?

_____

_____

_____

3. Suppose you are eager to attend a premiere, but when you get there you find a queue stretching around the block. Would you stay or leave? Explain.

_____

_____

_____

4. Why do so many émigrés from totalitarian regimes seek to settle in our country? Give two important reasons.

_____

_____

_____

5. Why is it advisable to know what the pièce de résistance is going to be before having any of the hors d'oeuvres?

_____

_____

_____

REVIEW 11: ANALOGIES

Write the *letter* of the expression that best completes the analogy.

1. *Parasol* is to *sun* as *variety* is to _____.
   a. queue *b.* fete *c.* ennui *d.* sky *e.* souvenir

2. *Regime* is to *revolutionists* as *custom* is to _____.
   a. elite *b.* connoisseurs *c.* devotees *d.* avant-garde *e.* conservatives

3. *Scene I* is to *climax* as *hors d'oeuvres* is to _____.
   a. entrée *b.* cuisine *c.* bonbon *d.* chef d'oeuvre *e.* bagatelle

4. *Passé* is to *a la mode* as *apropos* is to _____.
   a. appropriate *b.* stylish *c.* outmoded *d.* irrelevant *e.* pertinent

5. *Bottle* is to *neck* as *hotel* is to _____.
   a. facade *b.* cul-de-sac *c.* foyer *d.* suburb *e.* table d'hôte

6. *Nourished* is to *food* as *au courant* is to _____.
   a. exercise *b.* drink *c.* news *d.* rest *e.* rumor

7. *Star* is to *understudy* as *ambassador* is to _____.
   a. coterie *b.* valet *c.* entrepreneur *d.* chargé d'affaires *e.* protégé

8. *Bas-relief* is to *sculpture* as *genre* is to _____.
   a. palette *b.* painter *c.* sculptor *d.* baton *e.* painting

9. *Faux pas* is to *embarrassment* as *détente* is to _____.
   a. rapprochement *b.* impasse *c.* cul-de-sac *d.* pièce de résistance *e.* encore

10. *Ice* is to *thaw* as *hostility* is to _____.
    a. coup de grace *b.* détente *c.* coup d'etat *d.* tour de force *e.* denouement

CHAPTER 9

Italian Words in English

The Italian impact on English is especially important because Italy's rich contributions to the arts have profoundly influenced our cultural life. It is no wonder, then, that many English words that deal with music, painting, architecture, sculpture, and other arts are Italian loanwords.

1. Words for Singing Voices
(arranged in order of increasing pitch)

WORD	MEANING
basso (*n.*) 'bas-ō	lowest male voice; bass (pronounced bās)
baritone (*n.*) 'bar-ə-‚tōn	male voice between bass and tenor
tenor (*n.*) 'ten-ə(r)	adult male voice between baritone and alto
alto (*n.*) 'al-tō	1. highest male voice 2. lowest female voice, the contralto
contralto (*n.*) kən-'tral-tō	lowest female voice
mezzo-soprano (*n.*) ‚met-sō-sə-'pran-ō	female voice between contralto and soprano
soprano (*n.*) sə-pran-ō	highest singing voice in women and boys
coloratura (*n.*) ‚kəl-ə-rə-'t(y)ür-ə	1. ornamental passages (runs, trills, etc.) in vocal music 2. soprano who sings such passages, i.e., a *coloratura* soprano
falsetto (*n.*) fȯl-'set-ō	1. unnaturally high-pitched male voice 2. artificially high voice

EXERCISE 9.1

In each blank, insert the most appropriate word from group 1.

1. For her superb rendering of ornamental passages, the _____ was wildly acclaimed.

2. The lowest singing voice is *contralto* for women and _____ for men.

3. Yodeling is a form of singing that requires frequent changes from the natural voice to a(n)

   _____ .

4. Since Oscar's singing voice is between baritone and alto, he is classified as a(n) _____ .

5. The highest singing voice is soprano for women and _____ for men.

---

2. Words for Tempos (Rates of Speed) of Musical Compositions

(arranged in order of increasing speed)

grave (*adv.* or *adj.*)   slow (the slowest tempo in music)
'gräv-ā

largo (*adv.* or *adj.*)   slow and dignified; stately
'lär-gō

adagio (*adv.* or *adj.*)   slow; in an easy, graceful manner
ə-'däj-ō

lento (*adv.* or *adj.*)   slow
'len-‚tō

andante (*adv.* or *adj.*)   moderately slow, but flowing
än-'dän-‚tā

moderato (*adv.* or *adj.*)   in moderate time
‚mäd-ə-'rät-ō

allegro (*adv.* or *adj.*)   brisk; quick; lively
ə-'leg-rō

vivace (*adv.* or *adj.*)   brisk; spirited
vē-'väch-ā

presto (*adv.* or *adj.*)   quick
'pres-tō

prestissimo (*adv.* or *adj.*)   at a very rapid pace
pre-'stis-ə-‚mō

EXERCISE 9.2

In each blank, insert the most appropriate word from group 2.

1. A piece of music marked _____ moves more rapidly than one marked *presto*.

2. The slowest tempo in music, _____, is used in the opening measures of Beethoven's SONATE PATHÉTIQUE.

3. A ballad with a(n) _____ tempo has to be sung at a moderately slow but flowing pace.

4. The _____ movement of Dvořák's NEW WORLD SYMPHONY is played in a slow and dignified manner.

5. The term _____ over the opening notes of SWEET GEORGIA BROWN indicates that this tune should be played neither rapidly nor slowly, but in moderate time.

---

3. Words for Dynamics (Degrees of Loudness)

crescendo (*adv.*, *adj.*, or *n.*) kri-'shen-dō	gradually increasing (or a gradual increase) in force or loudness (*ant.* **decrescendo**)
decrescendo (*adv.*, *adj.*, or *n.*) ‚dā-krə-'shen-dō	gradually decreasing (or a gradual decrease) in force or loudness (*syn.* **diminuendo**; *ant.* **crescendo**)
dolce (*adv.* or *adj.*) 'dōl-chā	soft; sweet
forte (*adv.* or *adj.*) 'fȯr-‚tā	loud (*ant.* **piano**)
fortissimo (*adv.* or *adj.*) fȯr-'tis-ə-‚mō	very loud (*ant.* **pianissimo**)
pianissimo (*adv.* or *adj.*) ‚pē-ə-'nis-ə-‚mō	very soft (*ant.* **fortissimo**)
piano (*adv.* or *adj.*) pē-'än-ō	soft (*ant.* **forte**)
sforzando (*adv.* or *adj.*) sfȯrt-'sän-dō	accented

EXERCISE 9.3

In each blank, insert the most appropriate word from group 3.

1. The word _____ designates a familiar musical instrument, as well as a musical direction meaning "soft."

2. Ravel's BOLERO rises to a dramatic climax by a gradual increase in loudness; few pieces have such

an electrifying _____ .

3. When a chord is to be played with a strong accent, the composer marks it with the term

_____ .

4. Mendelssohn's SCHERZO has a _____ ending; it has to be played very
softly.

5. A degree of loudness higher than *forte* is _____ .

---

4. Words for Musical Effects

---

a cappella (*adv.* or *adj.*) ˌäk-ə-ˈpel-ə	(literally, "in chapel or church style") without musical accompaniment, as to sing *a cappella*, or an *a cappella* choir
arpeggio (*n.*) är-ˈpej-ō	1. production of the tones of a chord in rapid succession, rather than at the same time. (Normally, the tones of a chord are played simultaneously.) 2. a chord thus played
legato (*adv.* or *adj.*) li-ˈgät-ō	smooth and connected
pizzicato (*adv.* or *adj.*) ˌpit-si-ˈkät-ō	by means of plucking the strings instead of using the bow
staccato (*adv.* or *adj.*) stə-ˈkät-ō	with breaks between successive notes; disconnected; abrupt
tremolo (*n.*) ˈtrem-ə-ˌlō	rapid ("trembling") repetition of a tone or chord, without apparent breaks, to express emotion
vibrato (*n.*) vē-ˈbrät-ō	slightly throbbing or pulsating effect, adding warmth and beauty to the tone

EXERCISE 9.4

In each blank, insert the most appropriate word or expression from group 4.

1. By plucking the strings with the fingers, a violinist achieves a(n) _____ effect.

2. In Tchaikovsky's 1812 OVERTURE, the rapid and prolonged repetition of two tones produces a

"trembling" emotion-stirring effect known as _____ .

3. Some beginning piano students strike all the correct notes but fail to achieve a smooth and con-

nected effect because they do not play them _____ .

4. It is surely much easier to play the tones of a chord simultaneously than to play them as a(n)

_____ .

5. In Schubert's AVE MARIA, the notes are smoothly connected, but in his MARCHE MILITAIRE they are

mainly _____ .

---

5. *Words Dealing With Musical Compositions*

---

aria (*n.*)
'är-ē-ə
air, melody, or tune; especially, an elaborate, accompanied melody for a single voice in an opera

bravura (*n.*)
brə-'v(y)ùr-ə
1. piece of music requiring skill and spirit in the performer
2. display of daring or brilliancy

cantata (*n.*)
kən-'tät-ə
story or play set to music to be sung by a chorus, but not acted

concerto (*n.*)
kən-'chert-ō
long musical composition for one or more principal instruments with orchestral accompaniment

duet (*n.*)
d(y)ü-'et
1. piece of music for two voices or instruments
2. two singers or players performing together; duo

finale (*n.*)
fə-'nal-ē
close or termination, as the last section of a musical composition

intermezzo (*n.*)
‚int-ər-'met-sō
1. short musical or dramatic entertainment between the acts of a play
2. short musical composition between the main divisions of an extended musical work
3. short, independent musical composition

libretto (*n.*)
lə-'bret-ō
text or words of an opera or other long musical composition

opera (*n.*)
'äp-(ə)-rə
play mostly sung, with costumes, scenery, action, and music

oratorio (*n.*)
‚ȯr-ə-'tȯr-ē-‚ō
musical composition, usually on a religious theme, for solo voices, chorus, and orchestra

scherzo (*n.*)
'skert-sō
light or playful part of a sonata or symphony

solo (*n.*)
'sō-lō
1. piece of music for one voice or instrument
2. anything done without a partner

sonata (*n.*)
sə-'nät-ə
piece of music (for one or two instruments) having three or four movements in contrasted rhythms but related tonality

trio (*n.*)
'trē-ō
1. piece of music for three voices or instruments
2. three singers or players performing together

tutti (*adv.*)
'tüt-ē
all (a direction for all the instruments and/or voices to perform together)

tutti (*n.*)
'tüt-ē
section of a musical composition performed by all the performers

EXERCISE 9.5

In each blank, insert the most appropriate word from group 5.

1. To perform in a(n) _____, one must be gifted both as a singer and as an actor.

2. Roberta refuses to do a solo, but she is willing to join with someone else in a(n) _____.

3. From the opening selection to the _____, we enjoyed the concert thoroughly.

4. Though there is orchestral accompaniment in a piano _____, the pianist is the principal performer.

5. The selection you played is unfamiliar to me, but its light and playful character leads me to believe that it's a(n) _____.

6. Not a single instrument in the orchestra is silent in a passage marked _____.

---

6. Words Dealing With Arts Other Than Music

---

cameo (*n.*) 'kam-ē-ˌō	1. carved gem with a design higher and of a different color than its background (*ant.* **intaglio**) 2. brief role, usually limited to a single scene, by a prominent actor or actress 3. brief passage of exceptionally fine writing
campanile (*n.*) ˌkam-pə-'nē-lē	bell tower
canto (*n.*) 'kan-ˌtō	one of the chief divisions of a long poem
chiaroscuro (*n.*) kē-ˌär-ə-'sk(y)ù(ə)r-ō	1. distribution and treatment of light and shade in painting or sketching 2. painting or drawing that uses only light and shade
cupola (*n.*) 'kyü-pə-lə	1. rounded roof; dome 2. small dome or tower on a roof
fresco (*n.*) 'fres-ˌkō	1. art of painting with watercolors on damp fresh plaster 2. picture or design so painted
intaglio (*n.*) in-'tal-yō	design engraved by making cuts in a surface (*ant.* **cameo**)
majolica (*n.*) mə-'jäl-i-kə	enameled Italian pottery richly decorated in colors
mezzanine (*n.*) 'mez-ᵊn-ˌēn	intermediate story in a theater between the main floor and the first balcony

mezzotint (*n.*)   picture engraved on copper or steel by polishing or scraping away parts
'met-sō-ˌtint   of a roughened surface

patina (*n.*)   film or incrustation, usually green, on the surface of old bronze or copper
'pat-ə-nə

portico (*n.*)   roof supported by columns, forming a porch or a covered walk
'pōrt-i-ˌkō

rialto (*n.*)   1. marketplace
rē-'al-tō   2. theater district of a town

rotunda (*n.*)   1. round building, especially one with a dome or cupola
rō-'tən-də   2. large round room, as the *rotunda* of the Capitol

stucco (*n.*)   plaster for covering exterior walls of buildings
'stək-ō

tempera (*n.*)   method of painting in which the colors are mixed with white of egg or
'tem-pə-rə   other substances, instead of oil

terra-cotta (*n.*)   1. kind of hard, brownish-red earthenware, used for vases, statuettes,
'ter-ə-'kät-ə   etc.
                                    2. dull brownish-red color

torso (*n.*)   1. trunk or body of a statue without head, arms, or legs
'tȯr-sō   2. human trunk

EXERCISE 9.6

In each blank, insert the most appropriate word from group 6.

1. Because it is a large round room, the _____ of the Capitol in Washington, D.C., is ideal for an impressive ceremony.

2. The _____ my aunt wears has a carved ivory head raised on a light brown background.

3. A(n) _____ actually becomes a part of the wall on whose damp, fresh plaster it is painted.

4. The head of the statue was discovered not far from the place where its _____ had been found.

5. An antique increases in artistic value when its surface becomes incrusted with a fine natural _____ .

6. The white of egg or a similar substance is used for mixing colors in _____ painting.

7. Read the fifth _____ of Dante's INFERNO for a stirring account of the lovers Paolo and Francesca.

8. The _____ applied to exterior walls of buildings is a mixture of portland cement, sand, and lime.

9. In the morning we heard the sound of bells coming from the _____,
a tall structure right next to the church.

10. The main building and the annex are connected by a(n) _____
that facilitates traffic between the two, especially in bad weather.

11. A half hour before curtain time, the sidewalks of the _____ are thronged
with theatergoers.

---

7. Words Dealing With Persons

---

buffo (*n.*)
'bü-fō
male singer who plays a comic role in an opera; buffoon; clown

cognoscente (*n.*)
ˌkän-yō-'shent-ē
person who has a superior knowledge and understanding of a particular field; expert; connoisseur

dilettante (*n.*)
ˌdil-ə-'tänt(-ē)
person who follows some art or science as an amusement or in a trifling way

diva (*n.*)
'dē-və
principal female singer in an opera; prima donna

impresario (*n.*)
ˌim-prə-'sär-ē-ˌō
organizer, or director of an opera or ballet company or a concert series; manager; promoter

inamorata (*n.*)
in-ˌam-ə-'rät-ə
woman who loves or is loved

inamorato (*n.*)
in-ˌam-ə-'rät-ō
man who loves or is loved

maestro (*n.*)
mä-'e-strō
1. eminent conductor, composer, or teacher of music
2. master in any art

mountebank (*n.*)
'maún-ti-ˌbaŋk
boastful pretender; charlatan; quack

politico (*n.*)
pə-'lit-i-ˌkō
politician

prima donna (*n.*)
ˌprim-ə-'dän-ə
1. principal female singer in an opera
2. high-strung, vain, or extremely sensitive person

simpatico, *m.* (*adj.*)
sim-'pät-i-ˌkō
(**simpatica**, *f.*)
possessing attractive qualities; appealing; likable; congenial

virtuoso (*n.*)
ˌvər-chə-'wō-sō
one who exhibits great technical skill in an art, especially in playing a musical instrument

EXERCISE 9.7

In each blank, insert the most appropriate word or expression from group 7.

1. All eyes were riveted on the _____ as he raised his baton to begin the concert.

2. She hopes one day to take up the cello as a serious student rather than as a(n) _____.

3. The versatile young musician has won fame not only as a conductor and composer, but as a(n) _____ at the piano.

4. The gentleman sent a St. Valentine's greeting to his _____.

5. The owner is unpleasant to deal with, but the manager is very _____.

6. An event like a parade or a marathon needs a skillful and devoted _____ to organize and direct it.

7. The _____ in tonight's opera has won acclaim for his portrayal of comic roles.

8. Words for Situations Involving Persons

dolce far niente (*n.*) 'dol-chē-ˌfär-nē-'ent-ē	delightful idleness
fiasco (*n.*) fē-'as-kō	crash; complete or ridiculous failure
imbroglio (*n.*) im-'brōl-yō	1. difficult situation 2. complicated disagreement
incognito (*adv.*) ˌin-ˌkäg-'nēt-ō	with one's identity concealed
incognito (*n.*)	disguised state
vendetta (*n.*) ven-'det-ə	feud for blood revenge

9. Words Dealing With Food

antipasto (*n.*) ˌant-i-'pas-tō	appetizer consisting of fish, meats, etc.; hors d'oeuvres
Chianti (*n.*) ke-'änt-ē	a dry, red Italian wine
gusto (*n.*) 'gəs-ˌtō	liking or taste; hearty enjoyment

pasta (*n.*) 'päs-tə	1. wheat paste or dough—either dried, as for spaghetti or macaroni, or used fresh, as for ravioli 2. dish of cooked pasta
pizza (*n.*) 'pēt-sə	large, flat pie of bread dough spread with tomato pulp, cheese, meat, anchovies, etc.

---

10. Miscellaneous Common Words

alfresco (*adj.* or *adv.*) al-'fres-kō	in the open air; outdoor
brava (*interj.*) 'bräv-ə	(used to applaud a woman performer) well done; excellent
bravo (*interj.*) 'bräv-ō	(used to applaud a performance or a male performer) well done; excellent
gondola (*n.*) 'gän-də-lə	1. boat used in the canals of Venice 2. cabin attached to the underpart of an airship
grotto (*n.*) 'grät-ō	cave
piazza (*n.*) pē-'az-ə	1. open square in an Italian town 2. veranda or porch
portfolio (*n.*) pȯrt-'fō-lē-,ō	1. briefcase 2. position or duties of a cabinet member or minister of state
salvo (*n.*) 'sal-vō	1. simultaneous discharge of shots 2. burst of cheers, as a *salvo* of applause
sotto voce (*adv.* or *adj.*) ,sät-ō-'vō-chē	under the breath; in an undertone; privately, as a *sotto voce* remark

EXERCISE 9.8

In each blank, insert the most appropriate word or expression from groups 8–10.

1. My old briefcase can hold more books and papers than this new ———————————.

2. The host filled his guests' wineglasses from a freshly opened bottle of ———————————.

3. The complicated disagreement about this year's budget is similar to the ——————————— we had about last year's budget.

4. Philip's cold prevented him from eating his dinner with his usual ———————————.

5. The playwright attended the premiere ——————————— so that he would not be recognized.

6. Because of the ridiculous failure of the first performance, they have canceled tonight's show to avoid a repetition of that _____.

7. At last the feuding parties have ended their _____.

8. I did not hear what the mother said to the daughter, for they conferred _____.

9. The tourist relies on the taxicab in New York City and on the _____ in Venice.

10. While in prison, Edmond Dantès learned of an immense fortune concealed in an underground _____ on the island of Monte Cristo.

11. When the diva completed her first aria, the audience sprang to its feet and shouted ''_____.''

12. We had a delightful _____ lunch at a sidewalk cafe.

Review Exercises

REVIEW 1: MEANINGS

In the space before each word or expression in column I, write the *letter* of its correct meaning from column II.

COLUMN I	COLUMN II
_____ 1. rialto	*a.* trunk
_____ 2. canto	*b.* diva
_____ 3. cognoscente	*c.* promoter
_____ 4. grotto	*d.* division
_____ 5. buffo	*e.* hors d'oeuvres
_____ 6. sforzando	*f.* cave
_____ 7. torso	*g.* square
_____ 8. antipasto	*h.* connoisseur
_____ 9. piazza	*i.* dough
_____ 10. impresario	*j.* marketplace
_____ 11. prima donna	*k.* stressed
_____ 12. pasta	*l.* clown

REVIEW 2: SENTENCE COMPLETION

In the space provided, enter the *letter* of the choice that correctly completes the sentence.

1. A (an) _____ choir performs without accompaniment.

   a. a capella   *b.* cantata

2. A _____ is a musical composition requiring an entire orchestra, but featuring a solo instrument such as the piano or violin.

   a. sonata   *b.* concerto

3. When Ulysses returned _____ to his palace, he was recognized by his dog Argus.

   a. incognito   *b.* falsetto

4. The anchored fleet welcomed the chief of state with a thunderous _____.

   a. salvo   *b.* staccato

5. An impression made from an _____ results in a raised image.

   a. imbroglio   *b.* intaglio

6. The overworked executive longed for the _____ of a Caribbean cruise.

   a. sotto voce   *b.* dolce far niente

7. The orchestra and balcony seats are sold out, but a few _____ tickets are available.

   a. mezzanine   *b.* mezzotint

8. To achieve a smooth and flowing effect, I was advised to play the first two measures _____.

   a. tremolo   *b.* legato

9. For an example of a crescendo from pianissimo all the way to _____, listen to Grieg's IN THE HALL OF THE MOUNTAIN KING.

   a. prestissimo   *b.* fortissimo

10. A _____ sketch achieves its effects principally by its treatment of light and shade.

    a. chiaroscuro   *b.* terra-cotta

REVIEW 3: BRAINTEASERS

Fill in the missing letters.

1. While the spaghetti was boiling, our hostess served a delicious __ __ __ __ **p a s t** __.

2. The __ **r o t** __ __ had once been used to store stolen treasure.

3. Have you ever heard of the **v e n d** __ __ __ __ between the Hatfields and the McCoys?

4. Over the years a(n) __ __ **t i n** __ had formed on the surface of the copper vessel.

5. Responding to the __ __ __ __ __ **e n d** __ of applause, the violinist returned for an encore.

6. Though exhausted from crying, the child continued to punctuate the silence with occasional __ __ __ __ **c a t** __ sobs.

7. The ill-matched challenger's bid ended in a(n) __ __ **a s** __ __ in the opening seconds of the first round.

8. The **m o u n t** __ __ __ __ __ convinced gullible customers that his snake oil would cure their aches and pains.

9. My uncle paints as a(n) __ __ __ __ __ __ **t a n** __ __, not as a serious artist.

10. The __ __ **h e r** __ __ movement of that symphony is light and playful.

REVIEW 4: CONCISE WRITING

Express the thought of each sentence below in no more than four words.

1. The plotters arrived wearing disguises, so that they would not be recognized.

_____

2. This is a painting in watercolors that was done on damp fresh plaster.

_____

3. Is the section of the theater between the main floor and the first balcony crowded?

_____

4. They met the person who is doing the organizing and the promoting.

_____

5. We sang without the accompaniment of any musical instrument whatsoever.

_____

6. People respect someone who has a superior knowledge and understanding of a particular field.

_____

7. Play these notes by plucking the strings, instead of using the bow.

_____

8. This is the district in which the theaters of the city are concentrated.

_____

9. Here is a piece of music for two voices or instruments.

_____

10. The conversation that we took part in was conducted in an undertone.

_____

REVIEW 5: COMPOSITION

Answer in two or three sentences.

1. Explain why most people usually eat pizza with gusto.

_____

_____

2. Would a virtuoso enjoy being called a dilettante by a music critic? Explain.

_____

_____

3. Who contributes more to the success of an opera, the composer of the music, or the author of the libretto? Explain.

_____

_____

4. Why is an action taken on the advice of a mountebank likely to end in a fiasco?

_____

_____

5. What does a salvo of applause for the prima donna—even before she has sung a single note—tell us about the audience?

_____

_____

REVIEW 6: ANALOGIES

Write the *letter* of the word-pair that best expresses a relationship similar to that existing between the capitalized word-pair.

_____ 1. DESSERT : ANTIPASTO

    a. grave : prestissimo   *d.* play : denouement
    b. basso : soprano   *e.* finale : overture
    c. entrée : hors d'oeuvres

_____ 2. STAR : FILM

    a. composer : sonata   *d.* drama : protagonist
    b. soloist : concerto   *e.* actor : cast
    c. aria : vocalist

_____ 3. COGNOSCENTE : DILETTANTE

    a. uncle : aunt   *d.* ignoramus : connoisseur
    b. professional : amateur   *e.* artist : patron
    c. odor : aroma

_____ 4. INCOGNITO : IDENTITY

      a. novel : pen name   *d.* fiction : real
      b. masquerade : disguise   *e.* anonymous : known
      c. pseudonym : authorship

_____ 5. TORSO : STATUE

      a. trunk : tree   *d.* atom : nucleus
      b. dismember : intact   *e.* violinist : orchestra
      c. shard : vase

_____ 6. PATINA : AGE

      a. film : camera   *d.* mold : cheese
      b. hair : baldness   *e.* tarnish : silver
      c. blush : embarrassment

_____ 7. LENTO : TEMPO

      a. gondola : canal   *d.* piano : volume
      b. papers : portfolio   *e.* allegro : loudness
      c. Chianti : meal

_____ 8. ROTUNDA : EDIFICE

      a. gondola : canal   *d.* stucco : wall
      b. pizza : dough   *e.* portico : columns
      c. sole : fish

_____ 9. BUFFO : ZANY

      a. entrepreneur : risky   *d.* prevaricator : truthful
      b. mediator : partial   *e.* diplomat : tactless
      c. mentor : knowledgeable

_____ 10. PASTA : NOURISHMENT

      a. uncertainty : rumor   *d.* beverage : thirst
      b. instruction : enlightenment   *e.* ignorance : superstition
      c. shelter : domicile

CHAPTER *10*

Spanish Words in English

It should not surprise you that English has adopted many Spanish words. For centuries Spain governed many areas of this continent, including Florida and our vast Southwest. Despite the disintegration of the Spanish Empire, Spanish today is spoken in Mexico, virtually all of Central and South America (except Brazil), the Caribbean, the Philippines, and numerous other regions. As one of the world's principal languages, Spanish continues to exert its influence on English.

1. Words for Persons

WORD	MEANING
aficionado (*n.*) ə-ˌfis-ē-ə-ˈnäd-ō	devoted follower of some sport or art; fan; devotee
caballero (*n.*) ˌkab-ə-ˈler-ō	1. gentleman or gallant 2. horseman
Chicano (*n.*) chi-ˈkän-ō	American of Mexican descent
conquistador (*n.*) kȯŋ-ˈkēs-tə-ˌdȯ(r)	conqueror
desperado (*n.*) ˌdes-pə-ˈräd-ō	bold, reckless criminal
duenna (*n.*) d(y)ü-ˈen-ə	elderly woman chaperon of a young lady; governess

gaucho (*n.*)
'gaü-chō
Argentine cowboy of mixed Spanish and Indian descent

grandee (*n.*)
gran-'dē
1. nobleman of the highest rank
2. person of eminence

hidalgo (*n.*)
hid-'al-gō
nobleman of the second class (not so high as a *grandee*)

junta (*n.*)
'hùn-tə
1. council for legislation or administration
2. group of military officers controlling a government after a coup d'etat
3. junto

junto (*n.*)
'jənt-ō
group of persons joined for a common purpose; clique; group of plotters

Latino (*n.*)
la-'tēn-ō
Latin American; native of any western-hemisphere country where a Latin-derived language (Spanish, Portuguese, French) is spoken

Latino (*adj.*)
la-'tēn-ō
Latin-American; characteristic of Latinos

macho (*n.*)
'mä-,chō
man who exhibits **machismo** (strong sense of masculine pride); overly assertive, domineering, virile male

macho (*adj.*)
'mä-,chō
characterized by exaggerated masculinity; overly assertive, domineering, virile, etc.

matador (*n.*)
'mat-ə-,dȯ(r)
bullfighter assigned to kill the bull

mestizo (*n.*)
me-'stē-zō
man or person of mixed American Indian and European ancestry

peon (*n.*)
'pē-,än
1. common laborer
2. worker kept in service to repay a debt

picador (*n.*)
'pik-ə-,dȯ(r)
rider on horseback who irritates the bull with a lance

picaro (*n.*)
'pē-kä-,rō
adventurous rogue or vagabond

renegade (*n.*)
'ren-i-,gād
1. apostate (deserter) from a religion, party, etc.
2. turncoat; traitor

señor (*n.*)   Spanish or Spanish-speaking man; gentleman; Mr.; Sir
sān-'yȯ(r)

señora (*n.*)   married Spanish or Spanish-speaking woman; lady; Mrs.; Madam
sān-'yōr-ə

señorita (*n.*)   unmarried Spanish or Spanish-speaking woman; young lady; girl; Miss
ˌsān-yə-'rēt-ə

toreador (*n.*)   bullfighter, usually mounted
'tȯr-ē-ə-ˌdȯ(r)

torero (*n.*)   bullfighter on foot
tə-'rer-ō

vaquero (*n.*)   herdsman; cowboy
vä-'ker-ō

EXERCISE 10.1

In each blank, insert the most appropriate word from group 1.

1. The onetime Democrat who joined the Republican Party was regarded as a(n) _____ by some of his former Democratic colleagues.

2. In the Old West, it was common for a stagecoach to be robbed by a(n) _____ .

3. A(n) _____ is a nobleman of higher rank than a hidalgo.

4. Anyone who lacks an education or a skilled trade may earn little more than the wages of a(n)

    _____ .

5. The average fan attends two or three games a season, but the _____ goes to many more.

6. Hernando Cortes was the _____ who engineered the conquest of Mexico and destroyed the highly advanced civilization of the Aztecs.

7. The _____ was chaperoned by her duenna.

8. The ruler ordered the arrest of all members of the _____ involved in the plot against his regime.

9. The _____ who risks his life to kill the bull is idolized by his aficionados, but not by animal lovers.

10. Mexican Americans are proud of their fellow _____ Cesar Chavez for his contributions to the American labor movement.

11. For a long time, women were denied the right to vote because of a(n) _____ belief that they were weak and inferior.

12. The band played mainly _____ music, like cha-chas, mambos, and sambas.

2. Miscellaneous Words

adobe (*n.*)
ə-'dō-bē
1. brick of sun-dried clay or mud
2. structure made of such bricks

bolero (*n.*)
bə-'ler-ō
1. Spanish dance in ¾ time, with sharp turns, stamping, sudden pauses, and one arm arched over the head
2. music for this dance
3. loose waist-length jacket worn open at the front

bonanza (*n.*)
bə-'nan-zə
1. accidental discovery of a rich mass of ore in a mine
2. something yielding a rich return

bravado (*n.*)
brə-'väd-ō
1. boastful behavior
2. pretense of bravery

cabana (*n.*)
kə-'ban-(y)ə
beach shelter resembling a cabin

castanets (*n. pl.*)
ˌkas-tə-'nets
hand instruments clicked together to accompany music or dancing

fiesta (*n.*)
fē-'es-tə
saint's day celebrated with processions and dances; any festival or holiday

flotilla (*n.*)
flō-'til-ə
small fleet; fleet of small vessels

hacienda (*n.*)
ˌ(h)äs-ē-'en-də
1. large estate or ranch; plantation
2. main house in such an estate

incommunicado (*adv.*)
ˌin-kə-ˌmyü-nə-'käd-ō
deprived of communication with others, as a prisoner held *incommunicado*

mantilla (*n.*)
man-'tē-(y)ə
1. woman's light scarf or veil
2. cloak or cape

olio (*n.*)
'ō-lē-ˌō
mixture; hodgepodge; medley

patio (*n.*)
'pat-ē-ˌō
paved outdoor dining or lounging area adjacent to a house

peccadillo (*n.*)
ˌpek-ə-'dil-ō
slight offense

pimento (*n.*)
or **pimiento**
pə-'ment-ō
thick-fleshed pepper used for stuffing olives and as a source of paprika

poncho (*n.*)
'pän-chō
1. blanketlike cloak with a slit in the middle for the head, used mainly in Spanish America
2. similar garment made of waterproof material and used chiefly as a raincoat

pueblo (*n.*)   Indian village of southwestern U.S. built of adobe or stone
pü-'eb-lō

siesta (*n.*)   short rest or nap, especially at midday
sē-'es-tə

tortilla (*n.*)   thin, flat, round corn cake
tȯr-'tē-(y)ə

EXERCISE 10.2

In each blank, insert the most appropriate word from group 2.

1. Have you ever seen graceful Spanish dancers do the bolero to the accompaniment of clicking

   _____?

2. For every prospector who struck a(n) _____, there were countless others whose finds were disappointing.

3. Taking a bribe is not a(n) _____. It is a serious infraction of ethics.

4. You may be surprised to learn that a house made of _____ can last for more than a hundred years.

5. The ruffian's defiant challenge turned out to be mere _____, for when someone offered to fight him, he backed down.

6. Our Latino neighbors celebrate a(n) _____ by wearing brightly colored costumes and by singing and dancing.

7. By midafternoon, the whole _____ of fishing vessels had returned to port with the day's catch.

8. A gaucho uses his _____ both as a blanket and a cloak.

9. In regions where the afternoon heat is unbearably intense, one often takes a(n) _____ before resuming work.

10. _____s are made of cornmeal.

11. There were no plain olives on the shelves, only olives stuffed with _____.

12. Shall we stay indoors, or would you prefer to sit on the _____?

---

3. Additional Miscellaneous Words

---

      arroyo (*n.*)   watercourse; small, often dry, gully
      ə-'rȯi-ō

      barrio (*n.*)   Spanish-speaking neighborhood
      'bär-ē-ˌō

      bodega (*n.*)   small grocery store
      bō-'dä-gə

bronco (*n.*)
'bräŋ-kō
half-wild pony

burro (*n.*)
'bər-ō
small donkey used as a pack animal

canyon (*n.*)
'kan-yən
deep valley with high, steep slopes, often with a stream flowing through it, as the Colorado River in the Grand Canyon

indigo (*n.*)
'in-di-ˌgō
1. plant yielding a blue dye
2. deep violet-blue color

mañana (*adv.*)
mən-'yän-ə
tomorrow; in the indefinite future

mesa (*n.*)
'mā-sə
flat-topped, rocky hill with steeply sloping sides

mustang (*n.*)
'məs-ˌtaŋ
bronco

pampas (*n. pl.*)
'pam-pəz
vast, treeless, grassy plains, especially in Argentina

sierra (*n.*)
sē-'er-ə
ridge of mountains with an irregular, serrated (saw-toothed) outline

sombrero (*n.*)
səm-'brer-ō
broad-rimmed, high-crowned hat of felt or straw

taco (*n.*)
'täk-ō
fried, folded tortilla stuffed with chopped meat, cheese, shredded lettuce, etc.

EXERCISE 10.3

In each blank, insert the most appropriate word from group 3.

1. A Hopi village was secure against enemy attacks because it was built on top of a steeply sloping, flat-topped _____ .

2. The blue dye formerly obtained from _____ can now be made artificially.

3. Do today's work today; don't put it off to _____ .

4. In desert areas of Mexico and of our own Southwest, the _____ is used for carrying heavy loads.

5. The _____ in Argentina are famous for their cattle, corn, and wheat.

6. Most _____s are open late for the convenience of people who may need groceries.

7. At first, the newly arrived Latino immigrants lived in the _____ of a large American city.

8. Some of us like hamburgers for lunch; others prefer _____s.

Review Exercises

REVIEW 1: MEANINGS

In the space provided, write the *letter* of the word or expression in each group that has the *same meaning* as the italicized word.

_____ **1.** *duenna*   *a.* duet   *b.* junta   *c.* chaperon   *d.* twosome   *e.* fiancé

_____ **2.** *indigo*   *a.* hill   *b.* sugar   *c.* clay   *d.* native   *e.* violet-blue

_____ **3.** *peccadillo*   *a.* pepper   *b.* groundhog   *c.* alligator   *d.* petty officer   *e.* slight offense

_____ **4.** *olio*   *a.* grease   *b.* mixture   *c.* fuel   *d.* page   *e.* noise

_____ **5.** *macho*   *a.* reckless   *b.* domineering   *c.* excessive   *d.* roguish   *e.* eminent

_____ **6.** *aficionado*   *a.* zeal   *b.* connoisseur   *c.* fan   *d.* trifler   *e.* fictional hero

_____ **7.** *conquistadors*   *a.* discoverers   *b.* conquests   *c.* explorers   *d.* conquerors   *e.* bullfighters

_____ **8.** *renegade*   *a.* infidel   *b.* desperado   *c.* rogue   *d.* villain   *e.* turncoat

_____ **9.** *arroyo*   *a.* dart   *b.* gully   *c.* mesa   *d.* waterfall   *e.* bronco

_____ **10.** *siesta*   *a.* holiday   *b.* sojourn   *c.* fiesta   *d.* nap   *e.* sierra

REVIEW 2: SENTENCE COMPLETION

In each blank, enter the *letter* of the choice that best completes the sentence.

1. A section of Fifth Avenue will be closed to traffic tomorrow for a daylong _____.
   a. siesta   *b.* bonanza   *c.* bolero   *d.* fiesta   *e.* vendetta

2. To maintain anonymity, the leader of the junto employed a _____.
   a. lackey   *b.* grandee   *c.* pseudonym   *d.* poncho   *e.* peon

3. _____ are Argentine cowboys who inhabit the _____.
   a. Gauchos . . . pampas   *b.* Caballeros . . . mesas   *c.* Desperadoes . . . sierras
   d. Vaqueros . . . pueblos   *e.* Picaros . . . adobes

4. A famous painting by Murillo depicts a smiling señorita looking down from a window with her

   mantilla-clad _____ by her side.
   a. protégé   *b.* aficionado   *c.* duenna   *d.* grandee   *e.* fiancé

5. Benedict Arnold was the American _____ whose plot to surrender West Point resulted in a

   _____.
   a. patriot . . . vendetta   *b.* renegade . . . coup d'etat   *c.* grandee . . . junto
   d. turncoat . . . fiasco   *e.* apostate . . . détente

6. One cannot dine alfresco _____ .

   a. on the patio *b.* in the canyon *c.* on the mesa *d.* in the hacienda *e.* on the pampas

7. As a rule, a _____ does not offend anyone.

   a. macho *b.* desperado *c.* picaro *d.* caballero *e.* renegade

8. At the airport, we talked with some Chicanos from _____ .

   a. Spain *b.* Arizona *c.* Quebec *d.* Peru *e.* Portugal

9. The filling of a taco resembles but is not the same as the topping of a(n) _____ .

   a. croissant *b.* aperitif *c.* pizza *d.* tortilla *e.* bonbon

10. When you hear a(n) _____ , you are listening to Latino music.

   a. foxtrot *b.* waltz *c.* polka *d.* rumba *e.* lindy

REVIEW 3: BRAINTEASERS

Fill in the missing letters.

   1. A friend of ours has a **c a b** __ __ __ at the beach.

   2. Occasionally, a **m a t** __ __ __ __ is gored by an enraged bull.

   3. Several customers in the **b o d e** __ __ were waiting to be served.

   4. Her face was partly veiled by a(n) __ **a n t** __ __ __ __ .

   5. How many vessels were there in the __ **l o t** __ __ __ __ ?

   6. When the guests arrived, there was no one at the __ __ __ __ **e n d** __ .

   7. Reckless driving must not be treated as a(n) __ __ __ __ __ **d i l l** __ .

   8. There were fewer than a dozen conspirators in the __ **u n t o** .

   9. The blouse was pale yellow, and the slacks were deep __ __ **d i g** __ .

   10. Before dismounting, the __ __ **b a l l** __ __ __ removed his sombrero.

REVIEW 4: CONCISE WRITING

Express the thought of each sentence below in no more than four words.

1. Wear your loose jacket that comes up to the waist and is open at the front.

_____

2. This is an investment that will pay you very rich returns.

_____

3. I took a short nap in the middle of the day.

_____

4. Males who have an exaggerated sense of masculinity often behave in a boastful way.

_____

5. Hector was the bullfighter who was assigned to kill the bull.

_____

6. Elena respected the elderly lady who was acting as her chaperon.

_____

7. They were held without being given an opportunity to get in touch with anyone, or even to make a telephone call.

_____

8. The dancers used hand instruments that they clicked together to accompany the music.

_____

9. Some were wearing tall-crowned hats that had very wide brims.

_____

10. The group of military officers who engineered the coup d'etat and took over the government lacks experience.

_____

REVIEW 5: COMPOSITION

Answer in two or three sentences.

1. Suppose a security guard is discovered taking a siesta while on duty. Should the matter be treated as a peccadillo? Explain.

_____

_____

2. Why would it be wrongheaded for someone to exhibit his machismo when confronted by armed desperados?

_____

_____

3. Why is a fiesta usually a bonanza for local merchants? Explain.

_____

_____

4. Explain why a poncho is extremely valuable not only to a gaucho on the pampas, but to campers and hikers everywhere.

_____

_____

5. Why might the members of a junto hesitate to admit a renegade from a rival party?

_____

_____

REVIEW 6: ANALOGIES

Write the _letter_ of the word pair that best expresses a relationship similar to that existing between the capitalized word-pair.

_____ **1.** MATADOR : SWORD

      _a._ gaucho : poncho   _d._ desperado : loot
      _b._ picador : lance   _e._ toreador : bull
      _c._ torero : horse

_____ **2.** BONANZA : MINER

      _a._ legacy : heir   _d._ jackpot : gambler
      _b._ crop : farmer   _e._ bull's-eye : sharpshooter
      _c._ diploma : student

_____ **3.** ADOBE : PUEBLO

      _a._ settlement : Indian   _d._ seaport : flotilla
      _b._ cabana : beach   _e._ concrete : turnpike
      _c._ terra-cotta : clay

_____ **4.** OLIO : INGREDIENT

      _a._ concerto : instrument   _d._ entrée : dessert
      _b._ medley : tune   _e._ aria : opera
      _c._ potpourri : confusion

_____ **5.** SIERRA : CANYON

      _a._ zenith : nadir   _d._ grandee : hidalgo
      _b._ arroyo : mesa   _e._ monarch : retinue
      _c._ indigo : red

_____ **6.** MACHO : ASSERTIVE

      _a._ cognoscente : uninformed   _d._ renegade : loyal
      _b._ martinet : inflexible   _e._ peon : prosperous
      _c._ dipsomaniac : abstemious

_____ **7.** PONCHO : RAIN

      _a._ sombrero : shade   _d._ taco : nourishment
      _b._ mentor : guidance   _e._ parasol : sun
      _c._ antitoxin : immunity

CHAPTER *11*

Expanding Vocabulary Through Derivatives

Suppose you have just learned a new word—*ostentatious*, meaning "showy; done to impress others." If you know how to form derivatives, you have in reality learned not one new word, but several: you have learned *ostentatious* and *unostentatious*; *ostentatiously* and *unostenta-tiously*; *ostentatiousness* and *unostentatiousness*, etc.

This chapter will help you to get the most out of each new word learned, by teaching you how to form and spell derivatives.

What is a derivative?

A derivative is a word formed by adding a prefix, or a suffix, or both a prefix and a suffix, to a word or root.

PREFIX		WORD		DERIVATIVE
re	+	apply	=	rèapply
(again)				*(apply again)*

PREFIX		ROOT		DERIVATIVE
e	+	ject	=	eject
(out)		*(throw)*		*(throw out)*

WORD		SUFFIX		DERIVATIVE
ostentatious	+	ly	=	ostentatiously
(showy)		*(manner)*		*(in a showy manner)*

ROOT		SUFFIX		DERIVATIVE
ten	+	able	=	tenable
(held)		*(capable of being)*		*(capable of being held or defended)*

PREFIX		WORD		SUFFIX		DERIVATIVE
un	+	ostentatious	+	ly	=	unostentatiously
(not)						*(not in a showy manner)*

PREFIX		ROOT		SUFFIX		DERIVATIVE
un	+	ten	+	able	=	untenable
						(not capable of being held or defended)

See how many words you can form using only the prefixes, roots, and suffixes below. For example: ab + rupt = abrupt; cred + ible = credible; dis + tort + ion = distortion; etc.

PREFIXES	ROOTS	SUFFIXES
ab	cred, credit	able
ad	flex, flect	ible
con	fract	ion
de	monit	ive
dis	rupt	or, er
e, ex	strict	ory
in	ten, tent	ure
inter	tort	
re	vict	

A score of 75 words or more is excellent, 65–74 very good, 55–64 good, and 45–54 fair.

Terms used in this chapter

A derivative may be either a noun, an adjective, a verb, or an adverb.

A **noun** is a word naming a person, place, thing, or quality. In the following sentences, all the italicized words are nouns:

1. The dejected *motorist* very slowly drove his badly damaged *car* to the nearest *garage*.
2. *Health* is *wealth*.

An **adjective** is a word that modifies (describes) a noun or pronoun. The following words in sentence 1 above are adjectives: *dejected, his, damaged, nearest*.

A **verb** is a word that expresses action or a state of being. The verbs in the sentences above are *drove* (sentence 1) and *is* (sentence 2).

An **adverb** is a word that modifies a verb, an adjective, or another adverb. In sentence 1 above, *slowly* is an adverb because it modifies the verb "drove"; *badly* is an adverb because it modifies the adjective "damaged"; and *very* is an adverb because it modifies the adverb "slowly."

Vowels are the letters *a, e, i, o,* and *u*.

Consonants are all the other letters of the alphabet.

Forming Derivatives by Attaching Prefixes and Suffixes

1. Attaching Prefixes

Rule: Do not omit or add a letter when attaching a prefix to a word. Keep *all* the letters of the prefix and *all* the letters of the word.

PREFIX		WORD		DERIVATIVE
dis	+	similar	=	dissimilar
dis	+	organized	=	disorganized
un	+	natural	=	unnatural
un	+	acceptable	=	unacceptable
inter	+	related	=	interrelated
inter	+	action	=	interaction

EXERCISE 11.1

In column III, write the required derivatives. Be sure to spell them correctly.

I. PREFIX		II. WORD		III. DERIVATIVE
1. hypo	+	active	=	_____
2. in	+	opportune	=	_____
3. dis	+	service	=	_____
4. extra	+	ordinary	=	_____
5. dys	+	function	=	_____
6. re	+	entry	=	_____
7. mis	+	shaped	=	_____
8. pre	+	monition	=	_____
9. semi	+	annually	=	_____
10. de	+	emphasis	=	_____
11. mis	+	understood	=	_____
12. re	+	election	=	_____
13. dis	+	embark	=	_____
14. pre	+	eminent	=	_____
15. mis	+	statement	=	_____

16. sub   + basement   = _____

17. retro + actively   = _____

18. sub   + ordinate   = _____

19. un   + neighborly   = _____

20. pre   + arrange   = _____

21. in   + numerable   = _____

22. re   + unify   = _____

23. inter + relationship = _____

24. un   + equal   = _____

25. mis   + step   = _____

---

2. Attaching the Prefix UN or IN

You can give a negative meaning to a word by attaching the prefix UN or IN. Examples:

PREFIX		WORD		DERIVATIVE
un (not)	+	remunerative (gainful)	=	unremunerative (not gainful)
in (not)	+	tangible (capable of being touched)	=	intangible (not capable of being touched)

If you are not sure whether a word takes UN or IN, consult the dictionary.

Learn the different forms of IN:

1. Before *l*, IN changes to IL, as in *illegal*, *illiterate*, etc.
2. Before *b*, *m*, or *p*, IN changes to IM, as in *imbalance*, *immature*, *improper*, etc.
3. Before *r*, IN changes to IR, as in *irrational*, *irresistible*, etc.

Three less frequent negative prefixes are DIS, as in *disagreeable*; NON as in *nonstandard*; and A, as in *atypical*.

EXERCISE 11.2

Form the negative of the word in column II by writing *in*, *il*, *im*, or *ir* in column I. Then complete the new word in column III. (The first line has been done for you as an example.)

I. NEGATIVE PREFIX		II. WORD		III. NEGATIVE WORD
1. ___in___	+	considerate	=	inconsiderate
2. _____	+	moral	=	_____
3. _____	+	legibly	=	_____
4. _____	+	redeemable	=	_____

5. _____	+	decisive	=	_____
6. _____	+	patience	=	_____
7. _____	+	regularity	=	_____
8. _____	+	mobility	=	_____
9. _____	+	convenience	=	_____
10. _____	+	practical	=	_____
11. _____	+	eligible	=	_____
12. _____	+	responsibly	=	_____
13. _____	+	mortal	=	_____
14. _____	+	possible	=	_____
15. _____	+	accuracy	=	_____
16. _____	+	logical	=	_____
17. _____	+	revocable	=	_____
18. _____	+	perfection	=	_____
19. _____	+	completely	=	_____
20. _____	+	limitable	=	_____

3. Attaching Suffixes

Rule: Do not omit or add a letter when attaching a suffix to a word—unless the word ends in *y* or silent *e*. Keep *all* the letters of the word and *all* the letters of the suffix.

WORD		SUFFIX		DERIVATIVE
accidental	+	ly	=	accidentally
drunken	+	ness	=	drunkenness
banjo	+	ist	=	banjoist
ski	+	ing	=	skiing

EXERCISE 11.3

In column III, write the required derivatives. Be sure to spell them correctly.

I. WORD		II. SUFFIX		III. DERIVATIVE
1. soul	+	less	=	_____
2. ego	+	ism	=	_____
3. evil	+	ly	=	_____

4. solo	+	ist	=	_____
5. echo	+	ing	=	_____
6. barren	+	ness	=	_____
7. convivial	+	ly	=	_____
8. tail	+	less	=	_____
9. Hindu	+	ism	=	_____
10. hero	+	ic	=	_____

---

4. Attaching Suffixes to Words Ending in Y

Rule 1: If a consonant precedes the *y*, change the *y* to *i* before adding a suffix.

WORD		SUFFIX		DERIVATIVE
hurry	+	ed	=	hurried
spicy	+	est	=	spiciest
history	+	ic	=	historic
heavy	+	ness	=	heaviness
greedy	+	ly	=	greedily

Exception 1: Except before *ing*.

hurry	+	ing	=	hurrying
falsify	+	ing	=	falsifying

Exception 2: Drop the *y* before *ic*: historic, geographic, ironic, etc.

Exception 3: Learn these special exceptions: dryly, dryness, shyly, shyness, babyish, jellylike.

Rule 2: If a vowel precedes the *y*, do *not* change the *y* before adding a suffix.

betray	+	al	=	betrayal
convey	+	ed	=	conveyed
joy	+	ful	=	joyful

Exceptions: daily, laid, paid, said.

EXERCISE 11.4

In column III, write the required derivatives. Be sure to spell them correctly.

I. WORD		II. SUFFIX		III. DERIVATIVE
1. pacify	+	ing	=	_____
2. musty	+	ness	=	_____
3. arbitrary	+	ly	=	_____
4. controversy	+	al	=	_____

5. pray	+	ed	=	_____
6. calumny	+	ous	=	_____
7. accompany	+	ment	=	_____
8. vilify	+	ed	=	_____
9. earthy	+	est	=	_____
10. pay	+	less	=	_____
11. worry	+	some	=	_____
12. flay	+	ed	=	_____
13. colloquy	+	al	=	_____
14. vivify	+	ing	=	_____
15. pudgy	+	est	=	_____
16. cursory	+	ly	=	_____
17. paltry	+	ness	=	_____
18. coy	+	ly	=	_____
19. burly	+	er	=	_____
20. ignominy	+	ous	=	_____
21. bloody	+	ly	=	_____
22. mercy	+	less	=	_____
23. refractory	+	ly	=	_____
24. sully	+	ing	=	_____
25. photography	+	ic	=	_____

EXERCISE 11.5

Four derivatives have been omitted from each line. Insert the missing words in the spaces provided. When completed, each line should correspond to the first.

I. ADJECTIVE	II. ADJECTIVE ENDING IN *ER*	III. ADJECTIVE ENDING IN *EST*	IV. ADVERB	V. NOUN
1. quiet	quieter	quietest	quietly	quietness
2. _____	quicker	_____	_____	_____
3. _____	_____	happiest	_____	_____
4. _____	_____	_____	hastily	_____
5. _____	_____	_____	_____	dizziness
6. foxy	_____	_____	_____	_____

7. _____ craftier   _____   _____   _____

8. _____ _____ prettiest   _____   _____

9. _____ _____ _____ readily   _____

10. _____ _____ _____ _____ unsteadiness

---

5. Attaching Suffixes to Words Ending in Silent E

Rule 1: Drop the silent *e* before a suffix starting with a vowel.

WORD		SUFFIX		DERIVATIVE
desire	+	able	=	desirable
use	+	age	=	usage
produce	+	er	=	producer

Exception 1: Words ending in *ce* or *ge* keep the final *e* before a suffix beginning with *a* or *o*.

notice	+	able	=	noticeable
advantage	+	ous	=	advantageous

Exception 2: Learn the following additional exceptions: acreage, mileage, singeing, canoeing, hoeing, shoeing.

Rule 2: Keep the final *e* before a suffix starting with a consonant.

excite	+	ment	=	excitement
care	+	ful	=	careful
fierce	+	ly	=	fiercely
complete	+	ness	=	completeness

Exceptions: acknowledgment, judgment, argument, awful, duly, truly, wholly, ninth.

EXERCISE 11.6

In column III, write the required derivatives. Be sure to spell them correctly.

I. WORD		II. SUFFIX		III. DERIVATIVE
1. prosecute	+	or	=	_____
2. eulogize	+	ing	=	_____
3. induce	+	ment	=	_____
4. mature	+	ity	=	_____
5. blithe	+	ly	=	_____
6. contaminate	+	ion	=	_____
7. revive	+	al	=	_____

8. judge   +   ment   = _____

9. avarice   +   ious   = _____

10. remorse   +   ful   = _____

11. convalesce   +   ent   = _____

12. rationalize   +   ed   = _____

13. cursive   +   ly   = _____

14. versatile   +   ity   = _____

15. consecutive   +   ly   = _____

16. expedite   +   er   = _____

17. dispute   +   able   = _____

18. undulate   +   ion   = _____

19. courage   +   ous   = _____

20. nine   +   ty   = _____

21. belittle   +   ing   = _____

22. acre   +   age   = _____

23. abridge   +   ment   = _____

24. service   +   able   = _____

25. naive   +   ly   = _____

6. Attaching the Suffix LY

You can change an adjective into an adverb by adding the suffix LY.

ADJECTIVE		SUFFIX		ADVERB
brave	+	ly	=	bravely
calm	+	ly	=	calmly

Exception: If an adjective ends in *ic,* add *al* before attaching the suffix LY.

heroic   + al + ly =   heroically
specific   + al + ly =   specifically

However, do *not* add *al* to the adjective *public.*

public + ly = publicly

Note: Most adjectives ending in *ic* have an alternate form ending in *ical.* Examples: *philosophic* and *philosophical; historic* and *historical,* etc.

EXERCISE 11.7

Change the following adjectives to adverbs:

	ADJECTIVE	ADVERB
1.	fraternal	
2.	diabolic	
3.	solemn	
4.	scientific	
5.	fallacious	
6.	nostalgic	
7.	grave	
8.	public	
9.	partial	
10.	hermetic	

EXERCISE 11.8

For each noun in column I, write an adjective ending in *ic* in column II, and an adverb in column III. (As an example, the first question has been completed.)

I. NOUN	II. ADJECTIVE	III. ADVERB
1. biology	biologic	biologically
2. geology		
3. hero		
4. sociology		
5. idealist		
6. patriot		
7. philanthropy		
8. geometry		
9. economy		
10. biography		
11. egoist		
12. psychology		
13. meteorology		
14. microbiology		

15. socialist   _____   _____

16. technology   _____   _____

17. realist   _____   _____

18. despot   _____   _____

19. autobiography   _____   _____

20. physiology   _____   _____

---

7. Doubling Final Consonants When Attaching Suffixes

Rule 1: Double a final consonant in a one-syllable word before a suffix beginning with a vowel.

WORD		SUFFIXES		DERIVATIVES
run	+	ing, er	=	running, runner
stop	+	ed, age	=	stopped, stoppage
wet	+	er, est	=	wetter, wettest

Exception 1: If the final consonant is preceded by two vowels, no doubling occurs.

sail	+	ed, ing	=	sailed, sailing
kneel	+	ed, ing	=	kneeled, kneeling

Exception 2: If the final consonant is preceded by another consonant, no doubling occurs.

halt	+	ed, ing	=	halted, halting
ask	+	ed, ing	=	asked, asking

Rule 2: Double a final consonant in an *accented* syllable at the end of a word of two or more syllables before a suffix beginning with a vowel.

reFER'	+	ed, ing, al	=	referred, referring, referral
transMIT'	+	ed, ing, er	=	transmitted, transmitting, transmitter
readMIT'	+	ed, ing, ance	=	readmitted, readmitting, readmittance

Exception 1: The rule does not apply when the final consonant is in an *unaccented* syllable.

CRED'it	+	ed, ing, or	=	credited, crediting, creditor
LIM'it	+	ed, ing	=	limited, limiting
OF'fer	+	ed, ing, er	=	offered, offering, offerer

Exception 2: The rule does not apply when the final consonant is preceded by two vowels.

contain	+	ed, ing, er	=	contained, containing, container
recoil	+	ed, ing	=	recoiled, recoiling
appeal	+	ed, ing	=	appealed, appealing

Exception 3: The rule does not apply when the final consonant is preceded by another consonant.

condemn	+	ed, ing, able	=	condemned, condemning, condemnable
conduct	+	ed, ing, or	=	conducted, conducting, conductor

Exception 4: The rule does not apply if the accent shifts back to the first syllable.

reFER′	+	ence	=	REF′erence
deFER′	+	ence	=	DEF′erence
inFER′	+	ence	=	IN′ference

However, exCEL′ + ence, ent = EX′cellence, EX′cellent.

EXERCISE 11.9

In column III, write the required derivatives. Be sure to spell them correctly.

	I. WORD		II. SUFFIX		III. DERIVATIVE
1.	dispel	+	ing	=	_____
2.	occur	+	ence	=	_____
3.	accredit	+	ed	=	_____
4.	acquit	+	al	=	_____
5.	differ	+	ed	=	_____
6.	beget	+	ing	=	_____
7.	slip	+	ed	=	_____
8.	hot	+	est	=	_____
9.	suffer	+	ing	=	_____
10.	regret	+	able	=	_____
11.	confer	+	ence	=	_____
12.	excel	+	ing	=	_____
13.	gallop	+	ing	=	_____
14.	stoop	+	ing	=	_____
15.	defer	+	al	=	_____
16.	excel	+	ent	=	_____
17.	propel	+	er	=	_____
18.	inject	+	ed	=	_____
19.	commit	+	ee	=	_____
20.	libel	+	ous	=	_____
21.	fat	+	er	=	_____
22.	equip	+	ing	=	_____
23.	permit	+	ed	=	_____
24.	repel	+	ent	=	_____

EXERCISE 11.10

For each word at the left, complete the four derivatives indicated.

1. concur	_____ing	_____ed	_____ent	_____ence
2. defer	_____ing	_____ed	_____able	_____ence
3. retain	_____ing	_____ed	_____able	_____er
4. rebel	_____ing	_____ed	_____ious	_____ion
5. prefer	_____ing	_____ed	_____able	_____ence
6. ship	_____ing	_____ed	_____er	_____ment
7. differ	_____ing	_____ed	_____ent	_____ence
8. control	_____ing	_____ed	_____able	_____er
9. commit	_____ing	_____ed	_____ee	_____ment
10. excel	_____ing	_____ed	_____ent	_____ence

---

8. Troublesome Suffixes

There are no easy rules to tell you when to use *able* or *ible*, *er* or *or*, and *ant* or *ent*. Words ending in such troublesome suffixes have to be studied individually. Develop the habit of consulting the dictionary when in doubt about which suffix is right.

1. Adding *able* or *ible*. Study the following adjectives:

ABLE	IBLE
demonstrable	credible
impregnable	fallible
indisputable	flexible
memorable	illegible
navigable	incontrovertible
returnable	invincible
serviceable	plausible
tenable	reprehensible
unmanageable	resistible

Note: Adjectives ending in *able* become nouns ending in *ability*. Adjectives ending in *ible* become nouns ending in *ibility*.

ADJECTIVE	NOUN	ADJECTIVE	NOUN
impregnable	impregnability	flexible	flexibility
venerable	venerability	invincible	invincibility

2. Adding *er* or *or*. Study the following nouns:

ER	OR
consumer	aggressor
defender	censor
foreigner	creditor
mariner	debtor
observer	governor
philosopher	originator
reporter	possessor
subscriber	progenitor
sympathizer	speculator

Note: Verbs ending in *ate* usually become nouns ending in *or*, rather than *er*.

VERB	NOUN
demonstrate	demonstrator
liberate	liberator

Exception: debate, debater.

3. Adding *ant* or *ent*. Study the following adjectives:

ANT	ENT
brilliant	complacent
buoyant	decent
flamboyant	eloquent
flippant	eminent
fragrant	iridescent
malignant	obsolescent
nonchalant	pertinent
poignant	potent
relevant	recurrent
vacant	repellent

Note: Adjectives ending in *ant* become nouns ending in *ance* or *ancy*. Adjectives ending in *ent* become nouns ending in *ence* or *ency*.

ADJECTIVE	NOUN	ADJECTIVE	NOUN
nonchalant	nonchalance	eloquent	eloquence
vacant	vacancy	decent	decency
brilliant	brilliance, brilliancy	complacent	complacence, complacency

EXERCISE 11.11

Fill in the missing letter.

1. IRRESIST __ BLE   3. EXCELL __ NCE

2. MALIGN __ NCY   4. DEBT __ R

5. OMNIPOT __ NT

6. INCRED __ BLE

7. CONSUM __ R

8. LEG __ BILITY

9. UNNAVIG __ BLE

10. SPECULAT __ R

11. FLEX __ BILITY

12. VAC __ NCY

13. INFLEX __ BLE

14. OBSOLESC __ NCE

15. SERVICE __ BILITY

16. SUBSCRIB __ R

17. IMPERTIN __ NCE

18. DISPUT __ BLE

19. POIGN __ NCY

20. IRRELEV __ NT

EXERCISE 11.12

For each noun, write the corresponding adjective. (The first adjective has been filled in as an example.)

NOUN	ADJECTIVE
1. infrequency	infrequent
2. resistance	
3. visibility	
4. urgency	
5. dependability	
6. defiance	
7. negligence	
8. constancy	
9. unpredictability	
10. stringency	
11. self-reliance	
12. comprehensibility	
13. convalescence	
14. contingency	
15. diffidence	
16. preeminence	
17. hesitancy	
18. intangibility	
19. incompetence	
20. adolescence	

Review Exercises

REVIEW 1

In the following exercise, two derivatives have been omitted from each line. Insert the missing words in the spaces provided. The first line has been completed as a sample.

I. VERB	II. NOUN ENDING IN *ER* OR *OR*	III. NOUN ENDING IN *ION*
1. create	creator	creation
2. _____	_____	production
3. _____	elector	_____
4. possess	_____	_____
5. _____	_____	subscription
6. _____	promoter	_____
7. indicate	_____	_____
8. _____	_____	contribution
9. _____	liberator	_____
10. violate	_____	_____

REVIEW 2

In the following exercise, two derivatives have been omitted from each line. Insert the missing words in the spaces provided. The first line has been completed as a sample.

I. NOUN	II. ADJECTIVE	III. ADVERB
1. apathy	apathetic	apathetically
2. _____	vivid	_____
3. _____	_____	monotonously
4. fraternity	_____	_____
5. _____	hypersensitive	_____
6. _____	_____	lethargically
7. maladroitness	_____	_____
8. _____	weary	_____
9. _____	_____	controversially

10. euphemism   _____   _____

11. _____   pathetic   _____

12. _____   _____   eloquently

13. naiveté   _____   _____

14. _____   peripheral   _____

15. _____   _____   sheepishly

16. quarrelsomeness   _____   _____

17. _____   hypothetical   _____

18. _____   _____   avariciously

19. homogeneity   _____   _____

20. _____   heterogeneous   _____

REVIEW 3

In the following exercise, five derivatives have been omitted from each set. Insert the missing derivatives in the spaces provided. The first set has been completed as a sample.

ADJECTIVE AND OPPOSITE	ADVERB AND OPPOSITE	NOUN AND OPPOSITE
1. moral	morally	morality
immoral	immorally	immorality
2. _____	_____	_____
intemperate	_____	_____
3. _____	comprehensibly	_____
_____	_____	_____
4. _____	_____	_____
_____	dissimilarly	_____
5. _____	_____	fallibility
_____	_____	_____
6. _____	_____	_____
_____	_____	unostentatiousness
7. flexible	_____	_____
_____	_____	_____

8. _____   _____   _____

abnormal   _____   _____

9. _____   plausibly   _____

_____   _____   _____

10. _____   _____   _____

_____   incontrovertibly   _____

11. _____   _____   pertinence

_____   _____   _____

12. _____   _____   _____

_____   _____   untenability

13. rational   _____   _____

_____   _____   _____

14. _____   _____   _____

incredible   _____   _____

15. _____   mortally   _____

_____   _____   _____

16. _____   _____   _____

_____   unconventionally   _____

17. _____   _____   retentiveness

_____   _____   _____

18. _____   _____   _____

_____   _____   irrelevance

CHAPTER *12*

Sample Vocabulary Questions in Pre-College Tests

Vocabulary questions play a prominent and decisive role in pre-college tests. You will probably take one or more of these tests in high school if you expect to apply for college admission or college scholarship awards. Naturally, you will want to familiarize yourself with the types of vocabulary questions you are likely to encounter on such tests. For your guidance, therefore, this chapter will present officially released sample vocabulary questions for two widely administered pre-college examinations:

1. The Preliminary Scholastic Aptitude Test/ National Merit Scholarship Qualifying Test (PSAT/NMSQT)
2. The Scholastic Aptitude Test (SAT)

---

1. The PSAT/NMSQT

The sample vocabulary questions and explanations that follow are from the 1991 PSAT/ NMSQT *Student Bulletin*, published by the College Entrance Examination Board and the Educational Testing Service, which have graciously granted permission to reprint this material.

Sample Questions with Explanations

Antonyms (Opposites)

Antonym questions measure the extent and depth of your vocabulary. The words tested are ones that you are likely to find in your reading both in and out of school, although some may not be the kind you use in everyday speech.

These are the directions you will see on the test:

> **Each question below consists of a word in capital letters, followed by five lettered words or phrases. Choose the word or phrase that is most nearly <u>opposite</u> in meaning to the word in capital letters. Since some of the questions require you to distinguish fine shades of meaning, consider all the choices before deciding which is best.**
>
> **EXAMPLE:**
>
> GOOD: (A) sour (B) bad (C) red (D) hot (E) ugly

This sample question is very easy, but thinking about it may help you with other antonym questions. Remember that you are looking for the *best* answer given. Begin by eliminating **hot**

SAT questions selected from The 1991 PSAT/NMSQT Student Bulletin (1991) and Taking the SAT, 1991–92, (1991) College Entrance Examinations Board. Reprinted by permission of Educational Testing Service, the copyright owner of the test questions.

Permission to reprint the above material does not constitute review or endorsement by Educational Testing Service or the College Board of this publication as a whole or of any other questions or testing information it may contain.

and **red** because they don't have much to do with GOOD.

If you think that **sour** is the opposite of GOOD, you could ask yourself, ''What is the opposite of **sour**?'' You can eliminate **sour** because the opposite of **sour** is ''sweet,'' not GOOD. And you can eliminate **ugly** because the opposite of **ugly** is ''handsome,'' or ''pretty,'' or ''beautiful.''

Of course, the correct answer is (B). GOOD and **bad** are precise opposites. You probably did not have to go through this process to answer such an easy question, but you may want to try it when you are working on harder antonym questions.

---

1. RETRIEVE: (A) lose (B) believe (C) ask (D) strip (E) move

Some questions in the verbal section of the PSAT/NMSQT require that you have only a general understanding of the words being tested. To RETRIEVE an object means to get it back again. You had an object, a ball or book, in your possession once but misplaced it or lost it. Then, you **retrieved** it. The opposite meaning of RETRIEVE is (A) **lose**. (B) **believe** means to have faith in something, not to regain an object. (C), (D), and (E) have obvious definitions, none of which is the opposite of RETRIEVE.

---

2. FRIVOLITY: (A) notoriety
(B) dissonance (C) seriousness
(D) firm denial (E) mild manner

Sometimes it may help you to think of other forms of a word when you are looking for its opposite. In this case, **frivolous** is a more common form of the word FRIVOLITY. You probably know that **frivolous** means silly or lacking in seriousness. Be sure to look at all of the choices; don't take the first one that you think is right. In this question, both (C) and (E) may seem correct to you at first. However, a better opposite for (E) **mild manner** would be excitability or tempestuousness. The closest opposite for FRIVOLITY is solemn manner, or **seriousness**; therefore, choice (C) is the correct answer.

HINTS FOR ANTONYMS

1. Since you may have to distinguish between shades of meaning, be sure you read all the choices before you decide which is correct.

2. Choose the word that is *most nearly opposite* the word in CAPITAL letters.

3. Words often have several meanings, but only one meaning of a word has to be the ''opposite'' for that word to be the correct choice.

4. Most people can work faster on antonyms than on any other part of the test. However, don't go so fast that you make careless errors.

Sentence Completions

Sentence completion questions measure your ability to choose a word or words that fit logically with the other parts of a sentence. The sentences, taken from published material, cover a wide variety of topics of the sort you are likely to have encountered in school or in your general reading. Your understanding of the sentences will not depend on specialized knowledge in science, literature, social studies, or any other field.

These are the directions you will see on the test:

Each sentence below has one or two blanks, each blank indicating that something has been omitted. Beneath the sentence are five lettered words or sets of words. Choose the word or set of words that, when inserted in the sentence, best fits the meaning of the sentence as a whole.

EXAMPLE:

Although its publicity has been ---, the film itself is intelligent, well-acted, handsomely produced, and altogether ---.

(A) tasteless . . respectable
(B) extensive . . moderate
(C) sophisticated . . amateur
(D) risqué . . crude
(E) perfect . . spectacular

In many sentences with two blanks, one blank will be easier to figure out than the other. The blank in the first part of this sentence could be filled in with almost any description. The publicity could be **tasteless, extensive,** or any of the other choices given.

To get started on this question you should look at the second part of the sentence. The second blank is the last word of a list, so the word that fills the blank should fit with the other words in the list. **Intelligent, well-acted,** and **handsomely produced** are all complimentary, so the word that goes into the blank should also be complimentary.

Of the choices for the second word, **crude** and **amateur** are certainly not compliments, so you can eliminate (C) and (D). **Moderate** might be a compliment in some situations, but it does not work as well as **respectable** or **spectacular.** To decide which of these two is correct, you have to go back to the first part of the sentence.

Look for signals. The word **Although** is a signal that the first part of the sentence will contrast with the second part. Which word in the first part will make you surprised to read the second part? If the publicity were **perfect,** it wouldn't be much of a surprise to find out that the film itself was **spectactular. Tasteless** publicity, on the other hand, contrasts strongly with a **respectable** film and therefore fits the logic of the sentence.

The whole sentence works best with choice (A).

3. **With each retelling, the description the witness gave of the accident drifted further from reality, and the whole episode appeared more and more ---.**

   (A) persuasive (B) venerable
   (C) sarcastic (D) fictitious (E) infallible

Look for a *key word* or *phrase.* The word or phrase that best fills the blank is determined logically by the other parts of the sentence. "Drifted further from reality" indicates that the missing word should mean unreal. If the description "drifted further from reality," then the episode did not become more **persuasive** (A), or **venerable** (B), which means worthy of

respect. **Infallible** (E) means incapable of error. Choice (C) **sarcastic** means an unpleasant or mocking tone. None of these choices fits the blank as well as (D) **fictitious,** which means not real.

4. **Edgar wrote the conclusion to the novel with such --- that we began to suspect he was not an artist but a remarkable --- processing plots and characters with mechanical efficiency.**

   (A) emotion . . computer
   (B) awkwardness . . prodigy (C) hesitation . . wizard (D) dispatch . . automaton (E) difficulty . . plagiarist

Look for parts of the sentence that influence what words logically fill the blanks. The phrase "processing plots and characters with mechanical efficiency" controls the blanks. Find a word for the second blank that describes mechanical efficiency. The second words in (A) **computer** and (D) **automaton** describe machine-like behavior. (The second words in (B), (C), and (E) are inappropriate beause they do *not* describe machine-like behavior.) Now try both terms from choice (A). "Edgar wrote with such **emotion** that he seemed like a **remarkable computer** ..." **Emotion** and mechanical efficiency do not work together. Now try (D). "Edgar wrote with such **dispatch** that he seemed like a **remarkable automaton** ..." Since **dispatch** means with speed or mechanical efficiency, (D) is correct. Both **dispatch** and **automaton** support the idea of mechanical efficiency.

HINTS FOR SENTENCE COMPLETIONS

1. When you have to fill in two words, make sure *both* make sense in the sentence. Wrong answer choices often include one correct and one incorrect word.

2. Don't try to figure out both words at once. Narrow down the choices for one word, then use the other word to help you make your final decision.

3. Before you mark your answer, read the complete sentence with your choice filled in to be sure it makes sense.

Analogies

Analogy questions test your ability to see a relationship in a pair of words, to understand the ideas expressed in the relationship, and to recognize a similar relationship in another pair of words.

These are the directions you will see on the test:

> **Each question below consists of a related pair of words or phrases, followed by five lettered pairs of words or phrases. Select the lettered pair that best expresses a relationship similar to that expressed in the original pair.**
>
> **EXAMPLE:**
>
> YAWN : BOREDOM ::   (A) dream : sleep
> (B) anger : madness   (C) smile : amusement
> (D) face : expression
> (E) impatience : rebellion

The first step in answering an analogy question is to figure out the exact relationship between the words in CAPITAL letters. Many people find that it helps to *make up a short sentence that states the relationship*: "A YAWN is a physical sign or facial expression of BOREDOM." The second step is to look for the pair of words among the answer choices that fits your sentence best.

Choice (A), **dream : sleep**, is not correct. A **dream** is something you do when you **sleep**, but is not a "sign" or "expression" of **sleep** as closed eyes or a snore might be. In (B), **anger** means strong displeasure and **madness** refers to rage or insanity, but neither word is a "sign" or "expression" of the other. Choice (C), **smile : amusement**, fits the sentence since "a **smile** is a physical sign and a facial expression of **amusement**." Before you mark your answer, however, check the other choices. The words in (D) do not have the same relationship as YAWN and BOREDOM. You show an **expression** on your **face**, but your **face** is not a "sign" of an **expression**. In choice (E), **impatience** may lead to **rebellion** or be characteristic of a rebellious person, but **impatience** is not a "sign" or "expression" of **rebellion**. The choice that *best* expresses a relationship similar to the one between YAWN and BOREDOM is (C).

5. SQUABBLE : FIGHT ::
   (A) enlightenment : novel
   (B) glimmer : blaze   (C) drink : tavern
   (D) ship : port   (E) quiet : sound

First, make up a sentence stating the relationship between the pair of words in capital letters. A SQUABBLE is a small or not very serious FIGHT. Now, look for a pair of words among the choices that has the same or nearly the same relationship. **Enlightenment** may come from a **novel**, but it is not a kind of novel. **Glimmer** is a faint, or small, **blaze**, but check the other choices to see if another pair might fit even more closely than (B). Is **drink** a small **tavern**? No. Is **ship** a small **port**? No. Is **quiet** a small **sound**? No. **Quiet** is the absence of **sound**. A SQUABBLE is a small or not very serious FIGHT just as a **glimmer** is a small or not very serious **blaze**. (B) is the correct answer.

6. LIAR : MENDACIOUS ::   (A) culprit : naive
   (B) heretic : bogus   (C) dupe : illusory
   (D) seer : prophetic
   (E) resident : nomadic

A pair of words may have more than one relationship. Since MENDACIOUS means "given to deception or falsehood," you could say that "a LIAR indulges in the MENDACIOUS" is the relationship of the first pair of words above. Using this same rationale, you could then say of (C) "a **dupe** may indulge in the **illusory**," or of (D) "A **seer** indulges in the **prophetic**." However, since there can be only one correct answer, and since when you use the relationship given above it appears that you have two answers, you must return to the first pair of words and restate the rationale. Try "a LIAR is by definition MENDACIOUS." If you check the words in the dictionary, you will see that this new rationale is a correct one. Applying this rationale to the choices, you see that it fits only choice (D); "a **seer** is by definition **prophetic**" is the same relationship as "a LIAR is by definition MENDACIOUS." You could not say, using this rationale, that "a **dupe** is by definition **illusory**." The correct answer is choice (D), **seer : prophetic**.

HINTS FOR ANALOGIES

1. First make up a sentence that shows how the two words in CAPITAL letters work together. Then see what pair of words among the choices works best in your sentence.

2. Remember that you are not looking for words that are similar to the words in CAPITAL letters or that have the same meaning. Don't look for a relationship between the first word in CAPITAL letters and the first word in each of the choices. Look for a *pair* of words with the same relationship between them as the *pair* in CAPITAL letters.

3. Many words have more than one meaning, and many pairs of words have more than one relationship between them. You may have to try a few relationships before you find the one that helps you choose the best answer.

4. If you can eliminate two or three answer choices with the first relationship you find, you may be able to select the *best* answer by defining the relationship more precisely rather than by trying an entirely different one.

Sample Questions from PSAT/ NMSQT Practice Test—Section 1

Each question below consists of a word in capital letters, followed by five lettered words or phrases. Choose the word or phrase that is most nearly <u>opposite</u> in meaning to the word in capital letters. Since some of the questions require you to distinguish fine shades of meaning, consider all the choices before deciding which is best.

Example:

GOOD: **(A)** sour **(B)** bad **(C)** red **(D)** hot **(E)** ugly   (A) ● (C) (D) (E)

1. BIND: (A) lend (B) seek (C) free (D) measure (E) level
2. PENALIZE: (A) respect (B) reward (C) befriend (D) correct (E) release
3. EXAGGERATE: (A) comply (B) adapt (C) specialize (D) minimize (E) familiarize
4. ELEGANT: (A) coarse (B) manual (C) illegitimate (D) large (E) possible
5. BLOAT: (A) divide (B) fade (C) soften (D) dilute (E) shrink
6. ENTERPRISING: (A) unexpected (B) appropriate (C) well preserved (D) without initiative (E) in need of protection
7. GRAPHIC: (A) inconvenient (B) unjustified (C) not vivid (D) not satisfactory (E) not tolerable
8. TRIFLING: (A) mistaken (B) hidden (C) confused (D) tactless (E) significant

Each sentence below has one or two blanks, each blank indicating that something has been omitted. Beneath the sentence are five lettered words or sets of words. Choose the word or set of words that, when inserted in the sentence, <u>best</u> fits the meaning of the sentence as a whole.

Example:

Although its publicity has been ---, the film itself is intelligent, well-acted, handsomely produced, and altogether ---.

(A) tasteless .. respectable **(B)** extensive .. moderate **(C)** sophisticated .. amateur (D) risqué .. crude (E) perfect .. spectacular   ● (B) (C) (D) (E)

21. He writes like a man crossing a minefield— every word a --- step.

(A) rhythmical (B) weary (C) militant (D) brazen (E) hesitant

22. Some Native American organizations recently have been successful in defending legal land rights previously protected only by tradition and unenforced ---.

(A) debts (B) chronicles (C) testimony
(D) outposts (E) treaties

23. Although many women in politics are not feminists, research --- that there is a pronounced --- women's rights on the part of officeholders who are women.

(A) denies . . interest in
(B) supports . . neglect of
(C) confirms . . concern for
(D) obscures . . need for
(E) refutes . . consciousness of

24. As a scientist, Dr. Conti makes only --- predictions, for she does not believe that science can ever absolutely foretell the future.

(A) unquestionable (B) explicit
(C) categorical (D) conditional
(E) negative

25. The architects agree that it would be --- to reconstruct the mansion exactly because the few existing records provide only --- information about the structure.

(A) difficult . . unavailable
(B) efficient . . historical
(C) impossible . . sketchy
(D) important . . reclassified
(E) pointless . . detailed

31. CUT : CHISEL :: (A) eat : plate
(B) act : stage (C) kick : mule
(D) gore : bull (E) dig : shovel

32. BABY CARRIAGE : INFANT :: (A) bus : bus driver (B) taxi : passenger
(C) wheelchair : nurse (D) horse : groom
(E) car : auto mechanic

33. FLOWER : BOUQUET :: (A) blouse : suit
(B) dog : animal (C) finger : arm
(D) cow : herd (E) nail : hammer

34. LOCKER ROOM : ATHLETE ::
(A) barracks : soldier
(B) ballroom : debutante
(C) dressing room : actor
(D) concert hall : pianist
(E) reformatory : delinquent

35. MORTIFY : EMBARRASSMENT ::
(A) disillusion : fantasy
(B) infuriate : anger (C) chide : confusion
(D) assuage : pain (E) alienate : empathy

36. GREENHOUSE : PLANTS ::
(A) incubator : chicks
(B) smokehouse : meats
(C) refrigerator : ice (D) hold : cargo
(E) vault : jewels

Each question below consists of a related pair of words or phrases, followed by five lettered pairs of words or phrases. Select the lettered pair that **best** expresses a relationship similar to that expressed in the original pair.

Example:

YAWN : BOREDOM :: (A) dream : sleep
(B) anger : madness (C) smile : amusement
(D) face : expression
(E) impatience : rebellion Ⓐ Ⓑ ● Ⓓ Ⓔ

**ANSWER KEY FOR
PSAT/NMSQT PRACTICE TEST
SECTION 1**

1. C	21. E	31. E
2. B	22. E	32. B
3. D	23. C	33. D
4. A	24. D	34. C
5. E	25. C	35. B
6. D		36. A
7. C		
8. E		

2. The SAT

The following vocabulary questions and explanations are reprinted with permission from *Taking the SAT*, a 1991–1992 booklet published by the College Entrance Examination Board and the Educational Testing Service.

Sample Questions and Explanations

Antonyms (opposites)

Antonym questions primarily test the extent of your vocabulary. The vocabulary used in the antonym questions includes words that you are likely to come across in your general reading, although some words may not be the kind you use in everyday speech.

> **Directions: Each question below consists of a word in capital letters, followed by five lettered words or phrases. Choose the word or phrase that is most nearly opposite in meaning to the word in capital letters. Since some of the questions require you to distinguish fine shades of meaning, consider all the choices before deciding which is best.**
>
> **Example:**
> **GOOD: (A) sour (B) bad (C) red (D) hot (E) ugly**
>
> Ⓐ ● Ⓒ Ⓓ Ⓔ

You can probably answer this example without thinking very much about the choices. However, most of the antonyms in the verbal section require more careful analysis. When you work on antonym questions, remember that:

1. Among the five choices offered, you are looking for the word that means the *opposite* of the given word. Words that have exactly the same meaning as the given word are not included among the five choices.

2. You are looking for the *best* answer. Read all of the choices before deciding which one is best, even if you feel sure you know the answer. For example:

SUBSEQUENT: (A) primary (B) recent (C) contemporary (D) prior (E) simultaneous

Subsequent means "following in time or order; succeeding." Someone working quickly might choose (B) *recent* because it refers to a past action and *subsequent* refers to an action in the future. However, choice (D) *prior* is the best answer. It is more nearly the opposite of *subsequent* than is *recent*.

3. Few words have exact opposites, that is, words that are opposite in all of their meanings. You should find the word that is *most nearly* opposite. For example:

FERMENTING: (A) improvising (B) stagnating (C) wavering (D) plunging (D) dissolving

Even though *fermenting* is normally associated with chemical reactions, whereas *stagnating* is normally associated with water, *fermenting* means "being agitated," and *stagnating* means "being motionless." Therefore, choice (B) *stagnating* is the best of the five choices.

4. You need to be flexible. A word can have several meanings. For example:

DEPRESS: (A) force (B) allow (C) clarify (D) elate (E) loosen

The word *depress* can mean "to push down." However, no word meaning "to lift up" is included among the choices. Therefore, you must consider another meaning of *depress*, "to sadden or discouarge." Option (D) *elate* means "to fill with joy or pride." The best answer is (D) *elate*.

5. You'll often recognize a word you have encountered in your reading but have never looked up in the dictionary. If you don't know the dictionary meaning of a word but have a sense of how the word should be used, try to make up a short phrase or sentence using the word. This may give you a clue as to which choice is an opposite, even though you may not be able to define the word precisely.

INCUMBENT: (A) conscious
(B) effortless   (C) optional
(D) improper   (E) irrelevant

You may remember *incumbent* used in a sentence such as "It is incumbent upon me to finish this." If you can think of such a phrase, you may be able to recognize that *incumbent* means "imposed as a duty" or "obligatory." Of the five choices, (A), (B), and (D) are in no way opposites of *incumbent* and you can easily eliminate them. Choice (E) means "not pertinent" and choice (C) means "not compulsory." Although choice (E) may look attractive, choice (C) *optional* is more nearly an exact opposite to *incumbent*. Choice (C), therefore, is the answer.

Hints for Antonyms:

Answering antonyms depends on knowing the uses as well as the meanings of words, so just memorizing word lists is probably of little value. You're more likely to improve your performance on antonyms and other kinds of verbal questions by doing things that help you to think about words and the way they are used. So, it would be a good idea to:

✔ Read books or magazines on subjects with which you're not already familiar. This will give you an idea of how familiar words can have different meanings in different contexts.
✔ Use a dictionary when you come across words that you don't understand. This will help to broaden your vocabulary and could improve your performance on the tests.

Analogies

Analogy questions test your ability to see a relationship in a pair of words, to understand the ideas expressed in the relationship, and to recognize a similar or parallel relationship.

Directions: Each question below consists of a related pair of words or phrases, followed by five lettered pairs of words or phrases. Select the lettered pair that best expresses a relationship similar to that expressed in the original pair.

Example:
YAWN:BOREDOM:: (A) dream:sleep
(B) anger:madness   (C) smile:amusement
(D) face:expression
(E) impatience:rebellion

The first step in answering an analogy question is to establish a precise relationship between the original pair of words (the two capitalized words). In the example above, the relationship between *yawn* and *boredom* can best be stated as "(first word) is a physical sign of (second word)," or "(first word) is a facial expression of (second word)."

The second step in answering an analogy question is to decide which of the five pairs given as choices best expresses a similar relationship. In the example above, the answer is choice (C): a (smile) is a physical sign of (amusement), or a (smile) is a facial expression of (amusement). None of the other choices shares a similar relationship with the capitalized pair of words: a *dream* is something that occurs when you are asleep, but it is not usually thought of as being a sign of *sleep* as, for example, closed eyes or a snore might be; *anger* denotes strong displeasure and *madness* can refer to rage or insanity, but neither word is a physical sign of the other; an *expression* is something that appears on a *face*, but a *face* is not a sign of an *expression*; *impatience* may lead to *rebellion* or be characteristic of a rebellious person, but *impatience* is not a physical sign of *rebellion*.

For the analogy below, state the relationship between the original pair of words and then decide which pair of words from choices (A) to (E) has a similar or parallel relationship.

SUBMISSIVE : LED ::
(A) wealthy : employed
(B) intolerant : indulged
(C) humble : humiliated
(D) incorrigible : taught
(E) inconspicuous : overlooked

The relationship between *submissive* and *led* can be expressed as "to be submissive is to be easily led." Only choice (E) has the same relationship: "to be inconspicuous is to be easily overlooked." To be *intolerant* is not to be easily *indulged*, to be *humble* is not to be easily *humiliated*, and to be *incorrigible* (or incapable of being reformed) is not to be easily *taught*. With regard to choice (A), the statement "to be wealthy is to be easily employed" is an expression of opinion and not an expression of the relationship between the words according to their dictionary meanings.

You may want to practice describing precise verbal relationships. Below are some examples of the kinds of relationships that could be used.

SONG : REPERTOIRE :
(A) score : melody (B) instrument : artist
(C) solo : chorus (D) benediction : church
(E) suit : wardrobe

The best answer is choice (E). The relationship between the words can be expressed as "several (first word) make up a (second word)." Several (songs) make up a (repertoire) as several (suits) make up a (wardrobe).

REQUEST : ENTREAT ::
(A) control : explode (B) admire : idolize
(C) borrow : steal (D) repeat : plead
(E) cancel : invalidate

The best answer is choice (B). Although both of the capitalized words have similar meanings, they express different degrees of feeling; to (entreat) is to (request) with strong feeling as to (idolize) is to (admire) with strong feeling. To answer analogy questions, you must think carefully about the precise meanings of words. For instance, if you thought the word "entreat" meant only "to ask" instead of "to ask urgently," you would have trouble establishing the correct relationship between *request* and *entreat*.

FAMINE : STARVATION ::
(A) deluge : flood
(B) drought : vegetation (C) war : treaty
(D) success : achievement
(E) seed : mutation

The best answer is (A). The relationship can be stated as (famine) results in (starvation) as a (deluge) results in a (flood). None of the other pairs of words expresses a causal relationship. (C) is close, since a *treaty* often follows a *war*, but we do not think of a war "causing" a treaty in the same way that a famine "causes" starvation.

AMPLIFIER : HEAR ::
(A) turntable : listen
(B) typewriter : spell (C) platter : eat
(D) camera : feel (E) microscope : see

The best answer is choice (E). An (amplifier) magnifies in order to help a person (hear) in the same way that a (microscope) magnifies in order to help a person (see). Note that, in (A), while a *turntable* is part of a larger mechanism that allows a person to *listen*, the choice is not as good an answer as (E) because a *turntable* does not magnify anything. Choice (D) is also wrong for a similar reason: a *camera* produces pictures that may make a person *feel* something, but a *camera* does not magnify in order to help a person *feel*.

Some choices may have relationships that are close but not parallel to the relationship in the original pair. However, the correct answer has *most nearly* the same relationship as the original pair. Look at the following:

KNIFE : INCISION ::
(A) bulldozer : excavation
(B) tool : operation
(C) pencil : calculation
(D) hose : irrigation   (E) plow : agriculture

On the most general level, the relationship between *knife* and *incision* is that the object indicated by the first word is used to perform the action indicated by the second word. Since "a (knife) is used to make an (incision)," "a (bulldozer) is used to make an (excavation)," and "a (hose) is used for (irrigation)," there appear to be two correct answers. You need to go back and state the relationship more precisely. Some aspect of the relationship between the original pair exists in only one of the choices. A more precise relationship between *knife* and *incision* could be expressed as: "a knife cuts into something to make an incision" and "a bulldozer cuts into something to make an excavation." This relationship eliminates *hose : irrigation* as a possible answer. The best answer is choice (A).

Remember that a pair of words can have more than one relationship. For example:

PRIDE : LION ::   (A) snake : python
(B) pack : wolf   (C) rat : mouse
(D) bird : starling   (E) dog : canine

A possible relationship between *pride* and *lion* might be that "the first word describes a characteristic of the second (especially in mythology)." Using this reasoning, you might look for an answer such as *wisdom : owl*, but none of the given choices has that kind of relationship. Another relationship between *pride* and *lion* is "a group of lions is called a pride"; therefore, the answer is (B) *pack : wolf*, since "a group of wolves is called a pack."

Hints for Analogies

State the relationship between the two capitalized words in a sentence or phrase as clearly as you can. Next, find the pair of words that has the most similar or parallel relationship. Don't be misled by choices that merely suggest a vague association. Be sure that you can identify a specific relationship.

Always compare the relationship between the <u>pair</u> of capitalized words with the relationship between the <u>pair</u> of words in each of the choices. Don't try to set up a relationship between the first word in the original pair and the first word in each of the five choices.

Think carefully about the meanings of words. The words in analogy questions are used according to their dictionary definitions or meanings closely related to their dictionary definitions. The better you know the precise meanings of words, the less trouble you'll have establishing the correct relationships between them.

Don't be misled by relationships that are close but not parallel to the relationship in the original pair. The correct answer has a relationship that is <u>most nearly parallel</u> to the relationship between the capitalized words.

Sentence Completion Questions

Sentence completion questions test your ability to recognize relationships among parts of a sentence. In sentence completion questions, you have to know the meanings of the words offered as choices and you also have to know how to use those words properly in the context of a sentence. The sentences are taken from published material and cover a wide variety of topics. You'll find that, even if you're not familiar with the topic of a sentence, there's enough information in the sentence for you to find the correct answer from the context of the sentence itself.

Directions: Each sentence below has one or two blanks, each blank indicating that something has been omitted. Beneath the sentence are five lettered words or sets of words. Choose the word or set of words that, when inserted in the sentence, best fits the meaning of the sentence as a whole.

Example:
Although its publicity has been ---, the film itself is intelligent, well-acted, handsomely produced, and altogether ---.
(A) tasteless . . respectable (B) extensive . . moderate (C) sophisticated . . amateur (D) risqué . . crude (E) perfect . . spectacular

The word *although* suggests that the publicity gave the wrong impression of the movie, so look for two words that are more or less opposite in meaning. Also, the second word has to fit in with "intelligent, well-acted, handsomely produced." Choices (D) and (E) are not opposites. The words in choice (B) are somewhat opposite in meaning, but do not logically fulfill the expectation set up by the word *although*. Choice (C) can't be the correct answer, even though *sophisticated* and *amateur* are nearly opposites, because an "intelligent, well-acted, handsomely produced" film isn't amateurish. Only choice (A), when inserted in the sentence, makes a logical statement.

For a better understanding of sentence completion questions, read the following sample questions and explanations.

Nearly all the cultivated plants utilized by the Chinese have been of --- origin; even rice, though known in China since Neolithic times, came from India.

> **(A) foreign (B) ancient (C) wild (D) obscure (E) common**

To answer this question, you need to consider the entire sentence—the part that comes after the semicolon as well as the part that comes before it. If you only consider the first part of the question, all five choices seem plausible. The second part of the sentence adds a specific example—that rice came to China from India. This idea of origin supports and clarifies the "origin" mentioned in the first part of the sentence and eliminates (C), (D), and (E) as possible answers. The mention of Neolithic times makes (B) harder to eliminate, but the sentence is not logical when (B) is used to fill in the blank because the emphasis in the second part of the sentence—country of origin—is inconsistent with that in the first—age. Only choice (A) produces a sentence that is logical and consistent.

The excitement does not --- but --- his senses, giving him a keener perception of a thousand details.

> **(A) slow . . diverts (B) blur . . sharpens (C) overrule . . constricts (D) heighten . . aggravates (E) forewarn . . quickens**

Since the sentence has two blanks to be filled, you must make sure that both words make sense in the sentence. If you look for grammatical clues within the sentence, you will see that the word *but* implies that the answer will involve two words that are more or less opposite in meaning. If you keep this in mind, you can eliminate all of the choices except for (B) *blur . . sharpens*. Only the words in choice (B) imply opposition. Also, "sharpens his senses" is consistent with the notion that he has a "keener perception of a thousand details."

They argue that the author was determined to
--- his own conclusion, so he --- any information that did not support it.

    **(A) uphold . . ignored (B) revise . .
destroyed (C) advance . . devised
(D) disprove . . distorted (E) reverse . .
confiscated**

The logic of the sentence makes it fairly easy to
eliminate choices (B), (D), and (E). The first
word in choice (A), *uphold*, and the first word
in (C), *advance*, seem all right. However, the
second word in choice (C), *devised*, does not
make sense in the sentence. Why would an author who wished to advance his theory devise
information that did not support it? Only choice
(A) makes a logically consistent sentence.

She is a skeptic, --- to believe that the accepted opinion of the majority is generally
---.

    **(A) prone . . infallible (B) afraid . .
misleading (C) inclined . . justifiable
(D) quick . . significant (E) disposed . .
erroneous**

The words to be inserted in the blank spaces in
the question above must result in a statement
that is consistent with the definition of a skeptic. Since a skeptic would hardly consider the
accepted opinion of the majority as *infallible*,
justifiable, or *significant*, you can eliminate
choices (A), (C), and (D). A skeptic would not
be afraid that the accepted opinion of the majority is misleading; a skeptic would believe that
it was. Therefore, choice (B) is not correct. Only
choice (E), *disposed . . erroneous* makes a logical
sentence.

Hints for Sentence Completions

- Read the entire sentence carefully; make sure you understand the ideas being expressed.
- Don't select an answer simply because it is a popular cliché or "sounds good."
- In a question with two blanks, the right answer must correctly fill <u>both</u> blanks. A wrong answer choice often includes one correct and one incorrect word.
- After choosing an answer, read the entire sentence to yourself and make sure that it makes sense.
- Consider all the choices; be sure you haven't overlooked a choice that makes a better and more accurate sentence than your choice does.

Sample Questions from SAT Practice Test—Section 1

Each question below consists of a word in capital letters, followed by five lettered words or
phrases. Choose the word or phrase that is
most nearly <u>opposite</u> in meaning to the word
in capital letters. Since some of the questions
require you to distinguish fine shades of meaning, consider all the choices before deciding
which is best.

Example:

GOOD: (A) sour (B) bad (C) red
(D) hot (E) ugly

    Ⓐ ● Ⓒ Ⓓ Ⓔ

1. DRENCH: (A) extend (B) heat
   (C) search (D) dry out (E) pull apart
2. STIMULATE: (A) record (B) suppress
   (C) criticize (D) assemble (E) illuminate
3. CIVIL: (A) rude (B) inefficient (C) shy
   (D) lazy (E) proud
4. RUPTURE: (A) immensity (B) clamor
   (C) dejection (D) scrutiny (E) union
5. GROUNDLESS: (A) familiar
   (B) symmetrical (C) well-founded
   (D) deeply appreciated (E) carefully
   executed

Each sentence below has one or two blanks,
each blank indicating that something has been
omitted. Beneath the sentence are five lettered
words or sets of words. Choose the word or set
of words that, when inserted in the sentence,
best fits the meaning of the sentence as a
whole.

Example:

Although its publicity has been ---, the film
itself is intelligent, well-acted, handsomely
produced, and altogether ---.
(A) tasteless . . respectable (B) extensive . .
moderate (C) sophisticated . . amateur
(D) risqué . . crude (E) perfect . .
spectacular

---

11. Scientists have discovered that our sense of
    smell is surprisingly ---, capable of distin-
    guishing thousands of chemical odors.

    (A) rigid (B) inert (C) erratic (D) keen
    (E) innate

12. With these --- sites as evidence, it would
    be --- to draw definite conclusions as to the
    places typically selected as settlements by
    the people of the Neolithic age.

    (A) imperfect . . feasible
    (B) few . . unsound
    (C) complete . . ridiculous
    (D) abundant . . presumptuous
    (E) scattered . . prudent

Each question below consists of a related pair
of words or phrases, followed by five lettered
pairs of words or phrases. Select the lettered
pair that best expresses a relationship similar
to that expressed in the original pair.

Example:

YAWN: BOREDOM::
(A) dream: sleep
(B) anger: madness
(C) smile: amusement
(D) face: expression
(E) impatience: rebellion

---

16. NUTRIENTS: FOOD:: (A) oxygen: air
    (B) earth: plants (C) diet: health
    (D) disease: symptom (E) moon: night
17. LIE: UNTRUTHFUL::
    (A) steal: punished (B) exaggerate: retold
    (C) proofread: erroneous
    (D) pardon: forgiving (E) pray: kneeling
18. SHELL: WALNUT:: (A) coating: candy
    (B) peel: banana (C) icing: cake
    (D) loaf: bread (E) root: tree
19. RENOVATE: BUILDING::
    (A) revoke: contract (B) rejuvenate: age
    (C) restore: painting (D) repeat: sentence
    (E) relinquish: possession

Section 3

Each question below consists of a word in capital letters, followed by five lettered words or
phrases. Choose the word or phrase that is
most nearly opposite in meaning to the word
in capital letters. Since some of the questions
require you to distinguish fine shades of meaning, consider all the choices before deciding
which is best.

Example:

GOOD: (A) sour (B) bad (C) red
(D) hot (E) ugly

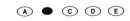

1. EXCESS: (A) response (B) modification
   (C) concealment (D) shortage
   (E) slenderness
2. DETESTABLE: (A) measurable
   (B) mature (C) agreeable (D) expensive
   (E) colorful
3. PREDETERMINED:
   (A) not encountered before
   (B) not decided in advance
   (C) not essential
   (D) imperfect
   (E) undesirable
4. COINCIDE: (A) diverge (B) hesitate
   (C) intend (D) remove (E) excite
5. VAPORIZE: (A) decrease (B) progress
   (C) immobilize (D) condense (E) dilute
6. DRAWBACK: (A) festivity (B) proposal
   (C) tabulation (D) sketch (E) asset

Each sentence below has one or two blanks,
each blank indicating that something has been
omitted. Beneath the sentence are five lettered
words or sets of words. Choose the word or set
of words that, when inserted in the sentence,
best fits the meaning of the sentence as a
whole.

Example:

Although its publicity has been ---, the film
itself is intelligent, well-acted, handsomely
produced, and altogether ---.
(A) tasteless . . respectable (B) extensive . .
moderate (C) sophisticated . . amateur
(D) risqué . . crude (E) perfect . .
spectacular

---

16. The athlete's insistence on self-discipline
    had become ---; rarely, it seemed, did he
    allow himself even a minor indulgence.

    (A) dilatory (B) obsessive
    (C) spontaneous (D) infectious
    (E) unemotional

17. All female red *Colobus* monkeys leave their

natal troops, but because these females are
---- by young females from other troops,
the practice has little effect on troop size and
composition.

(A) joined (B) replaced (C) ignored
(D) influenced (E) rejected

Each question below consists of a related pair
of words or phrases, followed by five lettered
pairs of words or phrases. Select the lettered
pair that best expresses a relationship similar
to that expressed in the original pair.

Example:

YAWN : BOREDOM :: (A) dream : sleep
(B) anger : madness (C) smile : amusement
(D) face : expression
(E) impatience : rebellion

---

36. HAMMER : CARPENTER ::
    (A) stone : mason (B) brush : painter
    (C) music : violinist
    (D) suspect : detective
    (E) bracelet : jeweler
37. EXPEL : SCHOOL :: (A) deny : entrance
    (B) banish : country (C) reject : offer
    (D) extricate : safety (E) abandon : enemy
38. SALUTATION : LETTER ::
    (A) greeting : conversation
    (B) message : telegram
    (C) goodwill : feeling
    (D) address : location
    (E) agreement : debate
39. PEPPER MILL : GRINDING ::
    (A) scale : weighing
    (B) grease : moving
    (C) detergent : scrubbing
    (D) engine : fueling
    (E) spice : seasoning
40. FACTION : POLITICS ::
    (A) geography : history
    (B) war : peace
    (C) sect : religion
    (D) taxes : income
    (E) duel : honor

ANSWER KEY FOR SAT PRACTICE TEST

SECTION 1			SECTION 3		
1. D	11. D	16. A	1. D	16. B	36. B
2. B	12. B	17. D	2. C	17. B	37. B
3. A		18. B	3. B		38. A
4. E		19. C	4. A		39. A
5. C			5. D		40. C
			6. E		

CHAPTER *13*

Dictionary of Words Taught in This Text

The following pages contain a partial listing of the words presented in this book. The words included are those likely to offer some degree of difficulty. The definitions given have in many cases been condensed.

The numeral following a definition indicates the page on which the word appears. Roman type (e.g., **abhor,** 25) is used when the word appears as a main entry. Italic type (e.g., **abase,** *66*) is used when the word appears as a sub-entry, such as a definition or a synonym of the main entry.

Use this dictionary as a tool of reference and review. It is a convenient means of restudying the meanings of words that you may have missed in the exercises. It is also a useful device for a general review before an important vocabulary test. Bear in mind, however, that you will get a fuller understanding of these words from the explanations and exercises in the foregoing chapters.

abase: lower *66*
abhor: utterly detest; loathe; hate 25
abhorrent: loathsome, repugnant 25
abiogenesis: spontaneous generation 111
abject: deserving contempt; sunk to a low condition 65, 168
aboard: on a ship, train, bus, *etc.*; on or into 191
abridge: shorten 202
abrupt: broken off; sudden 137, 164, *233*
abstemious: sparing in eating and drinking 76
abstinent: sparing in eating and drinking *76*
absurd: ridiculous 58, *86*
abysmal: profound; immeasurably great 65
abyss: bottomless, immeasurably deep space 65
a cappella: without musical accompaniment 233

access: way of entering 164
acclaim: welcome with approval 56
acclivity: upward slope 64
accredited: officially authorized or recognized 150
acme: highest point 64
acquit: pronounce not guilty 34
acrid: sharp in smell or taste *68*
acrophobia: fear of being at a great height 95
adagio: slow; in an easy, graceful manner 231
adherent: supporter; follower *209*
adieu: good-by 212
adjacent: lying near or next to 79
admonish: warn of a fault 25, 148
admonition: counseling against a fault or error 148
admonitory: conveying a gentle rebuke 148
adobe: brick of sun-dried clay or mud; structure made of such bricks 248
adolescent: growing from childhood to adulthood 73
adolescent: teenager 73
Adonis: very handsome young man 180
adulation: excessive praise 46
aegis: shield or protection; sponsorship 180
affidavit: sworn written statement made before an authorized official 151
affirmation: oath 203
aficionado: devoted follower of some sport or art; fan; devotee 245
afoul: in a state of entanglement 192
aggressive: disposed to attack 164
agoraphobia: fear of open spaces 95
à la carte: dish by dish, with a stated price for each dish 220
alacrity: cheerful willingness 63
a la mode: according to fashion; stylish 220
alfresco: in the open air; outdoor 239
allegro: quick 231
aloof: withdrawn 192
alto: highest male voice; lowest female voice (contralto) 230

altruism: unselfish concern for others 89

amazon: tall, strong, masculine woman 180

ambience: surrounding atmosphere 222

ambrosia: food of the gods *25, 180*

ambrosial: exceptionally pleasing to taste or smell 25, 180

ameliorate: become better; improve 7

amiss: wrong; imperfect; faulty 192

amoral: without sense of moral responsibility 101

amorphous: shapeless; without definite form; unorganized 87, 101, 123

amphibious: able to live both on land and in water 111

analogy: likeness in some respects between things otherwise different 84

anarchy: total absence of rule or government; confusion 101, 119

anatomy: dissection of plants or animals for the purpose of studying their structure; structure of a plant or animal 113

andante: moderately slow, but flowing 231

anemia: lack of a normal number of red blood cells 102

anent: about; concerning; in respect to 195

anesthesia: loss of feeling or sensation resulting from ether, chloroform, novocaine, etc. 102

anesthetic: drug that produces anesthesia 102

Anglophile: supporter of England or the English 97

Anglophobe: one who dislikes England or the English 96

Anglophobia: dislike of England or the English 95

anguish: extreme pain *44*

anhydrous: destitute of water 102

anomalous: not normal; abnormal 102

anomaly: deviation from the common rule 102

anon: soon; presently 195

anonymous: nameless; of unknown or unnamed origin 102

anoxia: deprivation of oxygen 102

antediluvian: antiquated; belonging to the time before the Biblical Flood 73

anthropology: science dealing with the origin, races, customs, and beliefs of man 110

anthropomorphic: attributing human form or characteristics to beings not human, especially gods 123

antibiotic: antibacterial substance produced by a living organism 111

anticlimax: abrupt decline from the important to the trivial; comedown 66

antidote: remedy for a poison or evil 54

antipasto: appetizer consisting of fish, meats, etc.; hors d'oeuvres 238

antipathy: strong dislike *63,* 122

antipodes: parts of the earth (or their inhabitants) diametrically opposite 114

anxious: fearful of what may come *167*

apathy: lack of feeling, emotion, interest, or excitement 122

apéritif: alcoholic drink taken before a meal as an appetizer 220

apex: farthest point opposite the base, as in a triangle or pyramid 65

aphelion: farthest point from the sun in the orbit of a planet or comet 124

apiary: place where bees are kept 53

aplomb: absolute confidence in oneself; poise 211

apnea: temporary cessation of breathing 102

apogee: farthest point from earth in the orbit of a heavenly body; highest point; culmination 64, 121, *124*

apostate: one who has forsaken the faith, principles, or party he supported earlier *246*

appellation: name 203

appendectomy: surgical removal of the appendix 113

apprehend: seize or take into custody; understand 167

apprehensive: fearful of what may come 167

appropriate: take for oneself 202

approximate: nearly correct 79

apropos: by the way; incidentally 222

apropos: appropriate; relevant; pertinent 222

aqueduct: artificial channel for conducting water from a distance 161

arbiter: a person having power to decide a dispute *85*

arbitrary: proceeding from a whim or fancy; autocratic; tyrannical 84

arbitrate: decide a dispute, acting as arbiter (judge); submit a dispute to an arbiter 85

arbitrator: judge *85*

archaic: no longer used, except in a special context; old-fashioned 73

aria: melody; an elaborate, accompanied melody for a single voice in an opera 234

aristocracy: class regarded as superior in some respect *209*

aroma: pleasant odor 68

aromatic: sweet-scented; fragrant 68

arpeggio: production of the tones of a chord in rapid succession and not simultaneously; a chord thus played 233

arrogant: haughty 89

arroyo: watercourse; small, often dry, gully 249

arthropod: any invertebrate (animal having no backbone) with jointed legs 114

ascetic: self-denying; person who shuns pleasures 43

aseptic: free from or keeping away disease-causing microorganisms 102

asinine: like an ass or donkey; stupid, silly 199

assertive: acting and speaking boldly *164*

assuage: ease or lessen 202

astringent: drawing (the tissues) tightly together; stern; substance that shrinks tissues and checks flow of blood by contracting blood vessels 54, 140

asunder: apart 192

asymmetrical: not balanced in arrangement 88

asymptomatic: showing no symptoms of disease 102

atheism: godlessness 102

atlas: book of maps 181

atom: smallest particle of an element 113

atomizer: device for converting a liquid to a fine spray 113

atrophy: lack of growth from want of nourishment or from disuse 102

attaché: member of the diplomatic staff of an ambassador or minister 208

attenuate: make thin; weaken 45

atypical: unlike the typical 102

au courant: well-informed; up-to-date 207

audiophile: one who is enthusiastic about high-fidelity sound reproduction 97

au revoir: good-bye till we meet again 212

auriferous: bearing or yielding gold 172

auroral: pertaining to or resembling the dawn; rosy 181

auspices: patronage and care *180*

austere: stern *140*

autarchy: rule by an absolute sovereign 119

autobiography: story of a person's life written by the person himself 111

avant-garde: experimentalists or innovators in any art 219

avarice: greed 203

averse: disinclined *63*

aversion: strong dislike 63, *122*

avert: turn away; prevent 169

aviary: place where birds are kept 53

avoirdupois: weight 223

axiom: self-evident truth; maxim 85

axiomatic: self-evident 85

bacchanalian: jovial or wild with drunkenness 181

bacchic: jovial or wild with drunkenness 181

bactericide: substance that kills bacteria 138

bacteriology: science dealing with the study of bacteria 110

badger: nag 53

baffle: bewilder 16

bagatelle: trifle 223

banter: playful teasing 57

baritone: male voice between bass and tenor 230

barrio: Spanish-speaking neighborhood 249

bas-relief: carving or sculpture in which the figures project only slightly from the background 219

bass: lowest male voice *230*

basso: lowest male voice 230

bathos: abrupt decline in dignity or importance at the end *66*

baton: stick with which a conductor beats time for an orchestra or band 219

beget: bring into life or into existence 201

begrime: make dirty 193

behest: command; order 195

beholden: bound in gratitude; indebted 195

behoove: be necessary for; be proper for 195

belittle: disparage 193

benediction: blessing 203

benighted: unenlightened; ignorant 193

benign: not dangerous; gentle 54

beset: attack on all sides; surround 192

besmirch: soil *79*

bête noire: object or person dreaded 213

betimes: early 195

bias: opinion formed before there are grounds for it; unthinking preference 85

bibliophile: lover of books 97

bibliophobe: one who strongly dislikes books 97

bigoted: narrow-minded 85

bigotry: views or behavior of a bigot 85

billet-doux: love letter 212

biochemistry: chemistry dealing with chemical compounds and processes in living plants and animals 111

biocidal: destructive to life 112

biocide: substance that destroys living micro-organisms 138

biodegradable: decomposable into harmless substances by living microorganisms 112

biogenesis: development of life from preexisting life 112

biography: story of a person's life written by another person 112

biology: science dealing with the study of living organisms 110, 112

biometrics: statistical analysis of biologic data 112

biometry: statistical calculation of probable duration of human life 112

biopsy: diagnostic examination of a piece of tissue from the living body 112

biota: the living plants (flora) and living animals (fauna) of a region 112

biped: two-footed animal 165

blandishment: word or deed of mild flattery; enticement 46

blasé: tired of pleasures; bored 207

bliss: perfect happiness 41

blithe: merry; joyous; heedless 41

bluster: talk or act with noisy violence *182*

boa constrictor: snake that crushes its prey in its coils 140

bodega: small grocery store 249

bolero: lively dance in ¾ time; the music for this dance; short, loose jacket 248

bombastic: using pompous language *172*

bona fide: made or carried out in good faith 151

bonanza: accidental discovery of a rich mass of ore in a mine 248

bonbon: piece of candy 220

bon mot: clever saying 212

bouffant: full; puffed out 221

bouquet: pleasant odor *68*

bourgeois: having to do with the middle class; lacking in culture or refinement   207

boutique: small shop specializing in fashionable clothes   221

bovine: cowlike or oxlike; sluggish and patient   199

bow: forward part of a ship   77

bowdlerize: remove objectionable material from a book   *78*

brava: (used to applaud a woman performer) well done   239

bravado: boastful behavior: pretense of bravery   248

bravo: (used to applaud a performance or male performer) well done   239

bravura: piece of music requiring skill and spirit in the performer; display of daring or brilliancy   234

brazen: shameless; made of brass or bronze; harsh-sounding   89

breach: a breaking gap; violation   *66,* 203

brine: salty water; ocean   77

brisk: lively   *231*

brochure: pamphlet   212

bronco: half-wild pony   250

buffo: male singer who plays a comic role in an opera   237

bugbear: object of dread   *213*

buoy: keep afloat; raise the spirits of   41

buoyant: cheerful; able to float   41

burly: strongly and heavily built; husky   45

burro: small donkey used as a pack animal   250

buxom: plump and attractive   45

caballero: gentleman or gallant; horseman   245

cabana: beach shelter resembling a cabin   248

cajole: persuade by pleasing words   46

cajolery: persuasion by flattery; wheedling; coaxing   46

callow: young and inexperienced   74

calumnious: falsely and maliciously accusing   56

calumny: false and malicious accusation   56

cameo: gem carved with a design higher and different in color than its background; brief role by a prominent performer; exceptionally fine brief passage   235

campanile: bell tower   235

canard: false rumor   212

canine: doglike; one of four pointed teeth   199

cantata: story or play set to music to be sung by a chorus, but not acted   234

canto: one of the chief divisions of a long poem; book   235

canyon: deep valley with high, steep slopes, often with a stream flowing through it   250

capitulate: yield   202

cardiology: science dealing with the action and diseases of the heart   110

caricature: drawing, imitation, or description that ridiculously exaggerates peculiarities or defects   57

carnivore: flesh-eating animal   140

carnivorous: flesh-eating   141

carousal: drinking party   77

carrion: decaying flesh of a carcass   78

carte blanche: freedom to use one's own judgment   213

Cassandra: one who prophesies doom; pessimist   181

castanets: hand instruments clicked together to accompany music or dancing   248

cause célèbre: famous case in law that arouses considerable interest   213

celestial: of the heavens   *64*

censure: adverse criticism   *140, 172*

centipede: small wormlike animal with many pairs of legs   165

chagrin: embarrassment; disappointment   43

changeling: infant secretly exchanged for another   194

chargé d'affaires: temporary substitute for an ambassador   208

chasm: wide gap   66

chef d'oeuvre: masterpiece in art, literature, etc.   219

chemise: loose-fitting, sacklike dress   221

cherub: angel in the form of a baby or child   *45*

cherubic: chubby and innocent-looking   45

Chianti: a dry, red Italian wine   238

chiaroscuro: style of pictorial art using only light and shade; sketch in black and white   235

chic: stylish   207

Chicano: American of Mexican descent   245

chimerical: fantastic   181

chiropodist: one who specializes in the care of the feet   114

cinema: movies; motion-picture industry   16

cinematography: art of making motion pictures   16

circumlocution: roundabout way of speaking   171

clairvoyant: clear-sighted; unusually perceptive   207

clamorous: noisy   *173*

claustrophobia: fear of confined spaces   95

cliché: trite or worn-out expression   212

climactic: arranged in order of increasing force and interest; of or constituting a climax   64

clique: small and exclusive set of persons   *209, 246*

cogitate: consider with care   85, 202

cognoscente: connoisseur   237

coiffure: style of arranging the hair; headdress   221

coincide: happen together   *163*

colloquy: conversation; conference   171

coloratura: ornamental passages (runs, trills, etc.) in vocal music; soprano who sings such passages   230

commendable: praiseworthy   *56*

commitment: consignment (''sending'') to prison, etc.; pledge   170

complacent: too pleased with oneself; smug   42

complaisant: willing to please; obliging   207

complex: complicated; intricate   34

complimentary: expressing a compliment; favorable   56

comprehensible: understandable   167

comprehensive: including very much 167
compunction: regret; misgiving 43
concave: curved inward, creating a hollow space 87
concerto: long musical composition for one or more principal instruments 234
concierge: doorkeeper; janitor 208
concise: expressing much in a few words *182*
concur: agree; happen together 163
concurrent: running together; occurring at the same time 163
condescend: bow; stoop 201
conducive: tending to lead to 161
conduct: lead; guide 161
confidant(e): one to whom secrets are entrusted 151
confident: having faith in oneself 151
confidential: communicated in trust 151
confine: imprison 25
conflagration: fire 203
confrere: colleague; co-worker 209
congratulate: express pleasure at another's success 158
coniferous: bearing cones 172
conjectural: of the nature of a guess or assumption *117*
conjecture: a guess *87*, 168
connoisseur: expert 209
conquistador: conqueror 245
consecrate: bless 201
consecutive: following in order 162
consequence: result; importance 162
conserve: keep from waste; save 7
consign: hand over 34
consignee: person to whom something is shipped 34
consommé: clear soup; broth 220
constrict: bind; draw together; render narrower; shrink 140
consume: eat 202
consummate: perfect; superb 64
contact: touching or meeting; connection 166
contaminate: make impure by mixture 78
contemporary: of the same period 74
contemporary: person living at same time as another 74
contend: strive in opposition 163
contiguous: touching; near 79, 166
contingent: dependent on something else; accidental 166
contort: twist out of shape *143*
contortionist: person who can twist or bend his body into odd postures 143
contour: outline of a figure 87
contralto: lowest female voice 230
contrariwise: on the contrary 193
contretemps: inopportune occurrence; embarrassing situation 214
contrite: showing regret for wrongdoing 43
contrition: regret for wrongdoing 43
controversy: dispute 169

convalesce: recover health after illness 54
convalescent: person recovering from sickness 54
conventional: generally accepted *86*
convex: rounded like the exterior of a circle 87
convict: prove guilty; person serving a prison sentence 144
conviction: state of having been judged guilty of an offense; strong belief 144
convince: persuade or show conclusively by argument or proof 144
convivial: fond of dining with friends; jovial 42, 142
conviviality: sociability 42
corporal: bodily 160
corporation: body authorized by law to carry on an activity 160
corps: organized body of persons; branch of the military 160
corpse: dead body 160
corpulent: very fat *45*, 160
corpus: general collection of writings, laws, etc. 160
corpuscle: blood cell; minute particle 160
corpus delicti: facts proving a crime has been committed; body of the victim in a murder case 160
corroborate: confirm 202
corrupt: change from good to bad 137
corsage: small bouquet worn by a woman 222
coterie: set or circle of acquaintances 209
countermand: issue a contrary order 149
coup de grâce: merciful or decisive finishing stroke 223
coup d'état: sudden, violent, or illegal overthrow of a government 218
coy: pretending to be shy 88
cravat: necktie 222
credence: belief 150
credentials: documents, letters, references, etc., that inspire belief or trust 150
credible: believable 150
credit: trust 150
credulous: too ready to believe 150
creed (credo): summary of principles believed in or adhered to 150
crescendo: gradually increasing (or a gradual increase) in force or loudness 232
criminology: scientific study of crimes and criminals 110
criterion: standard 85
croissant: rich, flaky crescent-shaped roll 220
crone: withered old woman 74
crux: essential part 85
cuisine: style of cooking 220
cul-de-sac: blind alley 214
culmination: highest point *65*
culpable: blamable *167*
cumbersome: burdensome 194
cupola: rounded roof; small dome or tower on a roof 235
current: now in progress; a running or flowing, as of water 163

curriculum: specific course of study in a school or college 163

curry favor: seek to gain favor by flattery 46

cursive: running or flowing 163

cursory: running over hastily 163

deadlock: stoppage produced by the opposition of equally powerful persons or groups *214*

debacle: collapse 214

debonair: affable and courteous 208

debut: formal entrance into society; first public appearance *209*

debutante: young woman who has just made her debut 209

decade: period of ten years 25

decapitate: behead 201

deceased: dead *74*

deceptive: misleading *86*

declivity: downward slope 66

decontaminate: rid of contamination 78

decrepit: weakened by old age 74

decrescendo: gradually decreasing (or a gradual decrease) in force or loudness 232

deduce: derive by reasoning 85

deduction: subtraction; reasoning from the general to the particular 161

defamatory: harming or destroying a reputation *56*

defective: flawed; incomplete; imperfect 166

defile: make filthy *79*

deflect: turn aside 146

defunct: dead; extinct 74

degrade: lower *66*

dejected: sad; in low spirits 43, 168

delectable: very pleasing 42

demarche: course of action, especially one involving a change of policy 218

demise: death, especially of a monarch or other important person 170

demitasse: small cup for, or of, black coffee 220

demure: falsely modest or serious; grave 89

denouement: solution of the plot in a play, story, or complex situation 219

denunciation: public condemnation *184*

dermatology: science dealing with the skin and its diseases 110

derogatory: expressing low esteem 56

desperado: bold, reckless criminal 245

despicable: worthy of contempt 16

despise: loathe 16

despotic: unjustly severe *84*

détente: a relaxing, as of strained relations between nations 218

detention: act of keeping back or detaining 147

detonate: explode; cause to explode 26

detriment: damage; disadvantage 7

devotee: ardent adherent *209, 245*

devour: eat greedily or ravenously; seize upon and destroy 141, 202

diabolic(al): devilish; very cruel; wicked; fiendish 199

dichotomy: cutting or division into two 113

diffident: lacking self-confidence 89, 151

digressive: rambling *167*

dilemma: situation requiring a choice between two equally bad alternatives 85

dilettante: person who follows some art or science as an amusement or in a trifling way 237

dimorphous: occurring under two distinct forms 123

dipody: verse (line of poetry) consisting of two feet 114

dipsomania: abnormal, uncontrollable craving for alcohol 77

disconsolate: cheerless 43

discredit: cast doubt on; disgrace 150

discursive: wandering from one topic to another 163

disgruntled: in bad humor; discontented 43

disharmony: discord; lack of harmony 8

disintegrate: break up 201

disrupt: break apart; cause disorder 138

distort: twist out of shape; change from the true meaning 87, 143

diva: principal female singer; prima donna 237

diversion: entertainment; amusement 169

divert: turn aside; amuse 169

docile: easily led *9, 161*

dogmatic: asserting opinions as if they were facts 85

dolce: soft; sweet 232

dolce far niente: delightful idleness 238

doldrums: calm, windless part of the ocean near the equator; listlessness 77

doleful: causing grief or sadness 43

dolorous: full of sorrow *43*

domicile: home 203

dour: gloomy *43*

Draconian: harsh 181

dregs: most worthless part; sediment at the bottom of a liquid 66

droll: odd and laughter-provoking 57

dross: waste; scum on the surface of melting metals 78

duckling: little duck 195

duct: tube or channel for conducting a liquid, air, etc. 161

ductile: able to be drawn out or hammered thin (said of a metal); easily led 161

duenna: elderly woman chaperon of a young lady; governess 245

duet: piece of music for two voices or instruments; two singers or players performing together 234

dysentery: inflammation of the large intestine 98

dysfunction: abnormal functioning, as of an organ of the body 98

dyslexia: impairment of ability to read 98

dyslogistic: expressing disapproval, uncomplimentary 98

dyspepsia: difficult digestion; indigestion 98
dysphagia: difficulty in swallowing 98
dysphasia: speech difficulty resulting from brain disease 99
dysphoria: sense of great unhappiness 99
dystopia: imaginary place where living conditions are dreadful 99
dystrophy: faulty nutrition 99

earthy: coarse, worldly 66
earldom: realm or dignity of an earl 193
ebullience: exuberance; high spirit 16
ebullient: overflowing with enthusiasm 16
echolalia: automatic repetition of what others say 181
éclat: brilliancy of achievement 211
eclectic: choosing (ideas, methods, etc.) from various sources 85
ecology: science dealing with the relation of living things to their environment and to each other 110
ecstasy: state of overwhelming joy 42
ecstatic: in ecstasy; enraptured 42
effrontery: shameless boldness 34
egoism: excessive concern for oneself; selfishness 89
egress: exit 164
eject: throw out 168
élan: enthusiasm 211
elate: lift up with joy *64*
elated: in high spirits 42
elite: group of individuals thought to be superior 209
elocution: art of speaking or reading effectively in public 171
eloquent: speaking with force and fluency 172
Elysian: blissful; heavenly 181
emaciated: abnormally lean because of starvation or illness 45
emancipate: free 202
émigré: refugee 209
eminence: high rank; lofty hill 64
eminent: standing out; notable; famous 64
emissary: person sent on a mission 170
emit: send out; give off 170
empathy: the complete understanding of another's feelings, motives, etc. 122
encomium: speech or writing of high praise; tribute; eulogy 56
encore: repetition of a performance; rendition of an additional selection 219
endocarditis: inflammation of the lining of the heart 119
endocrine: secreting internally 118
endoderm: membranelike tissue lining the greater part of the digestive tract 119
endogamy: marriage within the tribe, caste, or social group 118
endogenous: produced from within; due to internal causes 118

endomorphic: occurring within 123
endoparasite: parasite living in the internal organs of an animal 119
endophyte: plant growing within another plant 119
endoskeleton: internal skeleton or supporting framework in an animal 118
endosmosis: osmosis inward 118
ennui: boredom 211
en route: on the way 223
ensemble: complete costume of harmonious clothing and accessories 222
entente: understanding or agreement between governments 218
entourage: group of attendants accompanying a person 209
entrée: main dish at lunch or dinner 220
entre nous: between us 212
entrepreneur: one who assumes the risks and management of a business 209
environs: districts surrounding a place; suburbs 79
envoy: diplomatic agent; messenger 209
ephemeral: fleeting; short-lived 26
equanimity: evenness of mind *211*
equine: of or like a horse 199
eristic: prone to controversy; argumentative 181
erupt: burst or break out 138
esprit de corps: feeling of union and common interest pervading a group 160, 211
ethereal: of the heavens; delicate 64
ethnology: science dealing with the races of mankind, their origin, distribution, culture, etc. 110
etiquette: conduct and manners of polite society 223
eugenics: science dealing with improving the hereditary qualities of the human race 99
eulogistic: expressing praise *56*
eulogize: praise; extol; laud; glorify 56, 99
eupepsia: good digestion 99
euphemism: substitution of a "good" expression for an unpleasant one 99
euphonious: pleasing in sound 99
euphoria: sense of great happiness or well-being 99
euthanasia: illegal practice of painlessly putting to death a person suffering from an incurable, painfully distressing disease 100
euthenics: science dealing with improving living conditions 100
evict: expel 144, *168*
evince: show clearly 144
exaggerate: overstate 16
exalt: lift up with joy, pride, etc.; raise in rank, dignity, etc. 64
excoriate: flay, fleece, skin 202
excruciating: unbearably painful 34
exculpate: acquit 34
excursion: going out or forth; expedition 163
execrate: curse 201
execute: follow through to completion; put to death 162
exhort: urge 17

exhortation: urgent recommendation or advice   17

exocrine: secreting externally   118

exogamy: marriage outside the tribe, caste, or social group   118

exogenous: produced from without; due to external causes   118

exoskeleton: hard protective structure developed outside the body   118

exosmosis: osmosis outward   118

exoteric: external; readily understandable   119

exotic: introduced from a foreign country; excitingly strange   7, 119

expectorate: split   202

expedite: accelerate or speed up; make easy   165

expertise: expertness   17

expurgate: remove objectionable material from a book; purify   78

extinct: no longer in existence   74

extol: praise   64, 56

extort: wrest (money, promises, etc.) from a person by force   143

extraneous: not relevant; beside the point   88

extrovert: person more interested in what is going on around him than in his own thoughts and feelings   169

facade: face or front of a building, or of anything   223

facetious: in the habit of joking; said in jest without serious intent   57

facilitate: make easy   165

fait accompli: thing accomplished and presumably irrevocable   214

fallacious: based on an erroneous idea   86

fallacy: erroneous idea   86

fallible: liable to be mistaken   86

falsetto: unnaturally high-pitched male voice, artificial voice   230

farcical: exciting laughter   58

fatal: causing death   159

fathom: get to the bottom of; ascertain the depth of   66

fauna: animals of a particular region or period   181

faux pas: misstep or blunder in conduct, manners, speech, etc.   214

fawning: slavishly attentive   46

fealty: loyalty; faithfulness   151

feline: catlike; sly; stealthy   199

feminine: womanly   199

fester: form pus; rot   54

fete: to honor with a party; festival   223

fetid: ill-smelling   68

fiancé(e): person engaged to be married   209

fiasco: crash; complete or ridiculous failure   238

fidelity: faithfulness to a trust or vow; accuracy   151

fiduciary: held in trust; confidential   151

fiesta: saint's day; any festival or holiday   248

filament: thread   203

filet: slice of meat or fish without bones or fat   220

filial: of or befitting a son or daughter   67, 198

finale: close or termination, as the last section of a musical composition   234

finesse: skill in handling a difficult situation   211

finicky: hard to please   17

firmament: heaven   203

flamboyant: flamelike, showy   222

flex: bend   146

flexible: capable of being bent   146

flexor: muscle that serves to bend a limb   146

flippant: treating serious matters lightly   57

flora: plants of a particular region or period   181

flotilla: small fleet; fleet of small vessels   248

flotsam: wreckage of a ship or its cargo found floating on the sea; driftage   78

folly: lack of good sense   8

forbearance: leniency; patience   34

forebear: ancestor   74

forefather: ancestor   67, 74

formerly: previously   8

forte: loud   232

fortissimo: very loud   232

forum: medium or place of open discussion   182

foundling: infant found after being deserted by unknown parents   195

foyer: lobby; entrance hall   223

fraction: one or more of the equal parts of a whole   145

fractious: apt to break out into a passion   145

fracture: break or crack; breaking of a bone   145

fragile: easily broken   145

fragment: part broken off   145

fragrant: having a pleasant odor   68

Francophile: supporter of France or French   97

Francophobe: one who dislikes France or French   96

fraternal: brotherly; having to do with a fraternal society   67, 198

fratricide: act of killing (or killer of) one's own brother   138

fresco: art of painting with water colors on damp, fresh plaster; picture or design so painted   235

frivolity: trifling gaiety   58

frolic: play and run about happily   42

frolicsome: full of gaiety   42

frugivorous: feeding on fruit   141

frustrate: baffle   16

fulsome: offensive because of excessive display or insincerity   46, 194

fungicide: substance that kills fungi   138

fusty: stale-smelling; old-fashioned   68

gala: characterized by festivity   42

gall: brazen boldness; nerve   17, 34

gallant: man of fashion; lover   245

gastrectomy: surgical removal of part or all of the stomach   113

gauche: lacking social grace; awkward   208

gaucho: Argentine cowboy of mixed Spanish and Indian descent   246

gaunt: excessively thin   45

gendarme: policeman with military training 209

genealogy: account of the descent of a person or family from an ancestor 67, 110

generate: cause; bring into existence 201

genocide: deliberate extermination of a racial or cultural group 138

genre: kind; style 219

gentility: good manners; upper class, gentry 67

genuflect: bend the knee; touch the right knee to the ground, as in worship 146

geocentric: measured from the earth's center 120

geodesy: mathematics dealing with the earth's shape and dimensions 120

geodetic: pertaining to geodesy 120

geography: study of the earth's surface, etc. 120

geology: science dealing with the earth's history as recorded in rocks 110, 120

geometry: mathematics dealing with lines, angles, surfaces, and solids 121

geomorphic: pertaining to the shape of the earth or the form of its surface 121

geophysics: science treating of the forces that modify the earth 121

geopolitics: study of government and its policies as affected by physical geography 121

geoponics: art or science of agriculture 121

georgic: agricultural; poem on husbandry (farming) 121

geotropism: response to earth's gravity, as the growing of roots downward in the ground 121

Germanophilia: admiration of Germany or the Germans 95

Germanophobe: one who dislikes Germany or the Germans 96

Germanophobia: dislike of Germany or the Germans 95

germicide: substance that kills germs 138

gigantic: prodigious 35

glee: joy 57

glum: gloomy 43

goatish: goatlike; coarse; lustful 199

gondola: boat used in the canals of Venice; cabin attached to the underpart of an airship 239

gosling: young goose 195

gourmand: person excessively fond of eating and drinking 209

gourmet: connoisseur in eating and drinking 209

gracious: courteous 158

gradation: a change by steps or stages 164

grade: step; stage 164

gradient: rate at which a road, railroad track, etc., rises; slope 164

gradual: by steps or degrees 164

graduate: complete all the steps of a course and receive a diploma or degree 164

graduated: arranged in regular steps, stages, or degrees 164

grandee: nobleman of the highest rank; person of eminence 246

grandiloquent: using lofty or pompous words 172

graphic: clear-cut and lifelike *142*

grateful: thankful 158

gratify: give or be a source of pleasure or satisfaction 158

gratis: without charge or payment; free 158

gratitude: thankfulness 158

gratuitous: given freely; unwarranted 158

gratuity: present of money in return for a favor or service 158

grave: deserving serious attention 88

grave: slow (the slowest tempo in music) 231

grotto: cave 239

gruesome: horrifying and repulsive *55*

gull: deceive; cheat 26

gullible: easily deceived 26

gusto: liking or taste; hearty enjoyment 238

habeas corpus: writ requiring a detained person to be brought before a court to investigate the legality of that person's detention 160

hacienda: large ranch; landed estate; country house 248

haggard: careworn 45

haggle: argue over a price 26

halcyon: calm 53

hamper: interfere with 34

harlequin: clown 57

harmony: peaceable relations 8

heath: tract of wasteland 195

hector: to bully; to bluster 182

herbicide: substance that kills plants 139

herbivore: plant-eating animal 141

herbivorous: dependent on plants as food 141

Herculean: very difficult; having or requiring the strength of Hercules 182

herdsman: one who owns, keeps, or tends a herd *247*

heretical: rejecting regularly accepted beliefs or doctrines *86*

hermetic: airtight 182

heterochromatic: having different colors 115

heteroclite: deviating from the common rule; person or thing deviating from the common rule 115

heterodox: rejecting regularly accepted beliefs or doctrines 86, 115

heterogeneous: dissimilar 115

heterology: lack of correspondence between parts 115

heteromorphic: exhibiting diversity of form 115, 123

heteronym: words spelled like another, but differing in sound and meaning 115

hidalgo: nobleman of the second class 246

hierarchy: body of rulers or officials grouped in ranks, each being subordinate to the rank above it 120

hilarious: boisterously merry; very funny 57

hilarity: noisy gaiety 57, 203

hircine: goatlike, especially in smell 199

infantile: of or like a very young child; babyish 74, 198

infer: derive by reasoning *85*

inference: conclusion *168*

infernal: pertaining to the realm of the dead; hellish *185*

infidel: one who does not accept a particular faith 151

infidelity: faithlessness 151

inflection: change in the pitch or tone of a person's voice 147

inflexibility: rigidity 147

infraction: violation 145, 203

ingénue: naive young woman; actress playing such a role *209*

ingenuous: artlessly frank *208*

ingrate: ungrateful person 158

ingratiate: work (oneself) into another's favor 46, 158

ingratitude: ungratefulness 158

initiate: begin 201

inject: force or introduce a liquid, a remark, etc. 168

insatiable: incapable of being satisfied *141*

insecticide: preparation for killing insects 139

insectivorous: dependent on insects as food 141

insomnia: inability to sleep 26

insomniac: person suffering from insomnia 26

intact: kept or left whole 8, 166

intaglio: design engraved by making cuts in a surface 235

intangible: not capable of being touched *64,* 166

interject: throw in between 168

interlocutor: one who participates in a conversation; questioner 172

intermezzo: short musical or dramatic entertainment between the acts of a play; short musical composition between the main divisions of an extended musical work; a short, independent musical composition 234

intermittent: coming and going at intervals 171

interpose: place between *168*

interrupt: break into or between 138

intimidate: make fearful *182,* 202

intolerant: narrow-minded *85*

intoxicated: drunk 77

intractable: hard to manage *145*

intricate: complicated *34, 182*

introvert: person more interested in his own thoughts than in what is going on around him 169

invalid: having no force; void 8

invalidate: make valueless 201

invert: turn upside down 169

inveterate: firmly established by age; habitual 74

invigorate: give vigor, life, or energy to 202

invincible: incapable of being conquered 144

involuntary: not done of one's own free will 63

iridescent: having colors like the rainbow 182

ironic(-al): containing or expressing irony 58

irony: type of humor whose intended meaning is the opposite of the words used 58

irrational: senseless *86*

irrelevant: not pertinent; inapplicable 88

jetsam: goods cast overboard to lighten a ship in distress 78

jettison: throw (goods) overboard to lighten a ship or plane; discard 78

jocose: given to jesting; playfully humorous 58

jocular: given to jesting; done as a joke *58*

jocund: merry 42

jovial: jolly *182*

jubilation: rejoicing; exultation 42

junta: council for legislation or administration 246

junto: political faction; group of plotters 246

juvenile: of or for youth; immature 74

juxtapose: put side by side 79

juxtaposition: close or side-by-side position 79

kith and kin: friends and relatives 67

labyrinthine: full of confusing passageways; complicated, like the Labyrinth 182

lackey: follower who carries out another's orders like a servant; toady 46

laconic: using words sparingly 182

laissez-faire: absence of government interference or regulation 218

lament: mourn; deplore 43

lamentable: pitiable 44

languid: lacking in vigor; weak 142

lank: lean; ungracefully tall; lanky 45

lapse: cease being in force; become invalid 26

lapse: slip; error; interval 26

larceny: theft 203

largo: slow and dignified 231

Latino: Latin American 246

Latino: characteristic of Latinos 246

latter: later; second; last 8

laudable: praiseworthy 56

laudatory: expressing praise 56

lax: careless *171*

leeward: in the direction away from the wind 78

legato: smooth and connected 233

legerdemain: sleight of hand 211

legitimate: rightful; justifiable 84

lento: slow 231

lesion: injury 54

lethargic: unnaturally drowsy; sluggish 182

lettre de cachet: sealed letter obtainable from the King of France (before the Revolution) ordering the imprisonment without trial of the person named in the letter 218

levity: lack of proper seriousness 58

liaison: bond; coordination of activities 214

libel: false and defamatory written or printed statement 56

misanthrope: hater of humanity 97
misanthropy: hatred of humanity 98
misconception: erroneous belief *86*
misogamy: hatred of marriage 98
misogyny: hatred of women 98
misology: hatred of argument or discussion 98
misoneism: hatred of anything new 98
missile: weapon propelled to hit a distant object 171
missive: letter 171
mocking: ridiculing *58*
moderato: in moderate time 231
modest: humble; decent 66, 89
modesty: freedom from conceit or vanity 89
molt: shed feathers, skin, hair, etc. 53
momentous: very important *88*
monarchy: state ruled over by a single person, as a king or queen 103, 120
monitor: regulate the operation of a machine or process 148
monochromatic: of one color 103
monocle: eyeglass for one eye 103
monogamy: marriage with but one mate at a time 103
monogram: two or more letters interwoven to represent a name 103
monograph: written account of a single thing or class of things 103
monolith: single stone of large size 103
monolog(ue): long speech by one person in a group 103
monomania: derangement of mind on one subject only 103
monomorphic: having a single form 103, 123
monophobia: fear of being alone 95
monosyllabic: having but one syllable 103
monotheism: belief that there is but one God 103
monotonous: continuing in an unchanging tone; wearying 103
monument: a means of reminding us of a person or event; for example, a statue or tomb 148
morbid: having to do with disease; gruesome 55
moribund: near death 159
morose: ill-humoredly silent *44, 185*
morphology: branch of biology dealing with the form and structure of animals and plants 110, 123
mortal: human being; person; individual; destined to die 159
mortality: death rate; mortal nature 159
mortician: undertaker 159
mortification: embarrassment *43,* 159
mortify: humiliate, embarrass 159
mortuary: funeral home; morgue 159
mot juste: the exactly right word 212
mountebank: quack; boastful pretender 237
mournful: full of sorrow *43*
musicale: social gathering, with music as the featured entertainment 219
mustang: bronco 250
musty: moldy or stale *68*

myrmidon: obedient and unquestioning follower 183
mythology: account or study of myths 110

nadir: lowest point 66
naive: simple; unsophisticated 208
narcissistic: in love with onself 183
nautical: of the sea or shipping *78*
navigate: sail 202
necrology: register of persons who have died 110
nectar: something exceptionally delicious to drink 183
nemesis: due punishment for evil deeds; one who inflicts such punishment 183
nepotism: favoritism to relative to those in power 67
nettlesome: irritating 34
neurology: scientific study of the nervous system and its diseases 110
noblesse oblige: principle that persons of high rank or birth are obliged to act nobly 211
noisome: offensive to the sense of smell; unwholesome 68, 194
nom de plume: pen name; pseudonym 212
nonage: legal minority; period before maturity 75
nonagenarian: person in his 90's 75
nonbiodegradable: not readily decomposable by microorganisms *112*
noncarcinogenic: not cancer-producing 8
nonchalant: without concern or enthusiasm 208
nonpareil: person of unequalled excellence; paragon 210
nostalgia: homesickness; yearning for the past 44
notwithstanding: despite the fact that 192
nouveaux riches: persons newly rich 210
nowise: in no way 193
noxious: harmful *68*
nugatory: worthless 88
nuptials: wedding 203
nutriment: food 203

obese: extremely overweight; corpulent; portly 45
obesity: excessive body weight; corpulence 45
obligatory: required *149*
oblivion: condition of being forgotten or unknown 34
oblivious: forgetful 34
obloquy: a speaking against; public reproach 172
obsequious: showing excessive willingness to serve 46
obsolescent: going out of use 75
obsolete: no longer in use 75
obverse: front of a coin, medal, etc. 169
Occident: West 17
occidental: western 17
octogenarian: person in his 80's 75
odoriferous: yielding an odor, usually fragrant *68,* 172
odorous: having an odor, especially a sweet odor *68*

odyssey: any long series of wanderings or travels 184

offal: waste parts of a butchered animal; refuse 78

officialdom: those having the authority of officials 193

olfactory: pertaining to the sense of smell 68

oligarchy: form of government in which a few people have the power 120

olio: mixture 248

Olympian (Olympic): majestic; godlike; lofty 184

omnibus: bus; book containing a variety of works by one author; covering many things at once 145

omnifarious: of all varieties, forms, or kinds 146

omnific: all-creating 146

omnipotent: unlimited in power 146

omnipresent: present everywhere at the same time 146

omniscient: knowing everything 146

omnivore: person or animal that eats everything 141

omnivorous: eating everything; fond of all kinds 141, 146

opera: play mostly sung, all costumes, scenery, action, and music 234

opinionated: unduly attached to one's own opinion 85

optional: not compulsory; discretionary 149

oratorio: musical composition, usually on a religious theme, for solo voices, chorus, and orchestra 234

ornate: elaborate 222

ornithology: study of birds 53

orthodox: conforming to accepted doctrines, especially in religion 86

ostentatious: done to impress others 89

osteopath: practitioner of osteopathy 122

osteopathy: treatment of diseases by manipulation of bones, muscles, nerves, etc. *122*

oust: expel *144*

overweening: thinking too highly of oneself 89

ovine: of or like a sheep 200

pacify: calm 202

paean: song or hymn of praise, joy, or triumph 184

paleontology: science dealing with life in the remote past as recorded in fossils 110

palette: thin board on which an artist lays and mixes colors 219

palladium: safeguard or protection 184

paltry: practically worthless 88

pampas: vast, treeless, grassy plains, especially in Argentina 250

panic: unreasoning, sudden fright that grips a multitude 184

paradox: self-contradictory statement which may nevertheless be true 86

paradoxical: self-contradictory, yet possibly true 86

paramount: chief 88

parasite: animal, plant, or person living on others 53

parasol: umbrella for protection against the sun 223

par excellence: above all others of the same sort 223

parody: humorous imitation of a serious writing 58

parrot: repeat mechanically, like a parrot 53

parsimonious: stingy 8

partiality: special taste or liking *85*

parvenu(e): person suddenly risen to wealth or power who lacks the proper social qualifications 210

passé: old-fashioned; behind the times 223

pasta: wheat paste or dough 239

paternal: fatherly; inherited from or related to the father's side 67, 198

pathetic: arousing pity 44, 122

pathogenic: causing disease 122

pathological: due to disease 122

pathology: science dealing with the nature and causes of disease 110

pathos: quality in drama, speech, literature, music, or events that arouses pity or sadness 44, 122

patina: film or incrustation, usually green, on the surface of old bronze or copper 236

patio: paved outdoor dining or lounging area adjacent to a house 248

patriarch: venerable old man; father and ruler of a family or tribe; founder 75

patriarchy: form of social organization in which the father rules the family or tribe, descent being traced through the father 120

patricide: act of killing (or killer of) one's own father 139

peaceable: disposed to peace; not quarrelsome 145

peccadillo: slight offense 248

peculate: steal 202

pedal: lever acted on by the foot 165

pedestal: support or foot of a column or statue; foundation 165

pedestrian: foot traveler; commonplace 166

pedigree: an ancestral line *67*

penitent: feeling regret for wrongdoing 43

pensive: thoughtful in a sad way 44

peon: common laborer; worker kept in service to repay a debt 246

perfidious: false to a trust; faithless 151

perfidy: violation of a trust 151

pericardium: membranous sac enclosing the heart 124

perigee: nearest point to the earth in the orbit of a man-made satellite or heavenly body 121, 124

perihelion: nearest point to the sun in the orbit of a planet or comet 124

perimeter: the whole outer boundary or measurement of a surface or figure 124

periodontics: branch of dentistry dealing with bone and gum diseases 124

peripheral: on the periphery (outside boundary) 124

periphery: outside boundary *124*

periphrastic: expressed in a roundabout way 124

periscope: instrument permitting those in a submarine a view of the surface 124

peristalsis: wavelike contraction of the intestines which propels contents onward 124

peristyle: row of columns around a building or court; the space so enclosed 124

peritoneum: membrane lining the abdominal cavity and covering the organs *124*

peritonitis: inflammation of the peritoneum 124

persistence: perseverance *147*

pert: saucy 89

pertinacious: adhering firmly to a purpose or opinion 147

pertinent: bearing on the matter in hand *88*, 147

perusal: reading; study 17

peruse: read 17

perverse: turned away from what is right or good 170

pervert: turn away from right or truth; person who has turned from what is normal or natural *138*, 170

pesticide: substance that kills rats, insects, bacteria, etc. 139

pestiferous: infected with or bearing disease; evil 172

pestilential: morally harmful; pertaining to a pestilence 55, *172*

petrology: scientific study of rocks 111

petty: trifling *88*

philanthropist: lover of mankind 96

philanthropy: love of mankind 96

philatelist: stamp collector 96

philately: collection and study of stamps 96

philharmonic: pertaining to a musical organization 96

philhellenism: support of Greece or the Greeks 97

philippic: bitter denunciation; tirade 184

philogyny: love of women 97

philology: study of language 97

philosopher: lover of wisdom 97

phlebotomy: opening of a vein for the purpose of diminishing the supply of blood 113

phobia: fear; dread; aversion 96

photophobia: morbid aversion to light 96

physiology: science dealing with the functions of living things or their organs 111

pianissimo: very soft 232

piano: soft 232

piazza: open square in an Italian town; veranda or porch 239

picador: horseman who irritates the bull with a lance at the beginning of a bullfight 246

picaro: adventurous rogue; vagabond 246

piddling: trifling *88*

pièce de résistance: main dish; main item of any collection, series, program, etc. 221

pimento (pimiento): thick-fleshed pepper used for stuffing olives and as a source of paprika 248

pince-nez: eyeglasses clipped to the nose by a spring 223

pinnacle: highest point *64*

piscine: of or like a fish 199

pizza: large, flat pie of bread dough spread with tomato pulp, etc. 239

pizzicato: direction to players of bowed instruments to pluck the strings instead of using the bow 233

plaudit: applause; enthusiastic praise 56

plausible: apparently trustworthy 86

pliable: easily bent or molded; capable of adaptation 146

plight: unfortunate state 44

plumb: get to the bottom of; ascertain the depth of 66

plutocratic: having great influence because of one's wealth 184

podiatrist: chiropodist 114

podium: dais; low wall serving as a foundation 114

poignant: painfully touching 44

politico: politician 237

pollute: make unclean *78*

Pollyanna: irrepressible optimist 181

polyarchy: rule by many 103

polychromatic: showing a variety of colors 103

polygamy: marriage to several mates at the same time 103

polyglot: speaking several languages; person who speaks several languages 104

polygon: closed plane figure having many angles, and hence many sides 104

polymorphic: having various forms 104

polyphonic: having many sounds or voices 104

polysyllabic: having more than three syllables 104

polytechnic: dealing with many arts or sciences 104

polytheism: belief that there is a plurality of gods 104

poncho: large cloth, often waterproof, with a slit for the head 248

ponder: weigh in the mind *85*

portfolio: briefcase; position or duties of a cabinet member or minister of state 239

porcine: of or like a pig 200

portico: roof supported by columns, forming a porch or a covered walk 236

portly: imposing, especially because of size *45*

posthumous: published after the author's death; occurring after death 75

potpourri: mixture *214*

precipice: cliff 65

precipitous: steep as a precipice; hasty 65

précis: brief summary 213

precursor: forerunner 163

predecessor: one who precedes another *163*

predicament: unfortunate state *44*, *85*

predilection: inclination to like or choose something *85*

preeminent: standing out above others 65

prehensile: adapted for seizing 167

prejudice: unreasonable preference or objection *85*

premier: prime minister 218

premiere: first performance 223

premonition: forewarning 148

premonitory: conveying a forewarning 149

preposterous: senseless 86

prestissimo: at a very rapid pace 231

presto: quick 231

presumptuous: taking undue liberties *89*

pretentious: done to impress others *89*

prevaricate: lie 202

prima donna: principal female singer, as in an opera; highstrung, vain, or extremely sensitive person 237

primeval: pertaining to the world's first ages 75

primitive: characteristic of the original state of the world or of man 75

primordial: existing at the very beginning; first in order 76

pristine: in original state; uncorrupted 76

probe: investigation 26

prober: investigator 26

procreate: beget 201

procrustean: cruel or inflexible in enforcing conformity 184

prodigious: enormous 35

prodigy: person of extraordinary talent or ability 35

profound: very deep 66

progenitor: forefather 67

progeny: children; descendants 67

progress: act of going from a worse to a better state 165

progressive: going forward to something better 164

projectile: object designed to be shot forward; anything thrown forward 168

proliferous: producing new growth rapidly and extensively 172

propinquity: kinship; nearness of place 80

prosecute: follow to the end or until finished; conduct legal proceedings against 162

prostrate: lie face down 201

protean: exceedingly variable; readily assuming different forms or shapes 184

protégé(e): person under the care and protection of another 210

prow: forward part of a ship *77*

proximity: nearness *80*

pseudopod: temporary extension of the protoplasm, as in the ameba, to enable the organism to move and take in food 114

psychology: science of the mind 111

psychopathic: pertaining to mental disease; insane 122

puberty: physical beginning of manhood (age 14) or womanhood (age 12) 76

pudgy: short and plump; chubby 45

pueblo: Indian village built of adobe and stone 249

puerile: foolish for a grown-up to say or do; childish 76, 198

pungent: sharp in smell or taste; biting 68

purge: cleanse; rid of undesired element or person 79

putrefy: rot *54*

putrid: stinking from decay; extremely bad 68

Pyrrhic: gained at too great a cost 184

qualm: misgiving *43*

queue: line of persons waiting their turn 223

raconteur: person who excels in telling stories, anecdotes, etc. 210

raillery: pleasantry touched with ridicule *57*

raison d'être: reason or justification for existing 224

rancid: unpleasant to smell or taste from being spoiled or stale 68

rank: having a strong, bad odor or taste; extreme 69

rankle: cause inflammation *54*

rapport: relationship characterized by harmony, conformity, or affinity 211

rapprochement: establishment or state of cordial relations; a coming together *218*

rapture: state of overwhelming joy *42*

rash: overhasty *65*

ratiocinate: reason 202

rational: able to think clearly; based on reason 86

rationalize: devise excuses for one's actions, desires, failures, etc. 86

ravine: deep, narrow gorge worn by running water 66

raze: demolish 9

reactionary: resisting change; ultraconservative 164

rebuff: snub; insult 27

recuperate: recover health after illness *54*

recur: happen again 163

reek: emit a strong, disagreeable smell; be permeated with 69

reflect: throw back light, heat, sound, etc.; think *87*, 147

reflex: involuntary response to a stimulus 147

refract: bend a ray of light, heat, sound, etc., from a straight course 145

refractory: hard to manage 145

regicide: act of killing (or killer of) a king 139

regime: system of government or rule 218

regimen: set of rules to improve health 55

regressive: disposed to move backward 164

reimburse: indemnify *17*

reinvigorate: give new vigor to *35*

reject: refuse to take 168

rejuvenate: make young again 35

relevant: bearing upon the matter in hand 88

reluctant: disinclined *63*

remand: send back; recommit 149

remiss: negligent 171

remission: period of lessening of the symptoms of a disease 171

remit: send money due; forgive 171

remorse: regret for wrongdoing *43*

render: deliver; give 26

rendering: presentation; interpretation 26

rendezvous: meeting place; appointment to meet at a fixed time and place 224

renegade: deserter from a religion, party, etc.; traitor 246

repartee: skill of replying quickly, cleverly, and humorously; witty reply 213

repast: meal 27
repentant: showing regret for wrongdoing 43
repertoire: list of plays, operas, roles, compositions, etc., that a company or performer is prepared to perform 219
replenish: refill 27
reprehend: find fault with; rebuke 167
reprehensible: blamable 167
reproof: rebuke *148*
reprove: disapprove or criticize *148*
repugnance: strong dislike *63*
repulsive: offensive *46*
residual: remaining after a part is used or taken 35
residue: remainder 35
restrict: keep within limits 140
résumé: summary 213
retentive: able to retain or remember 147
reticent: inclined to be silent 9
retinue: group of followers accompanying a distinguished person 147
retire: withdraw from active duty; go to bed 9
retort: reply quickly or sharply in kind; quick, sharp reply 9, 143
retrograde: going backward; becoming worse 164
retrogression: act of going from a better to a worse state 165
retrogressive: disposed to move backward *164*
revere: regard with reverence 202
reverse: back part of something 169
revert: go back 170
revive: bring back to life 142
rialto: marketplace; theater district of a town 236
rift: crack or opening *66*
rigor mortis: stiffness of the body that sets in after death 159
riposte: quick retort or repartee; in fencing, quick return thrust after a parry 213
rogue: tricky, deceitful fellow *246*
rotund: rounded-out; full-toned 88
rotunda: round building, especially one with a dome or cupola; large round room 236
rout: state of confusion *214*
rueful: pitiable *44*
rupture: break; hostility 138, 203
Russophobe: one who dislikes Russia or the Russians 96

salubrious: healthful 55
salutary: beneficial 35
salvo: simultaneous discharge of shots; burst of cheers 239
sangfroid: coolness of mind or composure in difficult circumstances 211
sanguinary: bloody 200
sanguine: having a ruddy color; confident 200
sarcasm: sneering language intended to hurt a person's feelings 58
sarcastic: expressing sarcasm 58
sardonic: bitterly sarcastic 58

satire: language or writing that exposes follies or abuses by holding them up to ridicule 58
satiric(-al): expressing satire 58
saturnine: gloomy 185
savoir faire: knowledge of just what to do 211
scavenger: animal or person removing refuse, decay, etc. 53
scent: smell; perfume 69
scent: get a suspicion of 69
scherzo: light or playful part of a sonata or symphony 234
scintillate: sparkle; twinkle 202
score: twenty 27
scrupulous: painstaking; careful; upright 171
scrutinize: examine very closely 35
scrutiny: examination; inspection; review 35
scuffle: struggle; wrestle; grapple 17
sebaceous: greasy; secreting sebum (fatty matter) 55
sedate: of settled, quiet disposition *89*
seduction: act of leading astray into wrongdoing 161
senile: showing the weakness of age 76
señor: gentleman; Mr. or Sir 247
señora: lady; Mrs. or Madam 247
señorita: young lady; Miss 247
septuagenarian: person in his 70's 75
sequel: something that follows 162
sequence: the following of one thing after another 162
sequential: arranged in a sequence; serial 162
serpentine: winding in and out *88*
servile: befitting a slave or servant *66*
sforzando: accented 232
shard: fragment 203
sibling: one of two or more children of a family 67, 195
sierra: ridge of mountains with an irregular (saw-toothed) outline 250
siesta: short rest, especially at midday 249
silhouette: outline; shadow 224
simpatico (simpatica): likable; congenial 237
sinuous: bending in and out 88
siren: dangerous, attractive woman; woman who sings sweetly; apparatus for sounding loud warnings 185
skeptical: incredulous; disbelieving 150
slander: false and defamatory spoken statement 57, *162*
slanderous: falsely and maliciously accusing *56*
slatternly: untidy 79
sloven: person habitually untidy, dirty, or careless in dress, habits, etc. 79
snub: insult; rebuff 27
sober: not drunk; free from excitement or exaggeration 77
sobriety: temperance; abstinence 77
sobriquet: nickname 224
sociology: study of the evolution, development, and functioning of human society 111

solo: piece of music for one voice or instrument; anything done without a partner   234
solon: legislator; wise man   185
sombrero: broad-rimmed, high-crowned hat   250
somniferous: inducing sleep   173
sonata: piece of music (for one or two instruments) having three or four movements in contrasted rhythms but related tonality   234
sophistry: clever but deceptive reasoning   87
soprano: highest singing voice in women and boys   230
sordid: filthy   79
sororicide: act of killing (or killer of) one's own sister   139
sot: drunkard   77
sotto voce: in an undertone; privately   239
soup du jour: special soup served in a restaurant on a particular day   221
souvenir: keepsake   224
Spartan: marked by self-discipline, bravery, and ability to endure pain   185
specious: apparently reasonable, but not really so   87
speculate: reflect; buy or sell with the hope of profiting by price fluctuations   87
spurn: reject   18
squalid: filthy from neglect   79
squalor: filth; degradation   79
staccato: disconnected; with breaks between successive notes   233
staid: of settled, quiet disposition   89
starboard: right-hand side of a ship when one faces forward   78
starveling: one who is thin from lack of food   194
stentorian: very loud   185
stern: back part of a ship   77
stigma: mark of disgrace   57
stigmatize: brand with a mark of disgrace   57
stipend: fixed pay for services   18
stricture: adverse criticism   140
stringent: strict   140
stripling: lad   195
stucco: plaster for covering exterior walls of buildings   236
Stygian: dark; gloomy; infernal   185
subject: force (someone) to undergo something unpleasant   168
sublimate: redirect the energy of a person's bad impulses into socially and morally higher channels; purify   65
sublime: uplifting   65
subservient: useful in an inferior capacity; servile   66
subversion: sabotage; undermining   9
subvert: undermine   9
succession: the following of one thing after another: 162
successive: following in order   162
succumb: yield   202
suckling: child or animal that is nursed   194

suicide: act of killing one's self   139
sullen: resentfully silent; glum   44
sully: soil   79
summit: highest point   64
sumptuous: luxurious   182
superannuated: retired on a pension; too old for work   76
supersede: force out of use; displace   35
supersensitive: excessively sensitive   117
supplant: replace; supersede   35
supposition: a guess   117, 168
supreme: above all others   88
surveillance: close watch   18
survive: remain alive after   142
suture: stitch   27
svelte: slender   45
sweltering: oppessively hot   35
sycophant: parasitic flatterer   46
symbiosis: the living together in mutually helpful association of two dissimilar organisms   112
symmetrical: balanced in arrangement   88
symmetry: balance; harmony   88
sympathy: a sharing of ("feeling with") another's trouble   122

table d'hôte: describing a complete meal that bears a fixed price   221
taco: fried, folded tortilla stuffed with chopped meat, cheese, shredded lettuce, etc.   250
tact: sensitive mental perception of what is appropriate on a given occasion   166, 211
tactful: having or showing tact   166
tactile: pertaining to the sense of touch; able to be touched   166
tangent: touching; line or surface meeting a curved line or surface at one point, but not intersecting it   167
tangential: merely touching   167
tangible: touchable   166
tantalize: excite a hope but prevent its fulfillment; tease   185
tarnish: soil or dull   79
taurine: bullish   199
technology: use of science to achieve a practical purpose   111
tedium: boredom   211
teetotaler: person who totally abstains from intoxicating beverages   77
telepathy: transference of the thoughts and feelings of one person to another with no apparent communication   122
temerity: insolence; effrontery   34
tempera: method of painting in which the colors are mixed with white of egg or other substances, instead of oil   236
temperate: moderate in eating and drinking   77
tenable: capable of being maintained or defended   87

tenacious: inclined to hold fast *147*

tenacity: quality of holding fast 147

tenancy: period of a tenant's temporary holding of real estate 148

tenet: principle or doctrine generally held to be true 148

tenor: adult male voice between baritone and alto 230

tenure: period for which an office or position is held 148

tepid: lukewarm 18

tepidly: unenthusiastically; lukewarmly 18

terpsichorean: pertaining to dancing 185

terra-cotta: kind of hard, brownish-red earthenware, used for vases, statuettes, etc.; dull brownish-red 236

terse: free of unnecessary words *182*

tête-à-tête: private conversation between two persons 213

theology: study of religion and religious ideas 111

theory: a supposition supported by considerable evidence *86, 117*

therapeutic: curative 55

thespian: pertaining to the drama or acting 185

throes: pangs 44

titanic: of enormous strength, size, or power 185

tome: one volume of a work of several volumes; scholarly book 113

tonsillectomy: surgical removal of the tonsils 113

toreador: bullfighter, usually mounted 247

torero: bullfighter on foot 247

torrid: sweltering *35*

torsion: act of twisting; twisting of a body by two equal and opposite forces 143

torso: trunk or body of a statue without a head, arms, or legs; human trunk 236

tortilla: thin, flat, round corn cake 249

tortuous: full of twists or curves; tricky 143

torture: inflict severe pain upon 143

toupee: wig 222

tour de force: feat of strength, skill, or ingenuity 224

toxic: poisonous 55

tracheotomy: surgical operation of cutting into the windpipe 113

tractability: obedience 9

tractable: capable of being controlled *9, 146*

traduce: malign; slander; vilify *56, 162*

tranquillity: harmony *8*

transgress: step beyond the limits; break a law 165

transitory: fleeting; ephemeral *26*

travesty: imitation that makes a serious thing seem ridiculous 58

treatise: written account *212*

tremolo: rapid repetition of a tone or chord without apparent breaks, to express emotion 233

tribulation: suffering 44

tribute: speech or writing of high praise *56*

trio: piece of music for three voices or instruments; three singers or players performing together 234

tripod: utensil, stool, or caldron having three legs 114

truckle: submit servilely to a superior 46

turncoat: apostate *246*

tutti: all (direction for all to perform together) 234

tutti: section of musical composition performed by all the performers 234

tyrannicide: act of killing (or killer of) a tyrant 139

unfledged: without feathers; immature *74*

unflustered: calm *35*

unguent: ointment 55

unintentionally: unwittingly 27

unipod: one-legged support 114

unmanageable: unwieldy *35*

unrestricted: not confined within bounds; open to all 140

unruffled: not agitated 35

unsavory: unpleasant to taste or smell; morally offensive 69

untenable: incapable of being held or defended 148

unwieldy: bulky 35

unwittingly: inadvertently; by accident 27

ursine: bearish 199

utopia: imaginary place of ideal perfection 99

vagabond: one who wanders from place to place, having no fixed dwelling *246*

vain: conceited; worthless 89

vainglorious: excessively proud or boastful 90

valet: manservant who attends to the personal needs of his employer 210

valid: logically correct 86

vanity: condition of being too vain; conceit 90

vanquish: conquer 144

vaquero: cowboy 247

velocipede: child's tricycle 166

velocity: speed 203

vendetta: feud for blood revenge 238

venerable: worthy of respect because of advanced age, religious association, or historical importance 76

venerate: regard with reverence 202

veracity: truthfulness 203

verity: truth 203

versatile: having many aptitudes 170

verse: line of poetry 170

vertex: farthest point opposite the base, as in a triangle or pyramid; apex 65

vertigo: dizziness 170

veteran: person experienced in some occupation; ex-member of the armed forces 76

viaduct: bridge for conducting a road or railroad over a valley, river, etc. 162

vibrato: slightly throbbing or pulsating effect, adding warmth and beauty to the tone 233

victor: winner 144

vignette: a literary sketch; short verbal description 219